Colonial Algeria and the Politics of Citizenship

Colonial Algeria and the Politics of Citizenship

Avner Ofrath

BLOOMSBURY ACADEMIC
LONDON • NEW YORK • OXFORD • NEW DELHI • SYDNEY

BLOOMSBURY ACADEMIC
Bloomsbury Publishing Plc
50 Bedford Square, London, WC1B 3DP, UK
1385 Broadway, New York, NY 10018, USA
29 Earlsfort Terrace, Dublin 2, Ireland

BLOOMSBURY, BLOOMSBURY ACADEMIC and the Diana logo are trademarks of Bloomsbury Publishing Plc

First published in Great Britain 2023
This paperback edition published 2024

Copyright © Avner Ofrath, 2023

Avner Ofrath has asserted his right under the Copyright, Designs and Patents Act, 1988, to be identified as Author of this work.

For legal purposes the Acknowledgements on p. viii constitute an extension of this copyright page.

Cover image © French soldiers stand guard next to barbed wire, on 13 May 1961, rue Saint-Louis, one of the entrances to the Casbah of Algiers. Photo by Jean-Claude Combrisson / AFP via Getty Images.

All rights reserved. No part of this publication may be reproduced or transmitted in any form or by any means, electronic or mechanical, including photocopying, recording, or any information storage or retrieval system, without prior permission in writing from the publishers.

Bloomsbury Publishing Plc does not have any control over, or responsibility for, any third-party websites referred to or in this book. All internet addresses given in this book were correct at the time of going to press. The author and publisher regret any inconvenience caused if addresses have changed or sites have ceased to exist, but can accept no responsibility for any such changes.

A catalogue record for this book is available from the British Library.

A catalog record for this book is available from the Library of Congress.

ISBN: HB: 978-1-3502-6002-3
PB: 978-1-3502-6005-4
ePDF: 978-1-3502-6003-0
eBook: 978-1-3502-6004-7

Typeset by Deanta Global Publishing Services, Chennai, India

To find out more about our authors and books visit www.bloomsbury.com and sign up for our newsletters.

*In memory of my parents, Micky and Yehouda,
who are in every word of this book.*

Contents

Acknowledgements	viii
Note on transliteration	ix
List of abbreviations	x
Introduction	1
1 Creating a legal borderland	21
2 Subjects and citizens, 'Muslims' and 'Europeans'	41
3 'Taʿish al-République!' – 'À bas les Youdis!'	69
4 The levy of blood	91
5 A road not taken? The struggle for reform	115
6 Shifting horizons	137
Conclusion	159
Appendix	167
Bibliography	171
Index	186

Acknowledgements

Everything, Virginia Woolf wrote, is against the likelihood that a book will be written. 'Dogs will bark; people will interrupt; money must be made; health will break down.' The years of writing this book were no exception, and I am deeply grateful to the many people who made it possible nonetheless.

The Mellon Foundation, the Gerda Henkel Stiftung and the Society for the Study of French History funded my research with great generosity, and I am sincerely thankful for their support.

Robert Gildea has accompanied this book from day one with his rare combination of authority, wit, curiosity and good advice. Martin Conway read various chapter drafts, bravely struggling through my peculiar mixture of Germanic and Hebrew syntax. James McDougall and Martin Thomas were at once generous and uncompromising when urging me to turn my research into the book it should be. Abigail Green, Didier Guignard, Lisa Leff and Jennifer Sessions shared their thoughts and insights with me, and I am deeply grateful to them. The responsibility for the views and findings presented in this book is of course entirely mine.

Richard Ovenden has been extraordinarily helpful in identifying the right home for this book. At Bloomsbury, Maddie Holder, Megan Harris and Abigail Lane have been supportive all along the way. In Bremen, Claire Rostalski has been a tremendous help in preparing the manuscript for publication.

Much of the work on this book has been overshadowed by the untimely passing of my parents, Micky and Yehouda, and I am infinitely grateful to all those who never ceased to encourage me along the way. In Oxford, I owe a special debt to Robert Gildea, Martin Conway and Bruce Kinsey for their sympathy and good advice. Cornelius Torp went out of his way to make Bremen a pleasant new home as borders, archives and libraries closed during the pandemic. In person and remotely, Noam, Or, Assaf, Assaf, Simon and Norman have been and still are true friends. With my dear sisters, Shlomit and Na'ama, I have shared the hours and moments that made the past years what they were. To Sophia, who has made the world a place to call home again: *Bleib fest mein Haus im Weltgebraus*. And to Ima and Aba, Rest in peace; your love remains.

Note on transliteration

Translations from French, Arabic and Judeo-Arabic, unless stated otherwise, are mine. For reasons of simplicity, I have followed the simplified transliteration system of Maghribi Arabic (and Judeo-Arabic) that is now widely used in English-language scholarship. I have, therefore, omitted macrons on long vowels and diacritics on emphatic consonants. The Arabic consonant ʿ*ayn* is marked using the opening apostrophe, while *hamza* is denoted using the closing apostrophe (unless when at the end of a word). Arabic names are mostly spelled using the Gallicized transliteration that would be most recognizable to most readers: Abd al-Qadir, Abd al-Hamid Ben Badis and Ferhat Abbas. This also applies to place names, such as Algiers, Batna, Blida or Constantine.

Abbreviations

AUMA	*Association des 'ulama musulmans algériens*
CFLN	*Comité français de libération nationale*
ENA	*Étoile nord-africaine*
FLN	*Front de Libération nationale*
LDH	*Ligue des droits de l'homme*
OAS	*Organisation de l'armée secrète*
MTLD	*Mouvement pour le triomphe des libertés démocratiques*
PCA	*Parti communiste algérien*
PCF	*Parti communiste français*
PPA	*Parti du peuple algérien*
SFIO	*Section française de l'Internationale ouvrière*
UDMA	*Union démocratique du manifeste algérien*
UFSF	*Union française pour le suffrage des femmes*

Introduction

'Never, since 1830, did any measures of racial segregation exist in Algeria.' This astonishingly unequivocal claim was formulated in an official photo album produced by the delegation of the French government in Algeria in 1958, in the high days of the Algerian War. Depicting Algerians and Europeans sharing buses and public spaces, casting Algiers as the 'third French academic centre' and, not least, showing a group of Algerian men playing *pétanque*, this was a vivid depiction of the notion of a shared, republican public sphere.[1]

By any measure of legal theory or lived experience, this statement was of course simply and glaringly false. Though the French word *race* rarely featured in the corpus of legal documents that had constituted the colonial order, the regime that was established in Algeria had applied since its earliest days – and with increasing tenacity from the late nineteenth century onwards – different rules to different populations, demarcated along the lines of religion and descent. And yet, the claim that 'no measures of racial segregation existed in Algeria' reflected a widely shared conviction amongst French lawmakers, jurists and colonial administrators. The troubling and complex truth, this book argues, is that colonizing Algeria had shaped French concepts of equality, rights and belonging to the body politic – in short: citizenship – in a way that made the declaration above seem plausible to many a contemporary observer, and that legal writing and jurisprudence made 'racial segregation' illegible to much of the French political mainstream. The assumptions that underlay this illegibility, the policies it yielded and struggles around it are explored in this book.

Modern citizenship, the Algerian case demonstrates, was demarcated on the margins of sovereignty, in the legal and political grey zones between metropole and colonies. Declared to be an integral part of the national territory in 1848 yet governed by different laws and institutions throughout the colonial period, Algeria became a legal borderland between metropole and empire and a crucial battlefield for the definition of French citizenship. Since it was officially part of the national territory, upholding the colonial regime in Algeria required that any

---

1 Présidence du Conseil – Délégation en Algérie, *Documents algériens*, 1958, 49.

legislation concerning participation and rights in the metropole include special clauses explicitly limiting them across the Mediterranean. In a decisive turn during the second half of the nineteenth century, the colonial administration shifted its focus from settlement to jurisdictional politics as the main means of domination, seeking to provide a legal basis for settler political and economic privileges and the political exclusion of Algerians. The diversity of the settler population, which was mainly composed of French, Spanish and Italian nationals, led colonial authorities to demarcate rights and participation in a way that would include Europeans and exclude others, relying on religion and descent – and from the 1890s onwards on religion *as* descent – to delineate citizenship and subjecthood along the categories of Europeanness and Muslimness.

At the same time, colonial Algeria witnessed some of the most significant struggles to accommodate religious, social and linguistic difference within the republican body politic. Religion and above all religious legislation on matrimonial and sexual matters were construed as both the rationale and the fulcrum of the status of indigeneity in the colony. If they wished to obtain citizenship, Algerian Muslims and Jews were required to give up religious jurisdiction and the familial and communal structures associated with it. Yet, as this book argues, Algerian struggles for participation and rights rarely subscribed to this ideology of assimilation and acculturation. Rather, these were attempts to retain as much as possible of the societal structures, religious life and linguistic diversity of the Maghrib. As recent scholarship has established, the colonial endeavour of isolating Algeria from its centuries-old ties across the Maghrib, the Mashriq and the Mediterranean was only partly successful. Scholarly, commercial, and political ties prevailed and indeed flourished throughout the colonial period, bringing to Algerian Muslims and Jews impulses of religious and political reform movements, such as the Islamic *Islah*, the Arab *Nahda* and the Jewish *Haskalah*. In this vibrant political climate, this book argues, citizenship was never merely a legal tool of exclusion in the hands of the French administration but a promise or at least a horizon of political participation, a concept that was constantly negotiated and reimagined.

Drawing on French legal writing, political commentary and administrative correspondence, as well as on petitions, press articles and leaflets by Algerian Muslims, Jews and Europeans, this book explores the various mechanisms by which citizenship was demarcated along ethnoreligious lines, as well as the radicalism and innovation of struggles to accommodate difference within the *cité française*. It starts with the Second Republic's declaration of Algeria as part of the national territory in 1848 and ends with the collapse of the Fourth Republic in 1958. This was the time when the French state – most durably under the Third Republic (1870–1940) – created, consolidated and fought to maintain the legal and political borderland of Algeria. The story of citizenship, the following chapters argue, isn't merely or even primarily that of a legal-administrative institution but of the assumptions, norms and expectations associated with it and projected onto it as an emerging, powerful and strongly contested political concept.

Citizenship and empire

In exploring Algeria as a key battlefield for the shaping of the French body politic, this book builds on an explosion of research since the early 2000s that has thoroughly transformed how we think about citizenship. Frederick Cooper's statement from 2018 that 'the story of citizenship begins with empire' culminated a long scholarly shift away from the framework of the nation-state and the classical contrast between the ideal types of *jus sanguinis* (associated above all with Germany) and *jus soli* (associated with the Third French Republic).[2] This is not to say that earlier generations were oblivious to the global dimensions of citizenship. Gérard Noiriel, Mary Dewhurst-Lewis or Patrick Weil – to name but a few eminent historians – have all explored legislation and administrative measures created from the late nineteenth century onwards to demarcate the 'boundaries of the Republic' vis-à-vis labour and colonial migrants in the metropole.[3] But it is the vast and steadily expanding literature on citizenship in its colonial and imperial dimension that has recast political exclusion alongside ethnoreligious lines not as a side effect on the margins of mass political participation but as a core feature of modern political history. Emmanuelle Saada's work on French colonial Indochina has explored the presence and persistence of ethnicized and at times racialist tenets in the political thought of the late nineteenth century.[4] More specifically on colonial Algeria, Laure Blévis, Osama Abi-Mershed and Joshua Schreier have all studied the construction,

---

2   Frederick Cooper, *Citizenship, Inequality, and Difference: Historical Perspectives* (Princeton: Princeton University Press, 2018), 41.
3   Mary Dewhurst-Lewis, *The Boundaries of the Republic: Migrant Rights and the Limits to Universalism in France, 1918–1940* (Stanford: Stanford University Press, 2007); Gérard Noiriel, *Le Creuset Francais: Histoire de l'immigration (XIXe-XXe siècle)* (Paris: Seuil, 1988); Patrick Weil, *Qu'est-ce qu'un Français? Historie de la nationalité francaise depuis la Révolution* (Paris: Gallimard, 2004), esp. chapter 2.
4   Emmanuelle Saada, *Empire's Children: Race, Filiation, and Citizenship in the French Colonies*, trans. Arthur Goldhammer (Chicago: The University Press of Chicago, 2012), 100–13.

delineation and administration of religious and ethnic difference through jurisdictional politics.⁵

Moreover, recent scholarship has substantially widened our understanding of what citizenship in the age of empire was, and how it was shaped and negotiated. Michelle Campos's work on the late Ottoman Empire has explored not only the state endeavour of defining and standardizing Ottoman nationality from the 1850s to the 1870s, but the variety of ideas and forms of political participation that emerged around the turn of the twentieth century.⁶ The Ottoman attempt to incorporate heterogeneity into a newly defined body politic was in many ways a counter-model to the French republican model with its strong ancient Greek and Roman influence and its quest for uniformity.⁷ But as recent historiography demonstrates, the bottom-up struggle to retain and revive local culture, religion and language characterized much of the history of colonial Algeria. Historians now increasingly shift their focus from Algeria as seen, portrayed and governed by French scholars, generals, politicians and officials to the social, religious and intellectual life as shaped and experienced by Algerians during the nineteenth and twentieth centuries. The resilience and revival of information and communication channels throughout the Maghrib and the Mediterranean, religious reform movements and an emerging, politicized urban public sphere – all these played a crucial role in circulating ideas of participation, reform and equality before the law, as Fanny Colonna, Omar Carlier, James McDougall, Arthur Asseraf and Charlotte Courreye have shown.⁸

---

5   Joshua Schreier, *Arabs of the Jewish Faith: The Civilizing Mission in Algeria* (New-Brunswick: Rutgers University Press, 2010); Osama W. Abi-Mershed, *Apostles of Modernity: Saint-Simonians and the Civilizing Mission in Algeria* (Stanford: Stanford University Press, 2010); Laure Blévis, *Sociologie d'un droit colonial: citoyenneté en Algérie (1865-1947): une exception républicaine?* (Doctoral thesis, Institut d'Etudes politiques, Aix-en-Provence, 2004).

6   Michelle U. Campos, *Ottoman Brothers: Muslims, Christians, and Jews in Early Twentieth-Century Palestine* (Stanford: Stanford University Press, 2011).

7   As Emile Chabal notes, French republicanism since the late eighteenth century developed 'with little reference to the outside world.' See: Emile Chabal, *A Divided Republic: Nation, State and Citizenship in Contemporary France* (Cambridge: Cambridge University Press, 2015), 11. Nevertheless, references to ancient Greece and Rome informed much of the republican imagery. See: Henri van Effenterre, 'La cité grecque, modèle de la République des Républicains'; Claude Nicolet, 'Citoyenneté française et citoyenneté romaine. Essai de mise en perspective', in *Le modèle républicain*, ed. Serge Berstein and Odile Rudelle (Paris: Presses universitaires de France, 1992), 13-56.

8   Fanny Colonna, *Instituteurs algériens, 1883-1939* (Paris: Presses de la Fondation nationale des sciences politiques, 1975); Omar Carlier, 'Medina and Modernity: The Emergence of Muslim Civil Society in Algiers between the Two World Wars', in *Walls of Algiers: Narratives of the City through Text and Image*, ed. Julia Clancy-Smith et al. (Seattle: University of Washington Press, 2009), 62-84; James McDougall, *History and Culture of Nationalism in Algeria* (Cambridge: Cambridge University Press, 2007); Arthur Asseraf, *Electric News in Colonial Algeria* (Oxford: Oxford University Press, 2019); Charlotte Courreye, *L'Algérie des oulémas: une histoire de l'Algérie contemporaine, 1931-1991* (Paris: Éditions de la Sorbonne, 2020).

Surprisingly, the imprint of the Algerian legal borderland – its legislation, contradictions and political struggles – on the French idea of citizenship has never been systematically investigated. The story most commonly told in the rich and excellent scholarship on jurisdictional politics in colonial Algeria is that of construing difference as category of exclusion. Yet, construing and defining alterity invariably means defining the self. The French body politic of which Algerians – mostly Algerian Muslims – were to be excluded was itself a product of the colonial period.

Crucially, this imprint was not a late by-product of the Algerian War but belonged to the very essence of jurisdictional politics in the French 'trans-Mediterranean state' from early on.[9] Todd Shepard rightly highlighted the annulment of Algerian Muslims' recently obtained French citizenship in 1962 as a moment when the demarcation of within and without was played out with particular vehemence, as French politicians and intellectuals construed a narrative of history in which decolonization was inevitable. Yet, in terms of legal theory and administrative praxis, this moment was in no way revolutionary. Official rhetoric notwithstanding, jurisdictional politics in Algeria never sought 'to make real the principles of race-blind equality'.[10] The definition of rights and belonging along ethnoreligious categories was not a novelty of the Algerian War but a decades-long legal and political endeavour. A racialized idea of citizenship, this book argues, was the product not of colonial counterinsurgency or emergency but of the continuity and norm of colonial governance, not of the crisis of colonialism but of its very making.

Citizenship as institution, citizenship as ideology

One reason why struggles over citizenship were so stubborn and intense was that citizenship itself was in the process of definition and negotiation throughout the Mediterranean during the nineteenth century. In its modern form, citizenship regulates various areas of individual and collective life that were historically governed by a myriad of institutions. Place of residence, political participation, access to certain professions, land ownership, military service and the horizon of one's political belonging – these aspects were successively brought under the

---

9   I borrow the term from Jennifer E. Sessions, *By Sword and Plow: France and the Conquest of Algeria* (Ithaca: Cornell University Press, 2017), 267.
10 Todd Shepard, *The Invention of Decolonization: The Algerian War and the Remaking of France* (Ithaca: Cornell University Press, 2006), 15. See also: 1–15, 56–63, 82–90.

institution of citizenship during the nineteenth century.[11] As late as the 1880s, the *admission à domicile* (leave to reside) was of greater significance than citizenship – a fact that was particularly significant for the sizeable non-French European population in Algeria, and which the French government sought to replace with standardized citizenship.[12]

This was not a uniquely French tendency. As Jessica Marglin shows, throughout the 'Islamic Mediterranean', Ottoman, Tunisian and Moroccan statesmen sought to define imperial nationality in order to limit the reach of legal extraterritoriality and European capitulations that allowed individuals under European protection to be governed by the laws of their protecting country.[13] Previously of secondary significance – a French official in the 1880s estimated that many Spanish and Italian settlers in Algeria did not even know of which nationality they were – citizenship and nationality now became an increasingly central and tangible factor in the lives of individuals and communities. By the early twentieth century, the flexibility and negotiability of legal statuses that had long existed in the heterogenous cities of the Mediterranean vanished. As Will Henley writes, 'nationality was a matter of life and death.'[14]

Colonial Algeria, this book argues, was a crucial site of such developments. Its social reality and legal regime engendered a widely shared perception of French citizenship not as a political frame through which to negotiate questions of cohesion and difference but as a predefined, non-negotiable set of norms and mores that decided on what it meant to be a French citizen and what this status required from its holders. The idea of a deeper, abstract essence underlying the nation's laws had been famously and influentially articulated by Montesquieu in his seminal *The Spirit of Laws* (1748). In a section titled 'Of the laws in their relation with the principles that form the general spirit, the mores, and the manners of a nation', Montesquieu postulated: 'Several things govern people – climate, religion, laws, the government's principles [*maximes*], the examples

---

11 For a political analysis of French citizenship – and citizenship more generally – since 1789 see most notably Rogers Brubaker, *Citizenship and Nationhood in France and Germany* (Cambridge, MA: Harvard University Press, 1992).
12 See most notably proposals to collectively naturalise all non-French Europeans in Algeria: Archives nationales d'outre-mer, Aix-en-Provence (hereafter: ANOM), F80/2043: Projet de loi relatif à la naturalisation des étrangers en Algérie: Exposé des motifs (evidently March 1885); Chambres des Députés, no. 1490, quatrième législature, session de 1887: Proposition de loi ayant pour objet la naturalisation des étrangers en Algérie.
13 Jessica M. Marglin, 'Extraterritoriality and Legal Belonging in the Nineteenth-Century Mediterranean', *Law and History Review* 39, no. 4 (2021): 689–94.
14 Will Hanley, *Identifying with Nationality: Europeans, Ottomans, and Egyptians in Alexandria* (New York: Columbia University Press, 2017), 1. On the Ottoman nationality law see Campos, *Ottoman Brothers*, 60–4.

of past things, mores and manners – of which a general spirit forms itself and emerges.' His conclusion was clear: 'The costumes of an enslaved people are part of its servitude; those of a free people are part of its freedom.'[15] A century later, these assumptions on the centrality of mores and the futility of any attempt to alter them were loaded with legal and administrative substance by French legislation and jurisprudence on Algeria. Officials' and politicians' determination to include Europeans and exclude Algerian Muslims resulted in a tendency to rely on social norms and familial structures to define not only Islam and Muslimness but also what it meant to be a French citizen. The endeavour of defining otherness inevitably involved contrasting it with an increasingly fixed image of the collective self.

As Dipesh Chakrabarty has argued, the colonial quest to apply the assumptions and categories of modern European citizenship – above all the notion of political belonging and participation in the state as paramount – was inevitably and invariably an attempt to eradicate local forms of sociability and solidarity amongst colonized societies. As Chakrabarty aptly observes, the pivot of colonial politics of citizenship and subjecthood was the contrasting of the political community of the Enlightenment – a community composed of rational, self-reflecting individuals – with all other forms of social organization and political decision-making.[16] Therefore, while the 1860s witnessed the coming of local, decentralized forms of participation in metropolitan France, the coercive nature of colonial domination and the hostility to difference thwarted such a possibility in Algeria.[17]

Chakrabarty's observation informs a key argument of this book: that the legal practice of defining difference involved delineating the contours of the French citizen. Citizenship in its colonial dimension developed not as a political institution but rather as an ideology of belonging to which those seeking representation and rights were expected to adhere. It is for this reason that when Algerians began to contest this ideology and demand citizenship in significant numbers in the 1930s, their demand led to a ferocious opposition from Europeans in Algeria, resulting in a political crisis that all but paralysed the colonial administration.[18]

---

15 Montesquieu, *De l'esprit des lois*, in *Œuvres complètes*, vol. II (Paris: Gallimard, 1958), book XIX, chapters IV and XXVII, 558, 574.
16 Dipesh Chakrabarty, *Provincializing Europe: Postcolonial Thought and Historical Difference* (Princeton: Princeton University Press, 2008), 30–4.
17 Sudhir Hazareesingh, *From Subject to Citizen: The Second Empire and the Emergence of Modern French Democracy* (Princeton: Princeton University Press, 1998).
18 See Chapter 5.

The clearest manifestation of French citizenship as ideology was the definition by French jurists and officials of the Islamic *statut personnel* – a term that came to denote the fact of being governed by Islamic civil legislation. Deriving from the notion that France as an occupying force ought not to alter familial structures and religious traditions, French officials, scholars and jurists distinguished between French penal laws, which were applied to all subjects, and the area of Islamic civil legislation, where colonial authorities were far more hesitant. Officials and jurists stressed that matrimonial and sexual matters ought to remain in the realm of Islamic jurisdiction. The *sénatus-consulte* (imperial law) of 1865 institutionalized colonial subjecthood along this distinction, stating that the 'Muslim indigene', while considered to be a French national, was subject to Islamic civil legislation.[19] Crucially, as James McDougall notes, Islamic law and 'customs' were not simply tolerated but 'sharply differentiated from the properly civilised norms expected of citizens, especially in matrimonial and sexual matters.'[20] Cast as contrary to and irreconcilable with the French *Code civil*, the *statut personnel* was the most tangible and concrete formulation of the notion of being Muslim as anathema to being a French citizen.[21]

An important point of reference in the debates and struggles over citizenship and difference was the Algerian Jewish minority, whose significance in the colonial order far exceeded its proportion in Algerian society. At a certain level, this was certainly to do with a series of often competing or even contradicting French assumptions on the similarity and difference between Algerian Jews and Muslims. As Ethan Katz stresses, when French officials, politicians, and commentators thought about Algerian Jews, they often did so in relation to the political and legal status of Algerian Muslims, and vice versa.[22] More substantially, the Jewish minority disrupted the twin pairs of Europeanness-citizenship and indigeneity-subjecthood that emerged in the 1880s. As this book emphasizes, the famous Crémeiux Decree of 1870, by which French citizenship was collectively bestowed on the 34,000 Jews in Algeria at the time, was the product of a local Jewish campaign for citizenship, carried out through petitions in Judeo-Arabic and using a terminology quite different from that of assimilation and acculturation. Contrary to colonial expectations, Judeo-Arabic prevailed and flourished for decades thereafter. The inclusion of an Arabic-

---

19 See Chapter 2.
20 James McDougall, *A History of Algeria* (Cambridge: Cambridge University Press, 2017), 123.
21 For a succinct discussion see: Patrick Weil, 'Le statut des musulmans en Algérie coloniale', *Histoire de la Justice* 1 (2005): 93–109. See also below, Chapters 2 and 4.
22 Ethan B. Katz, 'An Imperial Entanglement: Anti-Semitism, Islamophobia, and Colonialism', *American Historical Review* 123 (2018): 1190–209.

speaking, 'indigenous' population in the *cité française* was the most powerful and constantly visible disruption of the ideology of citizenship.[23]

'It is one thing to want to make all citizens of Utopia speak Utopian, and quite another to want to make all Utopiphones citizens of Utopia. Crudely put, the former represents the French, the latter the German model of nationhood.'[24] This elegant juxtaposition, formulated by Rogers Brubaker in 1992, remains illuminating even as scholarship shifts its attention from the French/German and *jus soli/jus sanguinis* frame to the shaping of citizenship by colonial expansion. Most importantly, it highlights the cultural-ideological element in the demarcation of the French body politic. Rather than an ethnically grounded hierarchy, what guided the mainstream of French colonial thought was the idea of a hierarchy of 'civilizations' as they had developed throughout history. Alongside monogamy, the adoption of French language was repeatedly cast as a precondition of political rights in French colonial thought.[25]

While both the *jus sanguinis* and the *jus soli* principles assume a simple criterion for exclusion or inclusion, the regime of citizenship and naturalization as shaped in Algeria never adhered to such clear institutional definitions. Rather, it was conceived, portrayed and demarcated as a set of values and behavioural norms that colonial subjects were expected to embrace and to adopt if they wished to enter the *cité française*. Indeed, becoming a French citizen was cast as a choice and a process, an 'accession to rights', as legal parlance had it.[26] Consequently, being or in fact 'remaining' a colonial subject was equally portrayed as a choice. It was this notion of citizenship and subjecthood as choice that made the statement 'Never, since 1830, had any measures of racial segregation existed in Algeria' from 1958 conceivable.[27] The formal stipulation in the *séantus-consulte* of 1865 that 'the indigenous Muslim' could become full citizen simply by renouncing Islamic legislation (though itself a false promise, often obstructed by administrative and legal praxis) was the most tangible and durable manifestation of the ideology of citizenship.

---

23 See Chapter 3.
24 Brubaker, *Citizenship and Nationhood*, 8.
25 A still-relevant account of the concept of civilization is that of Lucien Febvre, 'Civilization: Evolution of a Word and a Group of Ideas', in *A New Kind of History. From the writings of Lucien Febvre*, ed. Peter Burke (London: Routledge, 1973), 225–38. See also discussion in Jay Berkovitz, *The Shaping of Jewish Identity in nineteenth-century France* (Detroit: Wayne State University Press, 1989), 47–9.
26 See e.g.: Claude Lazard, *L'Accession des indigènes algériens à la citoyenneté française* (Paris: Libraire technique et économique, 1938).
27 On the *Code noir* see most notably: Louis Sala-Molins, (ed.), *Le Code noir ou le calvaire de Canaan* (Paris: Presses universitaires de France, 2018). See also Chapter 1.

The *cité française*, therefore, emerged from the colonial period not as the sum of all its participants but as a predefined conception of the body politic – a conception which, as Achille Mbembe has aptly observed, negates the very process of the 'production and institution of the nation'.[28] The racialist policies implemented during the Algerian War were but the culmination of a process long in the making. What this culmination meant was that France entered the age of post-colonial migration and unprecedented ethnic, religious and linguistic diversity without a citizenship concept adequate for negotiating difference.

The legal borderland

In a sense, Algeria was to the French polity what Ireland was to Britain or the province of Posen in present-day western Poland was to the German unification movements in the nineteenth century: a geographically proximate territory, where waves of settlement had significantly altered societal, agricultural and demographic structures, whose political status remained ambiguous or unsettled and whose diverse population put the sweeping formal principles of political belonging as formulated in Paris, London or Frankfurt and Berlin into test. This somewhat daring comparison ought not to obfuscate the significant differences between the three cases. Rather, it intends to show that the emerging institution and ideology of citizenship was shaped above all not by philosophical elaboration but by the social and political circumstances of the moment, and that it was often at the margins of European nation-states that the demarcation lines of within and without were drawn and the most dramatic struggles took place.[29]

---

28 Achille Mbembe, 'La République et l'impensé de la « race »', in *La Fracture coloniale. La société française au prisme de l'héritage colonial*, ed. Nicolas Bancel, Pascal Blanchard and Sandrine Lemaire (Paris: La Découverte, 2005), 153.

29 On Germany, Poland, and the province of Posen see: Dieter Gosewinkel, *Einbürgern und Ausschließen: die Nationalisierung der Staatsangehörigkeit vom Deutschen Bund bis zur Bundesrepublik Deutschland* (Göttingen: Vandenhoeck & Ruprecht, 2001), 395–404; Wolfgang Wippermann, '"Gesunder Volksegoismus": Vorgeschichte, Verlauf und Folgen der Polendebatte in der Paulskirche', in *1848 Revolution in Europa: Verlauf, politische Programme, Folgen und Wirkungen*, ed. Heiner Timmermann (Berlin: Duncker&Humblot, 1999), 357–65. On Ireland see David Fitzpatrick, 'Ireland and Empire', in *The Oxford History of the British Empire: The Nineteenth Century*, ed. Andrew Porter (Oxford: Oxford University Press, 1999), 494–501; Kevin Kenny, 'Ireland and the British Empire: An Introduction', in *Ireland and the British Empire*, ed. Kevin Kenny (Oxford: Oxford University Press, 2005), 8–10. Benno Gammerl suggests a similar comparison with the Czech region of the Austro-Hungarian empire: Benno Gammerl, *Untertanen, Staatsbürger und Andere: Der Umgang mit ethnischer Heterogenität im Britischen Weltreich und im Habsburgerreich 1886–1918* (Göttingen: Vandenhoeck & Ruprecht, 2010), 67–8.

This legal borderland disrupted the otherwise clear-cut distinction between metropole and colonies, between parliamentarism and equality before the law on the one hand and sheer, arbitrary power on the other. In contrast to the dramatic struggles over participation, equality and rights that took place in the French slave colony of Saint-Domingue in the 1790s and culminated in the independence of Haiti in 1804, Algeria remained part of France's modern overseas empire throughout the colonial period; and unlike the smaller Caribbean colony of Guadeloupe, where citizenship was bestowed on former slaves in the mid-nineteenth century, colonial subjecthood was upheld in Algeria until the post-war era. Moreover, geographic proximity and dense administrative, political and economic ties across the Mediterranean meant that jurisdictional politics in Algeria shaped the French idea of citizenship far more deeply and lastingly than in such remote and legally separated colonies as Indochina.[30] In a similar vein to other settler societies, the settler population that started to develop in the 1830s and 1840s sought not only to exploit Algerians' land and labour but to institutionalize its privileges through the complete integration of the colony into the metropole.[31]

Due to Algeria's unique position within the French polity, excluding Muslims soon became a normative praxis of French lawmaking. With the formal recognition of Algeria as part of the national territory in 1848, the replacement of the military administration with a civilian one in 1870 and the representation granted to settlers in the French parliament, a powerful narrative of a colony-becoming-province was taking shape. Special legal dispositions designed to exclude Algerian Muslims were written into metropolitan law. This was particularly marked in 1889, when a major reform of French citizenship adopted the *jus soli* principle. While any European born on Algerian soil was automatically made French citizen, a separate article of the *Code civil* specified that separate legislation and 'special dispositions' applied in Algeria, thus excluding the native population.[32]

While the successive regimes in nineteenth-century France were all involved in establishing and cementing the colonial system, this book stresses a uniquely

---

30 On Guadeloupe vs. Haiti see: Laurent Dubois, *A Colony of Citizens: Revolution and Slave Emancipation in the French Caribbean, 1787–1804* (Chapel Hill: University of North Carolina Press, 2012), 7–9. On Indochina see: Saada, *Empire's Children*. See also Weil, *Qu'est-ce qu'un Français?*, 82–91.
31 Susan Pedersen and Caroline Elkins, 'Introduction: Settler Colonialism: A Concept and its Uses', in *Settler Colonialism in the Twentieth Century: Projects, Practices, Legacies*, ed. Susan Pedersen and Caroline Elkins (London: Routledge, 2005), 3–4.
32 'Loi sur la naturalisation, 27 juin 1889', *Journal officiel de la République française. Lois et Décrets*, 28 June 1889, 2977–8.

republican hostility to religious difference from the 1880s onwards. This is not to suggest an inherent anti-Islamism in French republican thought – a view which does not stand a thorough, nuanced inquiry, as Ian Coller has demonstrated.[33] Rather, it was as part of the quest to define the boundaries of participation in the age of mass politics that being Muslim was construed as a counter-model to being a citizen of the Republic. The Second Empire (1851–70) sought to administer religious difference in Algeria by maintaining certain vestiges of local social structures and applying different laws to different populations. Such policies were heavily criticized by the lawmakers of the Third Republic (1870–1940) who, as the work of Fanny Colonna has shown, replaced the caution of the former regime with a quest to standardize and assimilate.[34] By the late 1870s, early plans to colonize Algeria through a steady influx of European settlers were shattered by the small numbers of newcomers and the failure of rural settlement. With a local Muslim population of 2,125,000 in 1872, a French population of 129,000 and an Italian and Spanish population of 115,000, legislation was called for to create the societal and political order which warfare, settlement and demography had failed to deliver.[35] Alongside the 1889 law that made European foreigners French citizens, the 1880s saw a series of new measures designed to keep the Algerian Muslims outside the body politic.

Under the Third Republic, then, Algeria was governed through a permanent state of exception where universal rights were curtailed and reduced to settler privileges. The so-called *Code de l'indigénat*, an extensive body of legislation passed in parliament in 1881, systematized the myriad of semi-martial restrictions and ordinances which had been applied to the Algerian Muslim population since 1830.[36] Giving sweeping powers to administrators and mayors in Algeria and precluding any effective form of metropolitan oversight, the *Code de l'Indigénat* was considered excessive even by its supporters and included a clause requiring parliament to renew it every few years. It was reapproved time

---

33 Ian Coller, *Muslims and Citizens. Islam, Politics and the French Revolution* (New-Haven: Yale University Press, 2020), esp. 2–7.
34 Colonna, *Instituteurs algériens*, 20–1.
35 Kamel Kateb, *Européens, "Indigènes" et Juifs en Algérie (1830–1962): représentations et réalités des populations* (Paris: Institut national d'études démographiques, 2001), 30. To these figures must be added that of the indigenous Jewish population of 34,574.
36 The term *Code de l'indigénat* is somewhat misleading, yet too central to entirely avoid in this book. Unlike the *Code noir*, there was no single legal document officially called *Code de l'indigénat*. Rather, this was a collection of laws, decrees and administrative practices (Olivier Le Cour Grandmaison has aptly termed it a 'juridical monster'). However, due to the wide use of this term in contemporary language and in order to highlight the codification of the *indigénat* under the Third Republic, I do use this term in the following chapters. See: Olivier Le Cour Grandmaison, *De l'indigénat. Anatomie d'un «monstre» juridique: le droit colonial en Algérie et dans l'empire français* (Paris: La Découverte, 2010).

and again over the following decades and became the legal template for colonial policing throughout the French empire.[37]

The contradictions and conflicts of this legal borderland were hardly appreciated by French public opinion throughout much of the colonial period. Unlike the central role of Ireland in British public opinion of the same era, Algeria was absent from the grand narratives and contemporary debates that shaped republican France: the struggle between church and state, the social question, or France's relations with its European neighbours.[38] From the monarchist and conservative right to the revolutionary left, indifference to colonial matters and lack of knowledge of the situation in the colonies spanned – with a few individual exceptions – the entire political spectrum. As this book demonstrates, this silence is a crucial aspect of Algeria's place in French history. It explains not only the sweeping powers and considerable autonomy acquired by administrators, military commanders and settlers throughout the colonial period or the shock and confusion during the Algerian War, but also the limitations of public debates on the colonial legacy after 1962.

A key mechanism of this metropolitan blindness was the tendency to frame the coercion and injustices of the colonial order not as a matter of metropolitan politics or legislation – let alone responsibility – but of illegal 'abuse' by settlers in Algeria. In August 1881, just a few weeks after the National Assembly had passed the repressive laws of the *Code de l'indigénat*, Guy de Maupassant commented on the recent establishment of a *Société de protection des indigènes des colonies* in Paris: 'If the indigenes are in such need of protection, that means that they are oppressed. Who oppresses them? Surely it isn't me. It is therefore the Algerians [denoting the European population in Algeria at the time – the common terms for Algerian Muslims being *musulmans*, *indigènes* or the mostly derogatory *arabes*].'[39] The *Société de protection des indigènes* itself published highly critical accounts on settler society and politics in Algeria. 'The Algerian newspapers are hardly read in Europe', a society member wrote in 1882, 'and that is very fortunate, for [otherwise] we would have often blushed with shame.'[40] As Didier Guignard argues, the framing of 'abuses' and 'affairs' as sporadic excesses of corruption or violence in the late nineteenth and early twentieth centuries

---

37 Laure Blévis, 'La Situation coloniale entre guerre et Paix: enjeux et conséquences d'une controverse de qualification', *Politix* 4, no. 104 (Autumn 2013): 93–8.
38 On this absence and occasional exceptions see: Didier Guignard, *L'Abus de pouvoir dans l'Algérie coloniale (1880–1914): Visibilité et singularité* (Paris: Presses universitaires de Paris Ouest, 2014).
39 Guy de Maupasant, 'Lettre d'Afrique', *Le Gaulois* (20 August 1881), 1.
40 L.H. [Léon Hugonnet], 'Revue de la presse algérienne', *Bulletin de la Société française pour la protection des indigènes des colonies* 1, no. 1 (March 1882): 53.

played a crucial role in approving an otherwise allegedly well-functioning and just system.⁴¹ Metropolitan frustration over Europeans' politics and mentality in Algeria reached its peak in the early twentieth century, as the rise of settler anti-Semitism and thinly veiled autonomism coincided with a shift to indirect rule in the French empire. Senior ministers and colonial officials now referred to settlers as guided by 'chimeric anxieties' or by 'the same theories of inferior races' as those widely associated with Germany after the First World War.⁴² In the high days of the Algerian War, as the metropolitan consensus over Algeria was rapidly crumbling and the right-wing settler terrorist group *Organisation de l'armée secrète* ('Secret Army Organization' – widely known as the OAS) was conducting its last-ditch attacks to prevent Algerian independence, the young Pierre Nora provided a subtle yet damning judgement of settler mentalities in the first sentence of *Les Français d'Algérie*: 'The *Français d'Algérie* do not want to be defended by the metropole, but to be loved by it.'⁴³

It is no coincidence that the two rare exceptions of French commentators who traced the injustices in Algeria to the very structures of the colonial order were also the two most fatalistic ones. In 1882, a colonial administrator and advocate of reform by the name Henri de Lamothe wrote: 'It is a law of history that a state of exception tends to proceed incessantly towards the excesses of its own principles, thus accentuating with every day the antagonism between those who benefit from it and those who suffer. The persistence of abuses engenders interests that form alliances to prevent any reform, *until an internal or external catastrophe knocks down this edifice*.'⁴⁴ Five decades later, Maurice Viollette, the most prominent advocate of reforming the political regime in Algeria, used an astonishingly similar wording. A former governor of Algeria in the 1920s, Viollette was appointed state secretary in the left-leaning Popular Front cabinet and drafted the first official bill to allow for the political representation of Algerians in 1936. Alarmed by the violent opposition of the settler lobby, the inaction of his own government, and the apparent impossibility of implementing reforms in the colony, Viollette warned: 'We are heading towards a catastrophe.'⁴⁵

---

41 Guignard, *L'Abus du pouvoir*, 310–26, 480–93.
42 Adolphe Messimy, 'Les effectifs de l'armée et le service militaire des indigènes algériens (suite)', *Revue bleue* 10, 26 (26 December 1908): 776. For Lyautey's quotation see: Charles-Robert Ageron, *Les Algériens musulmans et la France, 1871–1919* (Paris: Presses Universitaires de France, 1968), 1208. See also Chapter 4.
43 Pierre Nora, *Les Français d'Algérie* (Paris: R. Julliard, 1961), 43.
44 Henri de Lamothe, 'De la Représentation des indigènes', *Bulletin de la société française pour la protection des indigènes des colonies* 1, no. 3 (September 1882): 153. Emphasis added.
45 Quoted in: Charles-André Julien, 'Léon Blum et les pays d'outre-mer', in *Léon Blum chef de gouvernement, 1936–1937*, ed. Pierre Renouvin and René Remond (Paris: A. Colin, 1967), 381–2.

Citizenship as promise – and its limits

'Imperial citizenship', Frederick Cooper has argued, 'was a concept that could capture the imagination of Africans and Europeans in the mid-twentieth century.'[46] Cooper's argument focuses on the reorganization of the French empire as a 'French Union' in 1946, by which former colonial subjects became members of a supranational polity with parliamentary representation in Paris.[47] But his interpretation reflects a wider wave of recent interest in colonial reform in the first half of the twentieth century. Studying 'colonial humanism' and *négritude* in French West Africa and the metropole in the 1920s and 1930s, Gary Wilder has made the case for moving 'beyond the analytic of failure' and exploring colonial reform as an attempt to redefine the relationship between the metropole and the empire an 'imperial nation-state'.[48] Lauren Benton has emphasized the 'legal pluralism' that had characterized European colonial expansion from the fifteenth to the late eighteenth century, deploying complex systems of jurisdictional politics to govern different populations by different laws. It was only by the late nineteenth century that a uniform and standardized legal model became the orthodoxy of colonial rule.[49]

Given the long history of colonial legal pluralism, it is tempting to view imperial citizenship and colonial reform as a prematurely terminated experiment. Yet, as this book argues, colonial rule in Algeria had closed off this possibility long before 1945. To understand citizenship as it was shaped by the colonial order, the following chapters move beyond legalist discussions to situate it within the broader context of sociability and visibility in an embattled public sphere. As Abdallah Laroui observed, 'the essence of the colonial process is in dissolving the indigenous society, only to admit individuals one by one.'[50] Indeed, the colonial principle that Algerians seeking to become citizens should renounce Islamic legislation in familial and matrimonial matters was an extremely high price that was viewed by most Algerians as apostasy and earned those naturalized the reputation of *mtournis* ('turncoats').[51]

---

46 Cooper, *Citizenship, Inequality, and Difference*, 8.
47 Frederick Cooper, *Citizenship between Nation and Empire: Remaking France and French Africa, 1945–1960* (Princeton: Princeton University Press, 2014), esp. chapters 2–4. See also below, Chapter Six.
48 Gary Wilder, *The French Imperial Nation-State: Negritude and Colonial Humanism between the Two World Wars* (Chicago: The University of Chicago Press, 2005), 76.
49 Lauren Benton, 'Colonial Law and Cultural Difference: Jurisdictional Politics and the Formation of the Colonial State', *Comparative Studies in Society and History* 41, no. 3 (1999): 563.
50 Abdallah Laroui, *The History of the Maghrib: An Interpretative Essay*, trans. Ralph Manheim (Princeton: Princeton University Press, 1977), 340.
51 McDougall, *A History of Algeria*, 130–1.

This is not to deny the significance of citizenship as promise, prospect or political horizon in the modern history of empire. As the following chapters argue, in specific historical moments, struggles for representation and rights and battles over the boundaries of citizenship were key to the political life of different groups in Algeria. Jewish petitions for citizenship in the 1860s and a struggle for reform led by various Algerian individuals and groups in the 1920s and 1930s radically contested the French ideology of citizenship-as-assimilation, while settler leaders fought to preserve the demarcation of within and without along ethnoreligious lines. But in order to appreciate the radicalism and the chances of such struggles, we must analyse them not only in their legal-theoretical dimension but rather situate them in the social and political context of the colonial order.

The colonial quest to 'assimilate' Algeria into the metropole was first and foremost an attempt to isolate Algerians from the Maghribi and broader Arab world and to create a French-modelled public sphere. Colonial authorities spent considerable efforts on regulating the movement of Algerian Muslims and Jews across the Maghrib, the Mashriq and the Hijaz. Alongside Muslims' pilgrimage to Mecca, the administration sought to limit the movement of Algerian Jews to the ancient centres of scholarship in Jerusalem, Hebron, Safed and Tiberias.[52] In 1936, Maurice Viollette, while suggesting granting the vote to some Algerian Muslims, warned his government over the alleged dangers of classical Arabic – the language of the Quran which, unlike Maghribi dialects, was understood by scholars throughout the Arab and Islamic world: 'I don't believe we have an interest in facilitating the spread of Arabic in Algeria, particularly of literary Arabic, which would establish direct communication between Algeria, Egypt and Syria.'[53]

Moreover, colonial rule thoroughly reshaped the urban spaces of interaction and exchange. As Zeynep Çelik shows, Algiers was the site of intrusive colonial urbanism which demolished much of the fragile social and economic equilibrium that had developed over centuries.[54] Spatially and politically marginalizing notable families and stripping them of their function as intermediaries between the provincial population and the imperial centres of power, colonial urbanism

---

52 See e.g.: ANOM: F80/1636, Pèlerinage à La Mecque (1842/1858); 81F 835, Pèlerinage à la Mecque, réglementation en matière d'hygiène publique et de transports: textes officiels, notes (1893–1937); GGA 3F 13, Mesure proposée à l'égard des habitants israélites allant en Syrie et en Palestine, 22 March 1845.
53 Archives nationales de France – Pierrefitte (hereafter AN): F/60/729, Maurice Viollette, Note pour le président du conseil [no date, evidently mid-1936].
54 Zeynep Çelik, *Urban Forms and Colonial Confrontations: Algiers under French Rule* (Berkeley: University of California Press, 1997), 26–43.

dismantled crucial mechanisms of political negotiation that had developed in the Ottoman era.⁵⁵ As further cities came under French rule and the influx of European settlers increased, the Algerian urban environment became the most important physical and political site of the nascent settler society. From Oran in the west to Bône and Constantine in the east, new boulevards, public gardens, docks and commercial streets were constructed. In the early twentieth century, French urbanists in Algeria advanced the idea of 'zoning' cities according to different social functions.⁵⁶ The symbolic appropriation of the built environment through the use of street names and monuments added a further level to the exclusion of the local population.⁵⁷ Around the turn of the twentieth century, the Algerian city became not only the setting but a constitutive element of settler politics, culture and identity, as David Prochaska and Peter Dunwoodie show.⁵⁸ Local popular culture celebrated the urban crowd and its distinct dialect as an emerging Mediterranean or Latin 'race' – a trope that had little to do with the (itself naive) cosmopolitanism of Albert Camus's reverie.⁵⁹

Starting in the 1920s, a slow reclaiming of urban space by Algerians was the most significant defiance of the French effort to reshape the public sphere, engendering new conflicts in the ongoing struggle over participation and sociability.⁶⁰ Colonial thinkers and officials now became particularly fixated on the veil as the most visible expression of the alleged seclusion and oppression of Algerian women. Allowing Algerian women to move in the public sphere yet remain unseen, French observers increasingly viewed the veil as a provocation. During the Algerian War, this disruption of the Europeanly shaped public sphere

---

55 James McDougall, 'A World No Longer Shared: Losing the *Droit de cite* in Nineteenth-Century Algiers', *JESHO*, no. 60 (2017): 33–4; Nora Lafi, 'Petitions and Accommodating Urban Change in the Ottoman Empire', in *Istanbul as Seen from a Distance: Centre and Provinces in the Ottoman Empire*, ed. E. Özdalga et al. (Istanbul: Swedish Research Institute, 2011), 73–7.
56 On Bône see: David Prochaska, *Making Algeria French* (Cambridge: Cambridge University Press, 1990). On Constantine and Oran see: Zeynep Çelik, *Empire, Architecture, and the City: French-Ottoman encounters, 1830-1914* (Seattle: University of Washington Press, 2008), 51–62, 75–9. On contemporary ideas of 'zoning' see e.g.: Tony Socard, 'Le zoning urbain', in *Chantiers* (August 1933): 807–12.
57 Jan C. Jansen, *Erobern und Erinnern. Symbolpolitik, öffentlicher Raum und französischer Kolonialismus in Algerien, 1830-1950* (Munich: Oldenburg Verlag, 2013), 243–66.
58 David Prochaska, 'History as Literature, Literature as History: Cagayous of Algiers', *Am Hist R* 101 (1996): 694–9; Peter Dunwoodie, *Writing French Algeria* (Oxford: Clarendon Press, 1999), 83–8. See also Patricia Lorcin, *Imperial Identities: Stereotyping, Prejudice and Race in Colonial Algeria* (Lincoln: University of Nebraska Press, 2014), 198–214.
59 See e.g.: Albert Camus, 'La Culture indigène, la nouvelle Culture méditerranéenne', in *Essais* (Paris: Gallimard, 1965), 1322–5. See also: Michael Herzfeld, 'Practical Mediterraneanism: Excuses for everything from epistemology to eating', in *Rethinking the Mediterranean*, ed. William Harris (Oxford: Oxford University Press, 2005), 45–8. On Europeans' politics in the interwar period see: Samuel Kalman, *French Colonial Fascism: The extreme right in Algeria, 1919-1939* (Basingstoke: Palgrave Macmillan, 2013).
60 Carlier, 'Medina and Modernity', 62–84.

became a veritable battlefield, as the psychiatrist, anti-colonial theoretician and member of the *Front de libération nationale* ('National Liberation Front' – hereafter FLN) Frantz Fanon famously observed: 'After it had been posited that the woman constituted the pivot of Algerian society, all efforts were made to obtain control over her. . . . In the colonialist programme, it was the woman who was given the historic mission of shaking up the Algerian man.'[61]

Against the backdrop of a decade-long effort to dismantle societal structures and isolate Algeria from its history and geography, Maurice Viollette's 1936 reform bill and the ensuing political confrontation between Algerians and Europeans appear as a defining moment in the history of French citizenship. Though Viollette's overall goal was to guarantee the future of the French empire amid mounting nationalism, his reasoning broke with key tropes of French colonial thought. Instead of stagnation and backwardness, he portrayed Algerian society in terms of innovation and change; instead of the common tropes of polygamy and the veil, he sought to deliver a more nuanced account of women in Algerian society.[62] It was during the turbulent years of 1936–8, when Algerians and Europeans in the colony bitterly fought over the boundaries and nature of the Algerian political community, that the scene for an all-out conflict was set. The ideology of French citizenship as shaped by decades of colonial rule precluded any meaningful political negotiation, leaving only one path open – that of total, uncompromising violence.

* * *

Neither the ideology nor the promise of citizenship was ever static. The political battlefield of Algeria in which ideas of inclusion and exclusion were shaped was itself the object of changing policies and approaches throughout the nineteenth and twentieth centuries. The following chapters seek to account both for continuities and turning points, exploring the complex legal entanglements, political ties and intellectual networks that bound the colony with the metropole and turned it into a crucial site in the making of French citizenship. They are arranged around six historical moments, shifts or crises that were particularly formative in the shaping of French citizenship. The first three chapters of this book explore the making of the Algerian legal and political borderland in

---

61 Frantz Fanon, *A Dying Colonialism*, trans. Haakon Chevalier (1959, repr., New York: Grove Press, 1965), 38–9.
62 Maurice Viollette, *L'Algérie vivra-e-elle? Notes d'un ancien Gouverneur général* (Paris: Alcan, 1931), 412–17. See also Chapter 5.

1848; the emergence of ethnoreligious categories of exclusion and inclusion between the 1860s and 1880s; and the dramatic struggle over the nature and boundaries of racialized citizenship during the anti-Semitic crisis of the 1890s. The latter three chapters discuss the growing contestations and deepening crisis of racialized citizenship in the first half of the twentieth century: the debates on conscription and rights of the Algerian population and changing conceptions of colonial governance around the First World War; the Algerian struggle for representation and rights and the French campaigns for colonial reform in the 1930s; and the passing of citizenship as promise in the post-war period.

1

Creating a legal borderland

On 6 March 1848, as the flag of the newly proclaimed Second Republic was hoisted in Algiers for the first time, a group of *ʿulama* (Islamic scholars) formulated a declaration welcoming the new government and expressing their hopes for a new chapter. Signed by *ʿulama*, *qadis* and members of the notability of Algiers, the declaration read:

> Oh God, make forever prosperous the days of the Republic and protect her!
> . . .
> All men are united in praising the people's sovereignty.
> How fortunate we are to live under a government that knows neither hatred nor envy,
> Under which no one is deprived of his rights,
> But where everyone is free! . . .
> We have long been neglected . . .
> Those of us who once lived in opulence today have almost nothing to exist; and those who, until recently, had the douceurs of comfort are now reduced to all the horrors of poverty.
> We hope, oh generous government, that you will lend us a compassionate glance,
> And that you will bring an effective remedy to our pains [maux]!
> We pray the great God to grant you immortal duration,
> And to crown with success all your endeavours![1]

With only a French translation of unknown source available to us, it is impossible to explore the nuances and exact terminology of this declaration. We do not know what were the Arabic terms which are translated here as 'Republic' or 'people's sovereignty', nor do we have any additional sources

---

1   Reprinted in French translation in *Le Nouvelliste*, 18 March 1848, 2.
On the republican flag being hoisted see report in *Le Moniteur algérien*, 5 March 1848, 1.

with which to contextualize the declaration.² Yet, the juxtaposition between a sinister past and hopes for a better future and the hundreds of signatures reportedly added to it by notables in the following day give us a glimpse into an atmosphere of uncertainty, excitement and indeed hope in Algiers following the fall of the July Monarchy.³ In the preceding eighteen years, colonial warfare and dispossession had brought unmeasurable destruction, repeated famines and a rapid population decline to Algeria.⁴ Just two months before the declaration of the Second Republic, Abd al-Qadir ibn Muhyi al-Din al-Hasani (commonly referred to in French sources and literature as 'emir Abdelkader'), who had led the strongest armed resistance to the French conquest in western Algeria since the early 1830s, surrendered, leaving the generals of the *Armée d'Afrique* with practically unchallenged military power over the country and its inhabitants.⁵ Drawing on the long political tradition of the *shikayat* (complaints) in Ottoman times – a form of direct communication between provincial elites in the Sublime Porte – the notables of Algiers portrayed this interplay of destruction, defeat and revolution as a moment out of which a new chapter may emerge.⁶

The government's position, however, could have hardly been more dismissive. In an address to 'the Arabs and Kabyles, grand and humble', the newly appointed governor Eugène Cavaignac warned: 'Do not listen to those who will tell you: things have changed for you, for this will only bring you misfortune.'⁷ Seeking to stress the continuity of government, Cavaignac portrayed the ousting of King Louis-Philipp as a smooth process by which 'the French nation . . . has changed in common accord its form of government'. A veteran of occupation warfare in Algeria and perpetrator of several massacres of civilians, Cavaignac had been personally engaged in the fighting against Abd al-Qadir. He now portrayed the enemy's surrender as a 'sign of God', adjuring Algerians to obey the new

---

2   One term that was in use in the Arab and Ottoman world at the time was *jumhur*. See: Wael Abu-'Uksa, 'Concepts of "Democracy" and "Republic" in Arabic in the Eastern and Southern Mediterranean', *Journal of the History of Ideas* 80, no. 2 (2019): 253–5. Another term, known from Judeo-Arabic writing, was *al-République*. See, for example, the Oran-based newspaper *La Voix d'Israël*, 15 November 1889, 1. See also Chapter 3.
3   *Le Nouvelliste*, 18 March 1848, 2.
4   Kateb, *Européens, 'indigènes' et juifs*, 60–5. See also William Gallois, *A History of Violence in the Early Algerian Colony* (New York: Palgrave Macmillan, 2013).
5   For a succinct discussion of Abd al-Qadir's 'Islamic sovereignty' see McDougall, *A History of Algeria*, 58–72. The next major revolt would break out in 1871. There were, of course, revolts on a smaller scale after 1848. See most notably Julia Clancy-Smith, *Rebel and Saint: Muslim Notables, Populist Protest, Colonial Encounters (Algeria and Tunisia, 1800–1904)* (Berkeley: University of California Press, 1997).
6   On the Ottoman *shikayat* and their afterlife in colonial Algeria see: McDougall, 'A World No Longer Shared'.
7   Émile Carrey (ed.), *Recueil complet des actes du Gouvernement provisoire (février, mars, avril, mai 1848)* (Paris: Auguste Durand, 1848), part II, text no. 215, 281–2.

government as they obeyed its predecessors: 'Like those who have preceded us, we wish to change nothing in your laws, your mores, your rituals [usages].'[8] Though promising that the new government would guarantee 'even better than in the past' the peace and prosperity of the country, the overall message was clear: In matters concerning the local population, the republican government had no intention to bring about any change.

This was a stark contrast to the Republic's promises to the European settlers. As early as 2 March 1848, the provisional government addressed the *colons* in Algeria in a declaration rejecting the toppled government's alleged indecision concerning the future of the colony. 'The Republic', the provisional government pledged:

> will defend Algeria as the very soil of France [comme le sol même de la France]. Your material and moral interests shall be studied and satisfied. The gradual assimilation of the Algerian institutions into those of the metropole is being considered by the [est dans la pensée du] provisional government; it shall be the object of serious deliberations at the National Assembly.[9]

These two declarations encapsulated the political order which the Second Republic was about to establish in Algeria and which, over the next decades, would turn it into the key legal borderland in which the boundaries of French citizenship would be drawn. In the National Assembly's debates on the legal status of Algeria, the grievances and hopes expressed so powerfully by the *'ulama* in the early days of the Republic found no echo at all. What was at stake in this fundamental debate over the character and modus operandi of French sovereignty was the franchise and liberties of French settlers, who demanded that the military administration be replaced by civilian laws and authorities and that Algeria be 'assimilated' into the metropole. In contrast to the abolition of slavery in the colonies and the granting of the vote to the 'indigenous' populations of the 'old colonies' in the Caribbean, Senegal and La Réunion, the governments of the Second Republic remained widely indifferent to the question concerning Algerians' political status.[10] Algerian society existed in this deliberation only as

---

8   Ibid. On Cavaignac's involvement in colonial warfare and massacres (*'enfumades'*) see: Frederick A. de Luna, *The French Republic under Cavaignac, 1848* (Princeton: Princeton University Press, 1969), 45–52.
9   Carrey (ed.), *Recueil complet des actes du Gouvernement provisoire (février, mars, avril, mai 1848)*, part I, text no. 62, 43.
10 Article 6 of the 1848 constitution stated: 'Slavery cannot exist on any French soil'. See: https://www.conseil-constitutionnel.fr/les-constitutions-dans-l-histoire/constitution-de-1848-iie-republique (accessed 14 March 2022). On Senegal and the other 'old colonies' see: Catherine Coquery-Vidrovitch, 'Nationalité et citoyenneté en Afrique occidentale française: Originaires et citoyens dans le Sénégal colonial'. *The Journal of African History* 42, no. 2 (2001): 285–305.

a menacing entity, a foreign element incompatible with republican sovereignty and thus a winning argument in the hands of those opposing the establishment of full civilian rule in the colony and fearing an imbalance of power between the metropole and the colony. With the return of popular participation mechanisms under the new republic and the government's pledge to 'assimilate' Algeria, the question of how to administer difference turned from a mere colonial issue into a matter of national interest.

The year 1848, then, was a key moment in the long history of Algeria as a terrain of exception within the French state. Historians have long referred to 1848 as an early impulse of the colonial 'assimilation' of Algeria into the metropole, mentioning above all the constitution of the Second Republic as the first legal document that declared Algeria to be part of the French national territory.[11] Yet, as we shall see, the constitution of November 1848 remained ambivalent on Algeria. Shaped by fears of secessionism and decades of debates on uniformity and difference in the French empire, the constitution represented a compromise between settler interests and fears of integrating a non-European territory into the Republic. Treating Algeria as *sui generis* alongside the metropole and the colonies and leaving it for future 'particular laws' to define the exact contours of its legal regime, the 1848 constitution created a pattern in defining Algeria's legal order as undefined and enshrined in law its position as a legal borderland between metropole and empire.

One and indivisible?

The Algerian legal-political order that this book analyses was in many ways the product of older patterns and tropes of French political thought. The questions debated by politicians and generals in 1848 concerning Algeria – settler representation, secessionism, the treatment of the local population – had preoccupied their predecessors in the early days of the French Revolution. Like earlier generations, the *quarante-huitards* declared the Republic to be 'one and indivisible' while avoiding any phrasing that would eliminate the jurisdictional distinction between the metropole and the colonies.[12] To understand the origins

---

11 See most notably Charles-André Julien, *Histoire de l'Algérie Contemporaine: La conquête et les débuts de la colonisation 1827–1871* (Paris: Presses universitaires de France, 1964), 353.
12 Constitution of 1848, préambule. See: https://www.conseil-constitutionnel.fr/les-constitutions-dans-l-histoire/constitution-de-1848-iie-republique (accessed 14 March 2022).

of the legal ambiguity institutionalized in Algeria by the Second Republic, we must go back to the revolutionary decade of the 1790s.

Different laws had applied to France and its colonies under the Old Regime since the late seventeenth century; the 1685 *Code noir* was legislated precisely for that goal, exempting the colonies from the ruling of French courts almost a century earlier that 'there are no slaves in France'.[13] Yet, the universalist language of the French Revolution and the definition of the French polity in all constitutions from 1791 onwards as 'one and indivisible' raised the question whether such distinctions ought to be upheld. The constitution of 1795 was the first legal document to abolish all particular laws in the colonies, declaring: 'The colonies are an integral part of the Republic and are subjected to the same constitutional law'.[14] Yet, the constitution was short-lived and was suspended following Napoléon Bonaparte's coup d'état of 1799. The tension between the attempt to create a 'one and indivisible' regime of legal uniformity, so central to French republican thought, and the social realities in the colonies would preoccupy French politicians for decades.

The most dramatic tensions between metropole and colonies were played out in France's largest slave colony of Saint-Domingue. The universality of rights, settler privileges and representation, fears of secession – all these had been bitterly fought over during the 1790s by the colony's different populations: slaves, free people of colour and slave-owning planters. In July 1789, a delegation of colonists set off to Paris and forced its way into the National Assembly. The most heated controversy at this stage concerned not Saint-Domingue's enslaved population – there were practically no voices in favour of immediate abolition, with even prominent abolitionists insisting this was a measure for the future – but rather settler franchise and the legal status of free people of colour. Creating a *fait accompli* of settler representation in the metropole, the Saint-Domingue delegation demanded that universal suffrage did not apply to the free people of colour in the colony, claiming that this would undermine whites' authority over slaves. At the same time, a second delegation, representing free people of colour,

---

13 See esp. articles 12, 13, 39, 58 and 59 regulating the legal status of slaves, free people of colour, and children born of mixed marriages in Sala-Molins' annotated edition: Sala-Molins, *Le Code noir ou le calvaire de Canaan*. On the legal questions around slavery in France und the Old Regime see: Sue Peabody, *There Are No Slaves in France: The Political Culture of Race and Slavery in the Ancien Régime* (Oxford: Oxford University Press, 1996), chapter 1.
14 Constitution of Year III (1795), Article 6. See: https://www.conseil-constitutionnel.fr/les-constitutions-dans-l-histoire/constitution-du-5-fructidor-an-iii (accessed 14 March 2022).

made its way to Paris and made the case for the political rights of non-white, slave-owning planters.[15]

In May 1791, after months of evasion and following uprisings in Saint-Domingue, the National Assembly carried a heated debate on the reach of universal principles and the colonies' legal status. 'The colonies do not resemble France; this truth cannot be misunderstood by anyone. They cannot have the same internal regime, nor the same organisation', argued the deputy for Martinique and would-be chronicler of Saint-Domingue Moreau de Saint-Méry.[16] The Radical deputy and future mayor of Paris Jérome Pétion de Villeneuve responded: 'Are the colonies a separate state? . . . If a part of the kingdom demanded the initiative of [making its own] laws and reduced you [the National Assembly] to the almost nil function of confirming them, wouldn't you say that such a demand aimed at the dissolution of the empire?'[17] Robespierre called the colonists' deputation a 'seditious faction which threatens to set your colonies aflame, to dissolve the bonds that unite them with the metropole if you do not approve their pretentions!'[18] The debate finally yielded a decree that gave political rights to free people of colour born to free parents but which excluded freedmen. It was not until April 1792 that the French government accorded full political rights to all free people of colour.[19] As for abolition, the first measure was taken as late as August 1793, when colonial officials in Saint-Domingue, in a desperate attempt to win over insurgent slaves who had sided with Spain, published on their own initiative a decree abolishing slavery in the colony – a decree which the National Convention approved six months later.[20] The uprisings, revolution and abolition in Saint-Domingue, followed by the 1804 declaration of the independent Republic of Haiti by former slaves, made the Caribbean the earliest site in which questions of citizenship and colonialism were negotiated.[21]

Of course, a lot had changed between the dramatic events in the Caribbean at the turn of the nineteenth century and the Second Republic's debates on Algeria half a century later. At a geopolitical level, after losing most of its possessions

15 Laurent Dubois, *Avengers of the New World: The Story of the Haitian Revolution* (Cambridge, MA: Harvard University Press, 2005), 80–5.
16 *Archives parlementaires de 1787 à 1860* (Paris, 1862–1896), vol. 25, 639. On Moreau de Saint-Méry see: Dubois, *Avengers of the New World*, 8–11.
17 *Archives parlementaires de 1787 à 1860* (Paris, 1862–1896), vol. 25, 641.
18 *Archives parlementaires de 1787 à 1860* (Paris, 1862–1896), vol. 26, 8.
19 David Geggus, 'Introduction', in *The Haitian Revolution: A Documentary History* (Indianapolis: Hackett, 2014), xvii–xix.
20 See documentation in Geggus, *The Haitian Revolution: A Documentary History*, 107–9, 112.
21 On debates on slavery and citizenship see: David Geggus, 'Racial Equality, Slavery, and Colonial Secession during the Constituent Assembly', *The American Historical Review* 94, no. 5 (1989): 1290–308.

in the Americas and the Caribbean, France had turned its attention to the Mediterranean, first through Napoléon's expedition to Egypt in 1798 and, thirty years later, through the conquest of Algiers. It was this reorientation and a sense of continuity that the provisional government sought to evoke in a proclamation to the soldiers of the *Armée d'Afrique* from 2 March 1848: 'The republican government which France has given itself had brought to the African soil half a century ago the colours under which you have fought eighteen years ago.'[22] At a political and intellectual level, the new colonial empire was portrayed as a contrast to that of the Old Regime. The 'turn to empire', to quote Jennifer Pitts, the endorsement of overseas expansionism by various liberal thinkers in Europe in the late eighteenth and early nineteenth centuries, dwelled precisely on contrasting the archaic and inhumane system of trans-Atlantic slave trade with a modern, efficient, liberal empire, one that would flourish due to the hard work and private capital of entrepreneurs and rural settlers.[23]

Moreover, it would be inaccurate to depict the assumptions and objectives with which politicians and generals approached the Algerian question in 1848 as part of a static or monolithic French orthodoxy concerning Muslims and Islam. As Ian Coller has shown, the eighteenth century witnessed, alongside exaggerations, prejudices and inaccuracies – most notably Montesquieu's caricatured depiction of Islamic 'despotism' in his *Persian Letters* – a flourishing of publications that elaborated on the progressive character of the Prophet Muhammad or the enlightened character of Islamic legislation. During the Revolution, deputies' views of Islam and the extent to which it was compatible with the liberties and institutions of the new political entity they were seeking to define varied from rejection and scorn to profound admiration. When the First Republic was proclaimed in 1791, the Regency of Algiers – itself referred to as 'republic' in some contemporary French accounts – was amongst the first powers to endorse it, a fact which was appreciated by several press articles in France.[24] The Algiers expedition in 1830 and the military and legal instruments of domination that followed were the product of specific political circumstances under the Restoration and the July Monarchy, as Jennifer Sessions has shown,

---

22 Proclamation du Gouvernement provisoire à l'Armée d'Afrique, 2 March 1848, in *Recueil des actes du Gouvernement de l'Algérie, 1830-1854* (Algiers: Imprimerie du gouvernement, 1856), 549.
23 Jennifer Pitts, *A Turn to Empire: The Rise of Imperial Liberalism in Britain and France* (Princeton: Princeton University Press, 2006), especially chapters 6-7. For an example from Algeria see, for example, E. Delpech de Saint-Guilhem, *Adresse de la délégation de l'Algérie aux Chambres* (Paris: Imprimerie de Rignoux, 1847), 7.
24 Coller, *Muslims and Citizens*, 17–20, 62–81, 125–7.

and not a linear continuation of the *Code noir* and the controversies over Saint-Domingue.[25]

Yet, the key questions on uniformity and difference between metropole and empire remained open on the eve of the Second Republic. Perhaps no political figure incorporated these ongoing controversies as the self-declared liberal essayist and parliamentarian Alexis de Tocqueville. Though his writings on Algeria were not as widely read as his famous celebration of American society and politics in *Democracy in America*, Tocqueville made Algeria a central issue of his political agenda, travelling there twice during his parliamentary career between 1839 and 1851 and becoming one of the Chamber of Deputies' experts on the colony. A staunch advocate of French presence in North Africa, Tocqueville initially envisioned a new civilization that would emerge out of an 'amalgamation' of Europeans and Algerians and argued that France should create a regime of legal pluralism during the first phase of its colonial rule in Algeria. This was much in line with the mainstream of colonial thought in the 1830s. In 1833, for instance, an inquiry commission warned the government from the 'dangerous illusion' that Algeria could be assimilated into the metropole.[26] During the 1840s, however, Tocqueville's interest shifted to the consolidation of a separate settler society as means of solidifying French sovereignty in the colony, rejecting the 'restricted occupation' strategy of the 1830s and propagating a total war against Abd al-Qadir. He argued that settlers' security and property – though not political liberties – must be protected against the arbitrariness of the military administration.[27] In a report commissioned by the Chamber of Deputies in 1847, Tocqueville insisted on the necessity and urgency to create legal clarity for the settlers in Algeria: 'The European population has arrived . . . Now, it is about deciding under which laws it should live and what should be done to accelerate its development.'[28]

Tocqueville's writings represented a broader controversy over the role of settlers and the extent to which landed property, nature resources and local labour should be subjected to their interests. What historians have long referred to as a clear-cut contrast between 'assimilation' and 'association' represented in fact in the 1840s different emphases of the modes of colonial governance in

---

25 Sessions, *By Sword and Plow*, esp. chapter 1.
26 Abi-Mershed, *Apostles of Modernity*, 38.
27 These remarks were made in an essay from 1841 which remained unpublished until 1962. See English translation in: Jennifer Pitts (ed.), *Alexis de Tocqueville: Writings on Empire and Slavery* (Baltimore: Johns Hopkins University Press, 2001), 56–66.
28 Alexis de Tocqueville, 'Rapport fait à la Chambre des députés (. . .), 1847', in *Œuvres complètes*, vol. 9 (Paris: Imprimerie Simon Raçon, 1866), 425. On Algeria's place in Tocqueville's political thought see: Jennifer Pitts, 'Introduction', in *Alexis de Tocqueville*, ix–xi, xxii–xxiv.

its encounter with difference.[29] While 'assimilation' denoted settlers' demand that French civil laws be applied to Algeria, thus giving them quasi-unlimited access to and power over land and natural resources, 'association' implied a more gradual mode of consolidating French sovereignty. Drawing on the philosophy of the French social reformer Saint-Simon, prominent officials and advisors such as Prosper Enfantin and Thomas Ismaÿl Urbain propagated a certain tolerance towards social, cultural and religious difference, arguing that only a regulated contact or 'association' between the French state and the Algerian population would eventually bring about the acculturation and 'civilization' of native society – a programme 'that aimed to enhance and invigorate the political and cultural autonomy of native Algeria merely to reduce it more completely in the end', as Osama Abi-Mershed has observed.[30] Recognizing the catastrophic consequences of French rule, Saint-Simonians sought to govern the colony through a caste of intermediaries and to shield Algerian society from some of the colonial state's most penetrative measures. This logic underlay the royal ordinance of 1845, which divided Algeria into civilian, military and mixed territories, barred Europeans (in most cases) from settling in the military zone and subordinated the military territories to the *Bureaux arabes*, still dominated at this time by Saint-Simonians.[31] The most notable exception to this policy was the Jewish population, which from 1845 onwards was subjected to direct French administration and 'assimilation' politics, culminating, as we shall see in the next chapter, in the collective bestowal of citizenship in 1870.[32]

That was the political legacy and administrative reality in March 1848: a political and military elite in deep, ongoing disagreement over the meaning of key legal concepts such as representation, sovereignty and territorial integrity, pledging to 'assimilate' a territory divided into three zones and subjected to different laws. Rather than clarifying these ambiguities, debates in Paris over the following months all but cemented them in the legal and political regime of Algeria.

---

29 See most notably: Raymond Betts, *Assimilation and Association in French Colonial Theory, 1890–1914* (New-York: Columbia University Press, 1961); Raoul Girardet, *L'idée coloniale en France de 1871 à 1962* (Paris: Editions de la Table Ronde), 1972.
30 Abi-Mershed, *Apostles of Modernity*, 118.
31 Ibid, 107.
32 Valérie Assan, *Les Consistoires israélites d'Algérie au XIXe siècle:L'alliance de la civilisation et de la religion* (Paris: Armand Colin, 2012); Schreier, *Arabs of the Jewish Faith*; Lisa Moses Leff, *Sacred Bonds of Solidarity: The Rise of Jewish Internationalism in nineteenth-century France* (Stanford: Stanford University Press, 2006).

Making settlers' Algeria

Ambivalent though it was, the 'gradual assimilation' policy nevertheless introduced settler participation in the Republic, thus shaping the relations between Algeria and the metropole for decades to come. Though short-lived – settler participation was abrogated following the coup d'état of 1851 – this was a symbolic milestone, a development that brought together the two strands that were now at work in Algeria: settler colonialism and republicanism. Yet, to some deputies and colonial officials, this represented an alarming development that might jeopardize French sovereignty in Algeria. After all, the late eighteenth and early nineteenth centuries were the age of settler secessionism in the Atlantic world, stretching from the Thirteen Colonies in North America to the series of independence wars against the Spanish and Portuguese empires in the south. The fears and warnings expressed in the 1848 debates of the National Assembly concerning power imbalance between the metropole and Algeria and even the scenario of secessionism foreshadowed some of the key controversies over citizenship and participation that would follow in the 1880s.

Settlers in Algeria greeted the new republican government with great expectations. The demand to be ruled by French civil laws and to participate in making them, which had predominated settler public opinion throughout the 1840s, was being articulated with great vigour on the eve of the 1848 revolution, with petitions urging the government to 'give Algeria civilian institutions', to establish a permanent Algerian delegation to the Chamber of Deputies, apply civil legislation and extend municipal and departmental organization to the colony, and even to naturalize European settlers as French.[33] The newly proclaimed republic, many now hoped, would usher in a new age. In the European cafés of Oran, petitions with the demand for an immediate 'reunion and assimilation of Algeria and France' were circulating in the first days of March.[34] In Algiers, Governor Cavaignac, himself an avowed republican, dissolved the former, 'Orleanist' municipality and convoked a new one with stronger republican representation. He allowed settlers to plant 'liberty trees' – a well-known symbol of the French republican tradition – but ordered that the massive equestrian statute of the Duc d'Orléans, a leading figure of the conquest war, be left intact at the *Place du gouvernement*.[35] In May, an 'Algerian congress' was founded as a

---

33 de Saint-Guilhem, *Adresse de la délégation de l'Algérie aux Chambres*, 6, 8–14. For further examples see: McDougall, *History of Algeria*, 102–3.
34 *La Liberté*, 19 March 1848, 3.
35 de Luna, *The French Republic*, 121–2.

forum in which Europeans in Algeria could discuss 'all political and financial questions concerning Algeria'.[36]

In late March, a delegation of *colons* from Algeria arrived in Paris to demand the immediate 'assimilation' of the colony. The delegation was received at the Hôtel de Ville by Adolphe Crémieux, the famous liberal Jewish lawyer and politician, now serving as Minister of Justice in the provisional government. Crémieux had been advocating the extension of French sovereignty to Algeria since the 1830s, not least through the assimilation of the local Jewish minority. His enthusiastic statement to the settler delegation encapsulated much of the reasoning, terminology and colonial fervour of the early days of the Second Republic:

> Citizens – I don't dare say of Algeria, for I would be lying to myself, but rather French citizens, residents of Algeria: none of you could doubt that the provisional government has the strongest and firmest intention to make you ... Frenchmen equal in rights to the Frenchmen of the continent ... France is Algeria, Algeria is France. It is the dream and intention of the provisional government to declare this assimilation, and rest assured that the decree proclaiming it will be for the government the accomplishment of a duty. It is not, citizens, because politics demand it, but because fraternity wants it ... It is not because necessity requires it, but because our hearts desire it. You are Frenchmen like us, we are brothers. And when the Republic proclaims fraternity, how should it forget a portion of our fellow citizens?[37]

Stressing that he had been calling for the 'assimilation' of Algeria long before the 'glorious revolution' of 1848, Crémieux asked the delegation to spread the word amongst settlers in Algeria that 'Paris is Algiers' and that 'the complete and absolute reunion of Algeria as a French *département* is the wish of France'.[38]

However, settlers in Algeria did not wait for the government's approval when founding a series of new newspapers once the Second Republic was proclaimed. The press landscape in Algeria had been evolving rapidly since 1839, when the first French-language newspaper, *L'Akhbar*, was founded. French-language press expanded with the growth of the settler population in the 1840s, leading to the foundation of *L'Echo d'Oran* and *La Seybouse* in Bône in 1844, which had a few hundreds of subscribers each. In 1847, the administration founded the first Arabic-language newspaper, *Mobacher* – a newspaper which emerged

---

36 Julien, *Histoire de l'Algérie contemporaine*, 350.
37 *Le Constitutionnel*, 31 March 1848, 3.
38 Ibid.

from officials' belief in the power of the printed word in the 'moral conquest' of Algeria, as Arthur Asseraf notes, but which, by the 1870s, was reduced to printing official decisions and decrees.[39] When, on 13 March 1848, Governor Cavaignac applied to Algeria the provisional government's laws on press freedom, he was merely 'regulating a *fait accompli*', as a governmental report from 1850 on the settler press put it.[40]

With the lifting of restrictions on the press and political gatherings, settler political activity in Algiers and Oran flourished in a series of new associations or *clubs*.[41] A crucial moment for this nascent settler public sphere was the first parliamentary election in colonial Algeria in April 1848. On 12 March 1848, the provisional government published its instructions concerning the upcoming parliamentary elections and their organization in Algeria. Mayors in the colony were instructed to put together the electoral lists which, like in the metropole, were to include all male French citizens (both by birth and by naturalization) aged 21 or older.[42]

Yet, as the newly constituted National Assembly began to debate the legal status of Algeria, the controversy concerning the colony's 'assimilation' surfaced again. On 15 June 1848, just before workers' protests in Paris directed the nation's attention once again to the social question, two deputies for Algeria proposed that the Assembly should adopt a decree reading: 'The territory of Algeria is an integral part of the French territory, and the French in Algeria are governed by the same Constitution as the French in the continent.'[43] But opposition to this motion – particularly concerning the more concrete application of laws to French nationals in Algeria – was very strong. The *rapporteur* of the committee debating Algerian affairs in the Assembly suggested referring this question to

---

39 Asseraf, *Electric News in Colonial Algeria*, 35-7.
40 Lettre du ministre de la Guerre au ministre de la Justice, 24 April 1850, cited in: J. Bonnardot, 'La presse algérienne sous la Seconde République (février 1848–décembre 1851)', *1848 et les révolutions du XIXe siècle*, 38, no. 180 (June 1948): 27. Newspapers founded in Algeria in 1848–1849 included the *Sentinelle républicaine*, *L'Afrique française*, *Le Journal de Constantine*, *Le Brûlot de la Méditerannée* (replaced by *L'Atlas* in 1849), *Le Démocrate de Blidah*, *Le Courrier d'Oran*, and *Le Courrier de Bône*. See: Bonnardot, 'La presse algérienne sous la Seconde République (février 1848–décembre 1851)', 31-3; Pierre Boyer, 'La Vie politique et les élections à Alger', in *La Révolution de 1848 en Algérie*, ed. Marcel Emerit (Saint-Deni: Éditions Bouchène, 2016 [Paris 1949]), 45. For Cavaignac's decree on press freedom see: 'Arrêté qui rend applicable à l'Algérie les lois et ordonnances qui régissent la presse en France', 13 March 1848, in *Recueil des actes du Gouvernement de l'Algérie, 1830-1854* (Algiers: Imprimerie du gouvernement, 1856), 553. Special clauses allowed him to censor news concerning military affairs.
41 Boyer, 'La Vie politique et les élections à Alger',, 43-5.
42 Bibliothèque nationale de France, FOL LE8 89 BIS: Instructions du Gouvernement provisoire pour l'exécution, en Algérie, du décret du 5 mars 1848, relatif aux élections générales.
43 'Assemblée nationale, présidence de M. Senard, séance du 15 juin', cited in *Journal des débats politiques et littéraires*, 16 June 1848, 2. The deputies were Louis Leblanc de Prébois and Alexandre Polagnie de Rancé.

the commission preparing the constitution and adopting a more declarative statement defining Algeria as an integral part of the national territory.[44] However, even this declarative statement was opposed by some deputies, most notably by Cavaignac, now serving as Minister of War, and his fellow veteran of the war of conquest in Algeria, Louis Juchault de Lamoricière (Lamoricière would soon come to replace Cavaignac as Minister of War, as the latter was made head of the executive power).

Cavaignac first mentioned the danger of secession. He argued that should the French population in the colony grow as one hoped and were to be subjected to the same laws as in France, Algeria would soon be sending 'forty, fifty, or a hundred' deputies to the Assembly – a development that would tip the balance of power between the colony and the metropole. 'We can certainly assume that different and perhaps hostile interests might emerge between the mother country and the colonies.'[45] Beside secessionism, Cavaignac expressed concern over integrating a colony into the Republic whose population was not purely European or even French. 'We cannot prevent . . . that the considerable foreign populations mix with our nationals. We cannot prevent . . . that with time the indigenes assimilate into the European population, either partially or entirely.'[46] As reactions to his speech showed, this was a widely shared concern in the Assembly.[47]

But the most interesting – and ambivalent – utterances were those made by Lamoricière, who reminded his fellow deputies that the debate on extending sovereignty and civil authority to Algeria could not ignore the presence of the Algerian population of two and a half million people. Drawing on his colleagues' historical reference to colonization in the Americas, he remarked, with a unique mixture of honesty and chillingly dispassionate cynicism:

> I ask what happened to the Indians. They were persecuted and massacred without pity; so much that they have disappeared completely from the American soil. . . . We do not want to destroy [écraser] or to break [broyer] the Arabs, thus we must keep them. And as they are almost as numerous as the European population, we will have in Algeria two sorts of citizens. The legislation must therefore be made appropriate for this condition . . . Without doubt, Algeria must have its

---

44 Ibid. The *rapporteur* was Christophe Bertholon.
45 Ibid., 3.
46 Ibid.
47 See for instance deputy Guichard: 'Let no one tell us that Algeria, this African soil, covered by barbarians, will be a French soil.' 'Assemblée nationale, présidence de M. Senard, séance du 16 juin', cited in *Journal des débats politiques et littéraires*, 17 June 1848, 3.

institutions and laws, but I do not want them to be the same institutions and the same laws as in France.[48]

Official rhetoric notwithstanding – the June 1848 debate resulted in the declaration that 'Algeria is forever a French territory' – the government's policies in the following months deepened the division of administration and attribution of responsibilities alongside ethnoreligious lines.[49] On 16 and 20 August, Cavaignac, now head of the executive power, issued a series of fiats that extended the authority of the Ministers of Public Instruction, Justice and Religious Affairs to the European and the local Jewish population in Algeria, while the Minister of War and the governor general retained their authority over the Algerian Muslims.[50] A further fiat from August 1848 created communes and established elected municipal councils in Algeria's civil territory. While Algerians and non-French Europeans residing in Algeria could elect and be elected alongside French citizens, their total number could not exceed a third of the municipal council and they were excluded from the posts of mayor and deputy mayor. But even such restrictions did not satisfy all settlers. In 1850, a member of the municipal council in Oran resigned in protest over the fact that 'the indigenous Jews, the Moors, the blacks and the foreigners' were allowed to elect and be elected without renouncing the 'habits of their past.'[51]

The constitution of November 1848 institutionalized this duality and made it permanent. It referred to three different types of French territories: the metropole, the colonies and Algeria, thus cementing Algeria as a legal exception in the French political system. Both Algeria and the colonies were given representation in the National Assembly, but only voters in Algeria were allowed to join those in the metropole in electing the Republic's president.[52] Most important, the 1848 constitution stated: 'The territory of Algeria and the colonies is declared to be a French territory *and will be ruled by particular laws until a special law will place them under the regime of the present constitution.*'[53] These 'particular laws' came in December in the form of decrees that redefined the administrative organization of Algeria. The division of the Algerian territory into civil and military territory was reaffirmed, giving civil prefects the authority

---

48 'Assemblée nationale, présidence de M. Senard, séance du 16 juin', cited in *Journal des débats politiques et littéraires*, 17 June 1848, 4.
49 Ibid.
50 Julien, *Histoire de l'Algérie Contemporaine*, 351.
51 Ibid., 352.
52 Constitution of 1848, articles 21 and 46, respectively. See: https://www.conseil-constitutionnel.fr/les-constitutions-dans-l-histoire/constitution-de-1848-iie-republique (accessed 14 March 2022).
53 Ibid., article: 109. Emphasis added.

over the newly created *départements* of Oran, Algiers and Constantine while leaving generals in charge of the corresponding military territories.[54]

This gap between solemn declarations and jurisdictional-administrative practices and particularities, between principles acknowledged in the present and measures to be taken in an always undefined future would dominate colonial thought and governance in Algeria for decades. In 1873, as yet another nascent republic was drafting its constitution, a settler representative from Algiers castigated the Second Republic for its indecision concerning the assimilation of Algeria. 'Let us hope', he wrote, 'that the new republican constitution will lead us out of this impasse in which the constitution of 1848 and that of the [Second] Empire have kept us for so long.'[55] Almost a century after the 1848 constitution was adopted, debates on citizenship and participation under very different circumstances would engender a strikingly similar formulation of temporality and exceptionalism. The 1946 Constitution of the Fourth Republic stated: 'All residents [ressortissants] of overseas territories (Algeria included) possess the quality of citizens ... *Particular laws will establish the conditions in which they will exercise their rights as citizens.*'[56]

The legacy and myth of 1848

Beyond legislation and political theory, the Second Republic played a crucial role in introducing Algeria into French popular imagery. Hundreds of workers and political convicts were transported and deported to Algeria in the autumn of 1848, giving rise to a legacy and above all a myth of ardent republicanism transplanted to the colony. Visions of a new society that would emerge on the southern Mediterranean shore had been an important feature of French popular culture throughout the 1830s and 1840s, as Jennifer Sessions stresses.[57] Algeria had been repeatedly described as a fertile land waiting to be salvaged from centuries of alleged desertion and degradation under Muslim and Ottoman influence and to restore its past Roman glory, while social reformers portrayed

---

54 Julien, *Histoire de l'Algérie Contemporaine*, 353.
55 Augustin Pierre Joseph Louis Liautaud, *La République de 1848 en Algérie* (Algiers: Juillet Saint-Léger, 1873), 36–7.
56 *Journal officiel de la République française – Lois et décrets*, 8 May 1946, 3888. Emphasis added. For a detailed discussion of the 1946 constitution see Chapter 6.
57 Sessions, *By Sword and Plow*, 179–206.

rural settlement in Algeria as remedy to the ailments of urban, industrial life.[58] With a new terminology of assimilation and settler participation, with political convicts expelled and workers setting off to the colony singing 'To the shores of Algeria, workers, let us turn our steps', the well-rooted tradition of colonial settlement as social reform received a renewed and strong impetus.[59]

During the turbulent summer and autumn of 1848, as workers took to the streets of Paris in protest over the closure of the National Workshops, which had provided work to many of them and were brutally repressed by troops led by the generals of the *Armée d'Afrique*, numerous petitions to the National Assembly turned to Algeria as a solution to the nation's social conflicts. Drafted by groups and individuals of diverse backgrounds and political inclinations, they elaborated on questions of sovereignty, citizenship and colonial settlement, foreshadowing the fundamental debates and eventually the major reform of French citizenship in the 1880s. A 'Plan to colonise Algeria by associations' from September 1848, for instance, presented some novel ideas concerning the relation between land, labour and rights: 'It should be decreed . . . that every emigrant [to Algeria], whichever nation he belongs to, will exercise in Africa the rights of French citizen and will become French once he has proved, after a certain period of residence, that he colonises, that is, that he cultivates.'[60] As the authors stressed, their vision was for the American model of *jus soli* to apply to Algeria rather than the *jus sanguinis*, which regulated French citizenship at the time:

> The nationality for the settlers, that is, a homeland rather than a foreign land; a fixed and durable residence [établissement] rather than a journey or an exploration; the condition and rights of citizen rather than the undefined, unsettled, repeatedly disrupted of the man who visits and only wishes to exploit a land which isn't his: that is the fundamental basis of colonisation, and the United States have recognised this, allowing every individual to the colonies to become American.[61]

---

58 Thomas Dodman, *What Nostalgia Was: War, Empire, and the Time of a Deadly Emotion* (Chicago: Chicago University Press, 2018); Diana K. Davis, *Resurrecting the Granary of Rome: Environmental History and French Colonial Expansion in North Africa* (Athens: Ohio University Press, 2007). This is of course a recurring trope with many sources. See for instance: *Note sur la colonisation de l'Algérie, présentant les moyens d'élever nos possessions d'Afrique à un haut degré de force et de prospérité, sans grever le budget. (Signé : M. Amarana. 15 décembre 1848)* (Saint-Quentin: Imprimerie de A. Moureau, s. d.), 14.
59 Bibliothèque nationale de France: Charles Bailly, 'Le Départ pour l'Algérie', Paris 1848. Reference: YE 55471–92.
60 *Pétition à l'Assemblée nationale. Projet de colonisation de l'Algérie par l'association (signé : E. de Solms, E. de Bassano)* (Paris: Imprimerie. de É. Proux, 1848), 7. Emphasis added.
61 Ibid., 8.

The wish to create a politically homogenous and committed settler population was also evident in a petition submitted by a certain aristocrat from the Pelet de Beaufranchet family, who suggested constructing dozens of new settlements, whose residents would all be subjected to conscription.[62]

In August 1848, a petition signed by fifteen engineers, entrepreneurs and land surveyors 'on behalf of 20,000 families' suggested colonizing Algeria by creating new, cooperative associations. Following the recent closure of the National Workshops, the signatories wrote, 'the eyes turn naturally to Algeria . . . as a promised land, to receive and save from despair all those who suffer today of famine.'[63] For those unemployed workers, the petitioners suggested creating groups of 200–50 families guided by experts and coordinated by the state who would create 'workshops of colonisation': 'Workshops today, in a few years they will become well-established villages [solidement établis], defended by an energetic militia, populated by laborious citizens, committed to order [attachés à l'ordre] by the lines of property and family, and glorifying with their gratitude the motherly benevolence of the Republic.'[64] Another petition, though less elaborate, also argued that by giving colonization a 'particular social character', the Second Republic would demonstrate the conquest of Algeria by France to be 'one of the greatest events' of the century.[65]

Inevitably, this republican-colonial fervour gave a renewed impetus to the dispossession of Algerians. A petition submitted to the National Assembly by a certain Faure-Daniels captured much of the outburst of popular enthusiasm that now sought to take hold of large swathes of land in Algeria. Calling to 'Colonise! Colonise!' the Mitidja, the author admitted with clear frustration that this region was not vacant:

> 'The state can only distribute land [to settlers] where no one made a claim of possessing it . . . We know that the toppled [déchu] government did not spare any measure to prevent the development of prosperity, that the colonisation has always been paralysed in the hands of certain rogues whose action was full of [couvert de] royal ordinances.'[66]

---

62 A. Pelet de Beaufranchet, *Projet de colonisation générale de l'Algérie* (Paris: Imprimerie de Poussielgue, 1848), 14.
63 Pétition et projet de colonisation en Algérie par associations temporaires, présentés au nom de 20,000 familles, Août 1848 (Paris: Typ. A. Appert, 1848), 'Exposition' (non-paginated).
64 Ibid.
65 A. Gardot, *De la Colonisation de l'Algérie par le concours politique de la France et de l'Espagne*, handwritten, 1848, 1.
66 *Projet de colonisation en Algérie, adressé aux citoyens Représentants du Peuple, par le citoyen Faure-Daniels*, Riom: E. Leboyer, 1848, 9.

The ordinance of 15 April 1845 did limit Europeans' settlement to the civil territories of Algeria. Yet, another ordinance from the same year, issued during the war against Abd al-Qadir, explicitly permitted the appropriation and colonization of land whose inhabitants had fled. It nevertheless defined some criteria and procedures that prevented an unlimited dispossession.[67] It was these remnants of protection of Algerians' rights over their land that the petitioner – evidently himself a *colon* – sought to eradicate: 'We men of the country ... have no doubt that when it will come to populating the entire Mitidja, the Republic will implement a reorganisation of the [ownership of] land that will guarantee the general prosperity.'[68] Needless to say, this 'general prosperity' was reserved for French settlers. In the early 1870s, a similar interplay of a recently quelled insurgency, a newly proclaimed Republic and a fervour to colonize would engender similar demands to lift restrictions on the use of sequestrated land. In the months following the brutal repression of Al-Muqrani's revolt in Kabylia in early 1871, the nascent Third Republic sought to settle hundreds of families from Alsace-Moselle, recently lost to Germany in the Franco-Prussian war, thus eliminating, ignoring, or circumventing the remaining legal protections of Algerians' rights.[69]

In September 1848, the National Assembly responded to these growing calls across the political spectrum to send unemployed workers to Algeria. On 19 September, the Assembly adopted a governmental plan that outdid all previous colonization schemes.[70] Presented by Lamoricière, the new plan sought to settle 12,000 workers in Algeria by the end of the year and to construct new colonial settlement over the next three years with a budget of 50 million francs. While the government avoided adopting the cooperative associations scheme presented on behalf of workers' families, the new plan was clearly a product of the revolutionary conditions, embracing much of the popular and social reform vocabulary of the time. Unlike previous schemes, all French citizens were eligible to participate in the 1848 scheme of state-sponsored colonization, regardless of whether or not they possessed any capital. The government committed to financing all costs and to lease to new settlers plots of 2–10 hectares, of which they could become the owners after three years. Within three weeks, no less than

---

67 Ordonnance de 1845, titre II, chapitre 4. See: *Le Moniteur algérien*, 25 Novembre 1845, 4.
68 Projet de colonisation en Algérie, adressé aux citoyens Représentants du Peuple, par le citoyen Faure-Daniels (Riom: E. Leboyer, 1848), 9.
69 See for instance debates within the Algerian administration: ANOM F80/1810: Extrait du procès-verbal du conseil du gouvernement, séance du 22 juin 1872.
70 Jennifer E. Sessions, 'Colonizing Revolutionary Politics: Algeria and the French Revolution of 1848', *French Politics, Culture & Society*, no. 1 (2015): 90–2.

36,000 workers in Paris alone applied for this scheme, leading the government to extend the number of participants to 13,500.[71] These rural settlers were joined, less than two years later, by hundreds of political convicts from the workers' uprising of June 1848, giving rise to a powerful historical myth. A century later, during the centenary celebrations of 1848, historian Marcel Emerit would note that 'when one interviews the descendants of the *colons* of 1848, it is rare for them not to claim that they descend from the "*déportés*". They are very proud of it. In reality, in almost all cases their ancestors were free settlers.'[72]

The first convoy, comprising 843 workers, left on 8 October 1848, from the quay of Bercy outside Paris, heading to the new agricultural settlement of Saint-Cloud near Oran. Minister of War Lamoricière, after handing a flag to the convoy's leader, praised the workers leaving for the 'new France'. The priest of Bercy gave the settlers his benediction, while a worker led the group with singing.[73] Though we do not know what exactly was sung on this occasion in Paris, other songs from 1848 give us a glimpse into a vocabulary of patriotism, republican conviction, worker radicalism and repeated emphases of Algeria now being part of France. 'Let us leave for Algeria, this beautiful land that is also our homeland', read a song titled 'The Departure to Algeria', praising 'a popular government respond[ing] to the wishes of the citizens, and abolish[ing] the misery of workers without property.'[74] Another song, entitled 'Song of the *colons*', read:

> You who, over there [là bas] offer us these swathes of land
> We swear to you that, worthy of such possessions,
> All of the children of our young companions,
> Sons of labour, shall be good citizens;
> They will grow up to become, one day, useful
> Like the seeds on the shores which we populate.[75]

Who were the unnamed addressees of these lines? Were these the soldiers of the *Armée d'Afrique* who, as the song's author wrote, 'had written their names with blood' on the Algerian soil? Were these settlers already residing in Algeria?

---

71 Julien, *Histoire de l'Algérie Contemporaine*, 364–7.
72 Marcel Emerit, 'Les Déportés du Juin', in *La Révolution de 1848 en Algérie*, ed. Marcel Emerit (Saint-Denis: Éditions Bouchène 2016 [Paris 1949]), 59. On the deportation of the June 1848 convicts see: Julien, *Histoire de l'Algérie Contemporaine*, 358.
73 *Journal de Toulouse*, 13 October 1848, 2–3. De Luna, *The French Republic*, 287–8.
74 Bibliothèque nationale de France: Charles Bailly, 'Le Départ pour l'Algérie', Paris 1848. Reference: YE 55471 92.
75 Bibliothèque nationale de France: Prosper Blanchemain, 'Chant des colons', Paris 1848. Reference: YE 55472 470.

Or was it a rare, implied recognition that the Parisian workers were about to settle in a land populated and cultivated by others? Like future generations of lawmakers, commentators and writers, the republicans of 1848 were well-aware – though mostly through simplifications and misconceptions – of the social, economic and agricultural structures in the colony they sought to colonize and 'assimilate'. The story of Algeria as a legal borderland is the story of scholarly, political, cultural – some might say psychological – mechanisms of overlooking the obvious reality of Algerians' presence and the various modes of commercial, agricultural, religious and political organization that underlay it. These mechanisms would become increasingly intricate in the following decades, as colonial governance shifted its focus from seizing the land to defining the boundaries of citizenship and subjecthood in Algeria.

2

Subjects and citizens, 'Muslims' and 'Europeans'

In September 1882, the journalist, colonial reform advocate and future colonial official Henri de Lamothe published an article on 'The Representation of the Indigenes'. Deploring the series of laws of exception adopted by the National Assembly a year earlier concerning Algeria and which would soon become known as the *Code de l'indigénat*, de Lamothe wrote:

> Wherever a privilege of one race exists, there exists hostility and the legitimate instinct of revolt amongst the victimised race . . . To counter the menacing eventualities which the upholding of an unnatural regime [régime contre nature] can bring about at any moment, we will [inevitably] feel compelled to incessantly augment the power of those holding authority, to multiply the laws of exception. Already now disciplinary powers have been decided upon, collective punishment is being demanded and the convicts of the Arab insurrections are denied amnesty; tomorrow, these means will be deemed insufficient. Some might recommend even more draconian propositions, like those we see surface from time to time in the columns of certain newspapers in Constantine. Later, one may come to advocate – as was done from 1832 in the entourage of the then governor general Duke of Rovigo – mass extermination or expulsion to the desert.[1]

Though neither a rebel nor an outsider – he would go on to become the governor of Senegal and a prolific commentator on questions of colonial governance – de Lamothe, nevertheless, grasped a legal-political development that most of his contemporaries failed to acknowledge. The myriad of intermediary categories and ever-extended 'temporary' clauses that had been put in place in Algeria since the 1860s, de Lamothe argued, amounted to nothing less than a permanent state of exception, one that was not a static situation but rather a constant escalation. 'Citizen or outcast [paria], that is the alternative we face. There is no middle, the indigene will inevitably be either the former or the latter', de Lamothe analysed

---

1 de Lamothe, 'De la représentation des indigènes', 153–6.

in a rare and widely overlooked recognition that subjecthood and citizenship could not be defined in disjunction from one another.[2] The simultaneous, interrelated construction of French citizenship and colonial subjecthood in the late nineteenth century is discussed in the following pages.

De Lamothe's analysis stemmed from a broader shift in the mode of colonial domination between the 1860s and 1880s: from settlement and land seizure to jurisdictional politics. The early 1870s had seen the last major scheme of 'official' colonization. In a nationalist replay of 1848, a major state-sponsored colonization scheme, propagated by the aristocracy and the high bourgeoisie, once again sought to introduce Algeria into the national imagery by resettling there the nation's suffering heroes – this time the 'war victims' from Alsace-Lorraine, annexed by Germany in 1871 following the Franco-Prussian war.[3] With a prospect of tens of thousands of new settlers, this new scheme meant a renewed wave of dispossession in the aftermath of the major revolt led by Al-Muqrani in the Algerian east in early 1871. By settling newcomers in strategic locations, the Algerian administration hoped to prevent future uprisings in the Algerian east.[4] Yet, the scheme failed to yield the expected influx of new settlers. With only a few thousand new arrivals from Alsace-Moselle, most of whom soon despaired and returned to France, even the leading figures behind the scheme became disillusioned with colonial settlement by the early 1880s.[5] In 1881, Governor Louis Tirman told the *Conseil supérieur* of the Algerian administration: 'As we no longer have any hope of augmenting the French population by means of official colonisation, we must seek the remedy in the naturalisation of foreigners.'[6]

The emergence of jurisdictional politics as a key instrument of colonial domination engendered new concepts of inclusion and exclusion. As this chapter argues, despite different modes of colonial governance applied by the Second Empire and the Third Republic, the years between 1865, when colonial subjecthood was legally defined, and the major citizenship reform of

2 Ibid.
3 For references to settlers from Alsace-Moselle as 'war victims' see most notably: Auguste Warnier, *L'Algérie et les victimes de la guerre* (Algiers: Imprimerie Duclaux, 1871).
4 See e.g.: ANOM, GGA L10: Extrait de la délibération du comité consultatif de colonisation, 26 October 1871.
5 On the Alsace-Lorraine settlement scheme see: Fabienne Fischer, *Alsaciens et Lorrains en Algérie: histoire d'une migration, 1830–1914* (Nice: Gandini, 1999), 105–14; Alfred Wahl, *L'Option et l'émigration des Alsaciens-Lorrains: 1871–1872* (Paris: Ophrys, 1974), 201–8; Charles-Robert Ageron, *Histoire de l'Algérie contemporaine*, vol. II (Paris: Presses Universitaires de France, 1979), 72–6. On leading figures of the project disillusioned by colonial settlement in the 1880s see Comte d'Haussonville, 'La colonisation officielle en Algérie – II', in *Revue des deux Mondes* 58, 1 July 1883, 102.
6 Cited in: Alfred Dain, *Étude sur la naturalisation des étrangers en Algérie* (Algiers: Adolphe Jourdan, 1885), 3–4, note 1.

1889 constituted a development by which the boundaries of within and without were increasingly drawn along the categories of Europeanness and Muslimness.[7] The 'republican renaissance' of the 1860s and the proclamation of the Third Republic in 1870 gave the politics of citizenship and participation renewed impetus.[8] With the Third Republic, a civilian colonial administration answering directly to the minister of the interior was established and a settler deputation to the parliament was restored. With the return of mass political participation in France re-emerged the urgency to demarcate the body politic.

Scholarship since the early 2000s has done much to explore the emergence of French republican hostility to Islam in the nineteenth and twentieth centuries. Todd Shepard has approached colonial legislation and politics as 'modes of representation' of deeply rooted tropes of 'sameness' and universality in French political thought since 1789.[9] Naomi Davidson has traced the legal and scholarly mechanisms of 'inscribing' difference onto the bodies of Muslims, thus construing a 'biologized' notion of Islam.[10] What remains surprisingly overlooked, however, is that the very meaning, conditions and implications of being a French citizen were equally the objects of ongoing negotiation in the age of nation-state building and colonial expansion.

To some extent, the 'invention of the "indigene"', as Laure Blévis has aptly described the creation of colonial subjecthood in 1865, represented a broader tendency in European colonial thought to cast Islam and Muslims in ethnic and even racialist terms.[11] This racialization of Islam, as Cemil Aydin has argued, was crucial in the emergence of the view of 'the Muslim world' as a coherent, clearly marked ethnic-religious entity.[12] It was indeed the support and sympathy of the entire 'Mohammedan races' with their 'solidarity amongst themselves . . . despite [geographic] distance' that Emperor Napoléon III hoped to gain when formulating the principles of what would soon become a cornerstone of

---

7   On the contrast between the Second Empire and Third Republic in Algeria, see e.g.: Charles-Robert Ageron, *L'Algérie Algérienne: De Napoléon III à de Gaulle* (Paris: Sindbad, 1980), esp. chapter 3; Gavin Murray-Miller, 'Bonapartism in Algeria: Empire and Sovereignty before the Third Republic', *French History* 32, no. 2 (2018): 249–70.
8   Gavin Murray-Miller, 'Imagining the Trans-Mediterranean Republic: Algeria, Republicanism, and the Ideological Origins of the French Imperial Nation-State, 1848–1870', *French Historical Studies* 37, no. 2 (2014): 303–30.
9   Shepard, *The Invention of Decolonisation*, 12. Shepard uses the word 'sameness' in inverted commas.
10 Naomi Davidson, *Only Muslim. Embodying Islam in twentieth century France* (Ithaca: Cornell University Press, 2012), 4–5.
11 Laure Blévis, 'L'invention de l'« indigène », Français non citoyen', in *Histoire de l'Algérie à la période coloniale*, ed. Abderrahmane Bouchène et al. (Paris: La Découverte, 2012), 212–18.
12 Cemil Aydin, *The Idea of the Muslim World: A Global Intellectual History* (Cambridge, MA: Harvard University Press, 2017), 3.

colonial governance: the *sénatus-consulte* (law ratified by the Senate in the First and Second Empire) of 1865.[13] Late nineteenth-century Algeria was certainly an important site of the racialization of Muslims and Islam.

Yet, at the same time, jurisdictional politics in colonial Algeria shed light on the mutual, dialectical process by which subjecthood and citizenship, exclusion and inclusion, Frenchness and foreignness were defined in relation to one another. While the *sénatus-consulte* of 1865 is rightly considered as the legal document which institutionalized colonial subjecthood, it also established certain, though deeply unequal legal plurality in Algeria: full French citizens, European nationals entitled to French citizenship, and colonial subjects, comprising 'indigenous' Jews and Muslims. By 1889, a series of laws and decrees replaced this plurality with the twin dichotomies of Europeanness/Muslimness and citizenship/subjecthood. Jurists, officials and commentators set to define and demarcate French citizenship in this way to prevent any claim for rights and participation from Algerian Muslims. While France in principle embraced *jus soli* in its new citizenship law of 1889, legal theory and jurisprudence in Algeria now cast 'European' versus 'Muslim' origin as central criteria of participation and inclusion. With its diverse population and ambiguous legal order, the Algerian borderland left a deep ethnic imprint on the modern French idea of citizenship.

Defining colonial subjecthood

The *sénatus-consulte* of 14 July 1865 set in motion a long political and legal development, by which citizenship and subjecthood were defined along religious and later ethnoreligious categories. Together with a *sénatus-consulte* from 1863 regulating the ownership and selling of land in Algeria, it was a cornerstone of the Second Empire's colonial policy and an important element of Emperor Napoléon III's 'Arab kingdom' programme of breaking away from the assimilationist tendencies of 1848 and governing Algeria through separate laws and institutions.[14] Yet, as we shall see, this attempt at governing Algeria separately was made impossible by the presence of a large European population

---

13 Napoléon III, *Lettre sur la politique de la France en Algérie: adressée par l'Empereur au Maréchal de Mac-Mahon . . . gouverneur général de l'Algérie* (Paris: Imprimerie Impériale, 1865), 23–4.
14 On the sénatus-consulte of 1863 see Didier Guignard, 'Conservatoire ou révolutionnaire? Le sénatus-consulte de 1863 appliqué au régime foncier d'Algérie', *Revue d'histoire du XIXe siècle*, no. 41 (2010).

and the growing pressure to demarcate the French body politic by defining the legal status of the different populations in Algeria.

The principles of the *sénatus-consulte* of 1865 were formulated by Napoleon III upon his return from a journey to Algeria in June of that year. In the preceding months, a series of revolts had broken out throughout the country. An estimated number of 8,000–10,000 Algerians took up arms against the French administration between February 1864 and the early months of the following year from Mostaganem in the west to Al-Milia in the east and from Algiers in the north to the Sahara in the south.[15] In a lengthy and damning account, Napoléon III summarized his impressions from his visit and outlined a series of legal and administrative reforms. 'It was a grave mistake to apply to Algeria laws made solely for countries such as France, where culture is advanced, the property [regime] is defined, and the population numerous', Napoléon wrote.[16] Instead, he argued, France must win Algerians' 'sympathy': 'What policy would be better suited for France than to give in its own estates to the Mohammedan races . . . the undeniable guarantees [gages] of tolerance, of justice, and of respect to difference in mores, religion and race?'[17] These 'guarantees' were formulated in a list of twenty-nine proposed measures to be taken, the first of which was to

> 'declare that the Arabs are French, for Algeria is a French territory, but that they will continue to be governed by their civil status, conforming to the Muslim law; that, nonetheless, the Arabs who will want to be admitted to the benefit [benefice] of the French civil law will be, upon their demand, without conditions of probation [conditions de stage], invested with the rights of French citizens.'[18]

This proposition was adopted with almost the exact same wording in the text of the *sénatus-consulte* that was ratified by the Senate on 14 July 1865. In three articles, this legislation divided the non-French population in Algeria into three distinct categories – Muslims, Jews and (European) foreigners – and defined their legal status:

> 1st Article: The Muslim indigene is French; nonetheless, he will continue to be governed by Muslim law. . . . He may, upon his demand, be admitted to exercising rights as French citizen [jouir des droits de citoyen français]; in this case, he is governed by the civil and political laws of France.

---

15 Annie Rey-Goldzeiguer, *Le Royaume arabe: La politique algérienne de Napoléon III, 1861–1870* (Algiers: Office des publications universitaires, 2014), 275–302.
16 Napoléon III, *Lettre sur la politique de la France en Algérie*, 23–4.
17 Ibid., 11.
18 Ibid., 33.

2nd Article: The Jewish indigene [l'indigène israélite] is French; nevertheless, he continues to be governed by his personal status [statut personnel] . . . He may, upon his demand, be admitted to exercising rights as French citizen [jouir des droits de citoyen français]; in this case, he is governed by the French law.

3rd Article: The foreigner who proves three years of residence in Algeria may be admitted to exercising all the rights of a French citizen.[19]

The jurists, officials and lawmakers of the Second Empire explained the upholding of Jewish and Muslim civil law as a measure of tolerance and respect towards religious difference, a fulfilment of France's commitment to allow its subject to practise their religion as formulated in the surrender treaties of the 1830s. The procedure of individual naturalization, for its part, was the product of the 'association' school of colonial governance, an option left open for those 'indigenes' willing to accept the full scope of French legislation in matrimonial and sexual matters. Louis-Hugues Flandin, the *rapporteur* who presented the *sénatus-consulte* to the senate, expressed these ideas neatly in his introduction to the legislation. On the one hand, he praised the new legislation as one that 'puts an end to all uncertainties, to all controversies' and contrasted the 'benevolent' government of Napoléon III with the disruptive Second Republic, claiming that 'the Arabs' in Algeria were taking notice of the stark difference between the two regimes. On the other hand, he described the new legislation as part of France's attempt to establish sovereignty in Algeria through the 'patient and continued work of assimilation, of progressive initiation into the benefits of civilisation'.[20]

Yet, what lawmakers and commentators described as 'respecting' difference was in fact a far more intrusive process of construing a hierarchy of laws and mentalities as the basis for a new legal regime in Algeria. As Michael Brett has argued, the *sénatus-consulte* of 1865 'on the one hand ascribed to the Muslim population an inferior status . . . [and] on the other hand . . . defined that inferiority as a product of Islam'.[21] In an introduction and explanation of the *sénatus-consulte* to the senate on behalf of the commission that examined the law, senator Delangle elaborated the question of religious difference in French legislation. Drawing on Montesquieu's argument that 'it is the folly of conquerors

---

19   ANOM, F80/2043: Bulletin des lois no. 1315: No. 13,504 – Sénatus-consulte sur l'état des Personnes et la Naturalisation en Algérie, 14 July 1865, 177–8.
20   Reprinted in: Charles-Louis Pinson de Ménerville, *Dictionnaire de la législation algérienne: code annoté et manuel raisonné des lois, ordonnances, décrets, décisions et arrêtés*, vol. II (Paris and Algiers: Challamel and A. Jourdan, 1877), 151, note 1.
21   Michael Brett, 'Legislating for Inequality in Algeria: The Senatus-Consulte of 14 July 1865', *Bulletin of the School of Oriental And African Studies* 51, no. 3 (1988): 441.

to wish to give their laws and customs to all peoples', Delangle argued: 'The same law cannot suit nations of different origin and mores . . . The dissemblance of minds [esprits] as they are shaped by education, climate, or the way of living cannot adapt to a same rule . . . In order not to slip into tyranny, one must respect the differences which nature and Providence themselves have created.'[22] But this 'respect' was a double-edged sword. For, as Delangle explained, if Algerian colonial subjects chose to solicit full citizenship according to the provision of the *sénatus-consulte*, this would mean losing any special 'rights' that Islamic law prescribes: 'From this moment, it is both the same rights and the same duties [that apply to them].' This, Delangle implicitly admitted, would mean a high price for Algerian Muslims and would affect their life both in the private and the public sphere:

> If the [Islamic] status they abandon engenders rights [droits] and traditions [usages] which are incompatible with the general propriety [pudeur publique], the morale or the proper structure of families, such rights are made null. The acceptance of French citizenship constitutes the most formal renunciation [abdiaction] of such rights. There cannot exist on the soil of the homeland citizens having contradictory rights.[23]

Such arguments were not uncontested. In a letter sent to Governor Patrice de MacMahon during the consultations preceding the *sénatus-consulte* of 1865, the president of the Imperial Court of Algiers, Alfred Pierrey wrote:

> Today, France has a single civil legislation for all subjects [régnicoles], but the time isn't distant when she counted as many different statuses as provinces. Prior to the accomplishment of the standardisation of our civil law, the inhabitant of Normandy, that of Brittany, of Bourgogne, of Auvergne, of Languedoc were French of the same status [titre], but each had his own civic law.[24]

Following this reasoning, Pierrey proposed in early 1865 the following regulation for a new law on citizenship and naturalization in Algeria: 'The Muslim indigène who will obtain the quality of French citizen will retain his civil rights [droits

---

22   Delangle, report on the *sénatus-consulte* of 1865, reprinted in: Pinson de Ménerville, *Dictionnaire de la législation algérienne*, 155. For original quote by Montesquieu see: *Considérations sur les causes de la grandeur des Romains et de leur décadence*, Texte établi par Édouard Laboulaye (Paris: Garnier, 1876), 174.
23   Delangle, report on the *sénatus-consulte* of 1865, reprinted in: Pinson de Ménerville, *Dictionnaire de la législation algérienne*, 155.
24   Report by Pierrey from 20 April 1865 as quoted in: ANOM, F80/2043: Premier président de la cour impériale d'Alger au Gouverneur général, 1 July 1867.

civils] as regulated by Muslim law. He will not be subjected to French civil law unless he formally expresses his wish in his naturalisation request.'[25]

Pierrey's propositions were a fascinating exception. His suggestion that France should return to a regime of legal pluralism ran counter to the fundamental principle of standardization as implemented and enshrined in the *Code civil* of 1804. Moreover, it implied the almost heretical idea of tolerating polygamy within the French community of citizens. Monogamy and the rejection of child marriage had long belonged to the very core of French civil legislation, as Judith Surkis notes. As early as 1801, during the preparatory debates on the *Code civil*, the jurist Jean-Marie Portalis stated that 'the multiplicity of husbands or wives may be authorised in certain climates, but is legitimate in none'.[26] While the Second Empire witnessed the coming of new ideas of decentralization and local forms of participation, as Sudhir Hazareesingh shows, such ideas were mostly confined to the metropole.[27] Pierrey's propositions were an unusual theoretical experiment attempting not merely to contain difference but to imagine a reorganization of the imperial body politic so as to accommodate it.

The debates on citizenship and naturalization in 1860s Algeria set in motion a long process by which religion, family structure, language and mores were codified and construed as criteria of political exclusion and inclusion. Already in 1862, the court of Algiers ruled that, even though a population conquered by France was in principle French with all rights and duties, exceptions may be made in case of profound differences between the conquering and the conquered population in the areas of 'religion, mores, the constitution of marriage [and] the organisation of the family'.[28] This ruling rested upon the interpretation of the surrender treaties of Algiers and Constantine, which guaranteed the right of the conquered to exercise their religion and was justified by the 'grand principle of equality before the law which the revolution of 1789 enshrined in our institutions and which may not be violated under any circumstances'.[29]

The *sénatus-consulte* of 1865 institutionalized the distinction between nationality and citizenship and the association of colonial subjecthood with Islam.

---

25 ANOM, F80/2043: Premier président de la cour impériale d'Alger au Gouverneur général, 17 March 1865.
26 Quoted in Judith Surkis, *Sex, Law and Sovereignty in French Algeria, 1830–1930* (Ithaca: Cornell University Press, 2019), 55.
27 Hazareesingh, *From Subject to Citizen*.
28 'Cour d'Alger – 24 février 1862', in *Bulletin judiciaire de l'Algérie. Jurisprudence algérienne de 1830 à 1876*, ed. Robert Estoublon (Algiers: A. Jourdan, 1890–1891), vol. III, 1862, 14.
29 Ibid., 15.

But this process operated in the other direction too. By basing the demarcation line between subjecthood and citizenship on sociocultural traits, the jurists, officials and statesmen of the late nineteenth century did not merely mark the boundaries of French citizenship but also redefined its nature and its role in the polity. The *sénatus-consulte* of 1865 was a crucial moment in the emergence of citizenship as an ideology – a view of citizenship not as frame within which to foster and negotiate cultural and social cohesion but a concept predefined by constructs of culture and collective identity. This tendency would become increasingly marked in the following decades, as the focus of colonial domination would shift from land seizure and settlement to jurisdictional politics.

Negotiating citizenship: The Jewish case

The *sénatus-consulte* of 1865 defined the legal status of Algerian Muslims and Jews in almost identical terms, referring to both groups as 'indigenous'. The reality, however, was more complex. Since the early days of French colonial rule in Algeria, the Jewish minority was subjected to a unique set of policies which sought to reshape it along the model of assimilation and 'regeneration' that had been at work in France since the late eighteenth century. This meant above all abolishing rabbinical jurisdiction and administering Jewish congregations through the system of official consistories.

By the 1860s, the interplay of resistance and accommodation with which Algerian Jewish elites sought to counter French and French-Jewish intervention resulted in a unique response to the challenges of colonial domination. In 1869, hundreds of Algerian Jews submitted to Napoléon III a bilingual petition requesting to be made full French citizens. Written in beautiful calligraphy and a large format, the petition consisted of parallel versions in Algerian Judeo-Arabic (a variety of Maghribi Arabic written in Hebrew script) and French. Pledging loyalty to the French state and its laws, the petition stated: 'Sire! An entire population asks for justice. Give us justice, and you shall render your reign glorious and fill us with joy and pride.'[30] Coining its own vocabulary of political participation and proudly demonstrating religious and linguistic difference, the petition was a most

---

30 ANOM, F80/2043, 'Pétition des Juifs d'Alger', 5 December 1869. Translated here from the French. All following quotations from the 1869 petition rely on this copy of the petition.

unique document in the history of French citizenship (italics denote Hebrew words used in the Judeo-Arabic text):[31]

French:	Judeo-Arabic:
We shall prove that, unwavering though we are in the religious convictions that we share with our coreligionists of France, we will, like them, be able to draw on the principles of Judaism and the teachings surrounding us to find the qualities and virtues that are appropriate for citizens and render them useful for their country.	We will show that our *faith* is as strong and true as *the faith of the members of our people*, the Jews of France. Like them, we shall learn from *our holy Torah* and from the people living amongst us the *good virtues* that are appropriate for acculturated residents and make them appropriate for their homeland to benefit from them.

The two versions – the Judeo-Arabic evidently translated from the French by an Algerian Jewish author – reveal the different perceptions of religion, citizenship and political belonging on both sides of the Mediterranean. Whereas the French version conveyed the idea of a single religious faith shared by communities on both sides of the Mediterranean, the Judeo-Arabic text implied the existence of two separate, if related, faiths. The notion of unity was thus abandoned in favour of a more complex relationship between two communities belonging to one and the same 'nation' or 'people', whose nature was left undefined. Moreover, the nature of religious faith and its role in the community's political life was articulated in very different terms. The French text conveyed both a rational mode of thinking – the scholarly term 'Judaism' implies through its suffix a well-defined system – and some room for interpretation and reform – for it is the 'principles' rather than commandments which are invoked. The Judeo-Arabic, by contrast, referred to the Torah as the source of wisdom and good conduct, precluding any claim for rationality, modernity or adaptability by describing it as 'holy'. While the French text evoked Judaism as a general source of moral guidance, then, the Judeo-Arabic version referred to the scripture as the absolute authority of good conduct.[32]

Articulating the concept of citizenship in Judeo-Arabic required a considerable effort, as this language did not feature equivalents for much of the European political terminology of the time. Having long served as a language of liturgy and everyday communication, Judeo-Arabic had only recently started to

---

31   Ibid.
32   I discuss the petition – which had long remained undiscovered – in more detail in: '"We Shall Become French": Reconsidering Algerian Jews' Citizenship, c. 1860–1900', *French History* 35, no. 2 (2021): 243–65. For a full translation of both versions see appendix.

emerge as a language of political writing. The first newspaper in Judeo-Arabic was founded in Algiers in July 1870 with the declared goal of supporting the cause of citizenship. Titled *L'Israélite algérien/ A-Daziri*, this bilingual weekly also sought to inform those members of the Jewish communities not fluent in French about developments in France. Seeking to prove Algerian Jews' worthiness of citizenship 'at a time when . . . the government plans to give us the glorious title of French citizens', founding editor and main contributor Nessim Benisti echoed much of the terminology and argumentation of the French text of the 1869 petition.[33] The newspaper's Judeo-Arabic part, by contrast, made ample use of loanwords such as *'naturalisation'*, *'citoyen'* and *'commerce'*.[34]

While few in France – Jews and non-Jews alike – would have been able to read the Judeo-Arabic text of the petition, the very act of submitting a request to become citizens in both French and Judeo-Arabic suited the core assumption of the 'Arab kingdom' policy that the contact between Europeans and 'natives' would eventually lead to the adoption of French language, culture and mores. 'Time is a mighty auxiliary of civilisation', wrote senator Delangle in his introduction to the *sénatus-consulte* of 1865, reiterating the guiding principal of the 'association' school of colonial governance. And while he argued that this may be an illusion in the case of Algerian Muslims, he assured the senate that 'some of the richest and most respected Jews' in Algeria were eager to become full French citizens.[35] Adolphe Crémieux had long believed in the power of 'revolutionary citizenship' as a tool of betterment amongst Algerian Jews, as Abigail Green puts it.[36] The elegance and eloquence of the petition all but affirmed such an assumption.

At a more practical level, bestowing full citizenship on the Jewish minority was viewed as a necessary step by a wide range of French jurists and officials. Ever since the 1830s, a series of fiats and decrees limited rabbinical jurisdiction in matrimonial and family matters, subjecting Algerian Jews to French civil legislation. The leaders of French Jewry, for their part, embarked on an ambitious mission to 'regenerate' Algerian Jewish life and thoroughly reshape it along the

---

33 Nessim Benisti, 'Chers lecteurs', *L'Israélite algérien*, 22 July 1870, 1. Only six issues were published – a common pattern in early Arabic press. On the newspaper and reactions to it in France see: Robert Attal, 'Ha-'Iton Ha-Yehudi Ha-Rishon Ba-Magreb: L'Israélite algérien (A-Dazeeri), 1870', *Pe'amim* (1983): 88–95.
34 Nessim Benisti, 'Naturalisasion', *L'Israélite algérien*, 5 August 1870, 1 of the Judeo-Arabic part, cul. 3. On loanwords in Judeo-Arabic: J. Chetrit, 'L'Influence du français dans les langues judéo-arabes d'Afrique du Nord', in *Judaïsme d'Afrique du Nord aux 19ᵉ-20ᵉ siècles: histoire, société et culture*, ed. M. Abitbol (Jerusalem, 1980), 144.
35 Delangle, report on the *sénatus-consulte* of 1865, reprinted in: Pinson de Ménerville, *Dictionnaire de la législation algérienne*, 156.
36 Abigail Green, *Children of 1848: Liberalism and the Jews from the Revolutions to Human Rights*, chapter 4, draft manuscript.

French model. From the 1840s onwards, they successfully advocated establishing in Algeria a consistorial system similar to that created in France by Napoléon I, creating a system of *écoles israélites françaises* and appointing French rabbis to oversee communal religious life in the colony.[37] The intrusion of Jewish life on the one hand and the interplay of resistance and accommodation with which Algerian Jews sought to counter such policies on the other soon resulted in legal chaos. Since many still chose to be wedded by their rabbis rather than the civil authorities, French courts dealing with inheritance and divorce disputes first had to rule whether the Jewish or the French law was applicable, often reaching contradicting conclusions.[38] A further ambiguity concerned the question of which public posts were open to Algerian Jews as nationals but not citizens.[39] By the 1860s, a widely shared view considered collective naturalization to be the best solution to the legal confusion concerning the Jewish population. This included Governor MacMahon and senior legal experts but also prominent settler representatives and French members of Algeria's three departmental councils.[40] At the *Corps législatif* in Paris in early 1870, count Le Hon, an outspoken advocate of settler interests in Algeria, called on the government to allow Algerian Jews to 'return into the great French family'.[41]

While the *sénatus-consulte* of 1865 theoretically allowed Jewish and Muslim individuals to solicit citizenship, the demand that applicants renounce religious civil legislation and freely accept French jurisprudence was an insuperable obstacle for the vast majority. Only 125 Algerian Jews requested to be naturalized between 1865 and 1869 (the numbers amongst the Muslim population were even

---

37   For recent scholarship on this subject see most notably: Lisa Moses Leff, *Sacred Bonds of Solidarity: The Rise of Jewish Internationalism in Nineteenth-Century France* (Stanford: Stanford University Press, 2006), esp. chapter 4; Michael Shurkin, 'French Liberal Governance and the Emancipation of Algeria's Jews', *Fr Hist Stud* 33 (2010): 259–80; Schreier, *Arabs of the Jewish Faith*; Assan, *Les Consistoires israélites*, esp. chapters 8–9.

38   An important dispute involved the Algerian Jew Jacob Seyman. The case reached the *cour impériale* in Algiers, and one of the lawyers was Crémieux himself. See: ANOM, F80/2043: Supplément à *l'Algérie française*, 25 June 1870.

39   Brett, 'Legislating for Inequality in Algeria', 451–2.

40   For governor MacMahon see report in the Algerian daily *l'Akhbar* on 22 October. 1869, cited in: S. Bloch, 'La question israélite algérienne', *L'Univers israélite* 25, no. 7 (1 December 1869): 214–17. For legal experts see study by the president of the Sétif tribunal: Casimir Frégier, *Les Juifs algériens [. . .]: leur naturalisation collective* (Paris: Lévy frères, 1865), 374–8, 383. Further expressions of support for some form of Jewish naturalization came from the attorney at the civil court of Oran and from legist Jules Delsieux from Algiers. See: Assan, *Les Consistoires israélites*, 318; Schreier, *Arabs of the Jewish Faith*, 164. For settler representatives see: *Cahiers algériens* (Algiers: Duclaux, 1870), 13–14. For departmental councillors see: Assan, *Les Consistoires israélites*, 316–19.

41   Cited in: S. Bloch, 'La question israélite algérienne', *L'Univers israélite* 25, no. 15 (1 April 1870): 471–2.

smaller).⁴² It was amid the resounding rejection of the individual naturalization procedure that the consistory of Algiers launched the 1869 petition. Interpreting the extension of French civil law to Algerian Jews and the limitation of rabbinical jurisdiction in the previous decades as a sign of France's assimilationist intentions, the petition bemoaned the procedure of individual naturalization as established by the *sénatus-consulte* of 1865 as evidence 'that the gates of naturalization will not be opened to us but with discretion and reserve'. The main copy, signed by notables from Algiers, contained both the Judeo-Arabic and the French text. Further copies, written in Judeo-Arabic only, were circulated in Blida, Aumale, Dellys and Orléansville.⁴³

Though the 1869 petition pledged to 'accept with no regret and no reserve the authority of French legislation', French officials expressed concern whether Algerian Jews were indeed prepared to renounce rabbinical jurisdiction. The Algerian consistories were thus requested to repeat the model of the 'Grand Sanhedrin' of 1807, a congregation of rabbis convoked by Napoléon I from across his European empire to abolish Jewish jurisdiction and enforce the *Code civil* upon the Jewish population.⁴⁴ Like the 'Grand Sanhedrin', the assembly envisioned by the government for Algeria was expected to declare Jewish law to be abolished in the colony.⁴⁵ In response, the Algerian consistories evoked the Halakic maxim that 'a state's law is the law' – an ancient principle that had for centuries 'governed Jewish history in exile', to quote Pierre Birnbaum.⁴⁶ This pillar of Jewish law, the consistory members argued, required its followers to abide by the laws of their country of residence.⁴⁷ Furthermore, they emphasized that the 'Grand Sanhedrin' of 1807 had relied precisely on this maxim when declaring that the Jews in the Napoleonic empire had to accept the *Code civil*. Since a precedent had been set and Jewish law entailed the acceptance of a ruling state's legislation, there was no need for a new 'Grand Sanhedrin'.

French officials, for their part, interpreted the campaign for citizenship as an expression of the willingness of Algerian Jews – at least their elite – to fully embrace the idea of assimilation. Responding to a questionnaire circulated

---

42 ANOM, F80/2043, Grand Rabbin d'Oran au Ministre de Justice, 12 October 1869; Ministre de la Justice au Grand Rabbin, 8 November 1869. See also Assan, *Les consistoires israélites*, 323–5.
43 ANOM F80/2043, Correspondence between consistory's president and envois in Aumale, Dellys, Orléansville, and Blida, 17–28 December 1869.
44 Simon Schwarzfuchs, *Napoleon, the Jews and the Sanhedrin* (London: Routledge & Kegan Paul, 1979), 93–5.
45 ANOM, F80/2043, Président de Conseil d'État au Ministre de la Justice, 18 March 1870.
46 Pierre Birnbaum, *L'Aigle et la Synagogue: Napoléon, les Juifs et l'État* (Paris: Fayard, 2007), 116.
47 ANOM F80/2043, Consistoire central au Ministre de la Justice, 19 November 1869; Président du Consistoire israélite d'Alger au Préfet, 19 April 1870.

amongst them by the government in early 1870, most *préfets* and generals in the colony were confident that naturalizing the Algerian Jews could even buttress French authority over the Muslim majority.[48] Such, for instance, was the view of the general commanding the French army in Algiers Joseph Pourcet, a veteran of colonial warfare in Algeria who would later become a right-leaning senator.[49] Encouraged by the willingness expressed in the 1869 petition to accept French civil legislation, Pourcet described the naturalization of local Jewry as a precursor of a more ambitious colonial effort, aiming to eradicate Islamic law and communal structures in Algeria:

> Our progressing action in this country will lead us with certainty to lay our hand on all those Islamic institutions that are different or contradictory to ours and that do not seem to belong inseparably to [Islamic] law ... The fact that the Jews accept this distinction and do not believe their religion to be threatened by the adoption of French law could be a good example for the Muslims.[50]

Such confidence was crucial. As Joshua Schreier points out, administrators and jurists had long evoked the reluctance of Jews and Muslims to accept the *Code civil* to justify their political exclusion.[51] The view expressed by Pourcet – though certainly unique in its unequivocal judgement – shows just how effective the Jewish campaign was in convincing French officials of its adherence to the idea of cultural and religious assimilation while still conveying a strong sense of local, collective identity. Such views of the Jewish campaign as a sign of the success of French colonial policies led to the preparation in March 1870 of a decree aiming to collectively naturalize the Algerian Jewish minority.[52]

The actual naturalization act was issued as a decree by the Government of National Defence during the Franco-Prussian war and after the fall of the Second Empire. It would soon become synonymous with Adolphe Crémieux, the most prominent French-Jewish statesman of the nineteenth century, a champion of European-Jewish philanthropy amongst the communities of the Middle East and North Africa, and, as we have seen in the previous chapter, an advocate of *rattachement* and civil administration in Algeria since the

---

48 ANOM F80/2043, Gouverneur général au Ministre de la Guerre, 14 June 1870.
49 Ministère de la Guerre, *Annuaire militaire de l'Empire français pour l'année 1870* (Paris: Veuve Berger-Levrault & fils, 1870), 28.
50 ANOM F80/2043, Avis du Général commandant la province d'Alger au sujet de la naturalisation collective des indigènes israélites, 17 April 1870.
51 Schreier, *Arabs of the Jewish Faith*, 146.
52 ANOM, F80/2043: Conseil d'État: No. 2963, distribution du 8 mars 1870. Project de décret relatif à la naturalisation collective de tous les Israélites indigènes du territoire algérien. See also Michel Ansky, *Les Juifs d'Algérie du décret Crémieux à la libération* (Paris: Éditions du Centre, 1950), 38.

1840s. On 24 October 1870, Crémieux, serving as interim Minister of Justice in the Government of National Defence, issued a series of decrees that replaced the military administration of Algeria with a civilian one. Amongst them was the decree which collectively bestowed full French citizenship and civil legislation on Algerian Jews, and which would become one of the most important and contested legal documents in the history of colonial Algeria. By bestowing French citizenship and civil legislation on the Algerian Jews, it created a one-to-one correlation between the category of 'indigène' as defined by the *sénatus-consulte* of 1865 and 'Muslim'. Before long, the third population referred to in this legislation – non-French Europeans residing in Algeria – would also become governed by separate laws and considerations, yielding the twin dichotomies of European/Muslim and citizen/subject.

An ethnic *jus soli*

By the 1880s, the various means at the disposal of the colonial administration – military force, land seizure and jurisdictional politics – effectively consolidated the political regime in Algeria vis-à-vis the local population. A decade after the repression of the Kabylian revolt, the Algerian administration was confident enough in its grip over Algerian Muslim society to turn its attention to the sizeable non-French European population. In Algeria, as in the metropole, politicians and officials were alarmed by the presence of a growing migrant population and a perceived threat to national sovereignty. In Algeria, only slightly more than 50 per cent of an overall settler population of 377,000 were French nationals in 1881, and commentators agreed that their share was declining.[53] Such concerns over a perceived 'foreign peril' were the main driving force behind a major reform of French citizenship, in which the *jus sanguinis* ('right of blood') principle, introduced to the *Code civil* by Napoléon in 1804 and granting citizenship according to descent, was to be replaced by the *jus soli* ('right of land') principle, granting citizenship according to birth in the French territory. By shifting the criterion of political belonging from descent to territory, the lawmakers of the 1880s sought to integrate migrant populations

---

53 Figures cited in: ANOM, F80/2043: Projet de loi relatif à la naturalisation des étrangers en Algérie: Exposé des motifs, evidently from 1885. See also: d'Haussonville, 'La colonisation officielle en Algérie – II', 80. On decline see: Paul Leroy-Beaulieu, *L'Algérie et la Tunisie* (Paris: Guillaumin et cie, 1897), 32–3.

into the nation through the republican institutions of citizenship, standardized education system and conscription.

What was born out of the intensive debates on French citizenship throughout the 1880s was not merely a technical change to the terms of naturalization but a new identification between society and polity. Even before the citizenship reform of 1889, the colonial administration exerted pressure on non-French Europeans residing in Algeria to take French citizenship by banning them from voting in municipal elections in 1883.[54] The 1889 citizenship reform, Charles-Robert Ageron has argued, constituted the 'birth certificate' of *l'Algérie française*.[55] Put more critically, this was a decisive step in defining the legal status of the non-French European population, a step that brought about the twin dichotomies of European/Muslim and citizen/subject and a crucial moment in the racialization of the French idea of citizenship. In the course of these debates, the tenet of Mediterranean, 'Algerian' or 'European' origin would gain ground as a criterion of inclusion. Whereas prior to 1889 a myriad of social groups and political statuses had existed in the colony, the 1889 law demarcated much more clearly – and increasingly using ethnoreligious categories – the rigid boundaries of citizenship versus subjecthood. And while the *sénatus-consulte* of 1865 sought to define the legal meaning of being Muslim in French-ruled Algeria, debates in the 1880s sought to coin a new legal category: Europeanness.

The 1880s were, therefore, an important moment of demarcation, a moment when religion and descent – indeed religion *as* descent – were institutionalized as legal criteria of within and without in the Algerian colonial order. Rogers Brubaker has rightly noted that the 1889 citizenship reform was one of the clearest political manifestations of an expansive idea of citizenship as an instrument with which to integrate foreign communities.[56] Yet, this statement requires some qualification. What the 1880s showed and indeed sharpened were the limits of this expansive idea and its delineation along ethnoreligious categories. As discussions on a new, territory-based citizenship law gained pace, Alfred Dain, a senior legal advisor to the colonial administration in Algeria warned: 'We must not forget that France, unlike England, does not accept a colonial nationality. The status of French, if obtained in Algeria, confers the same rights everywhere. The acquisition of this status must

---

54 Leroy-Beaulieu, *L'Algérie et la Tunisie*, 36, note 2.
55 Ageron, *Histoire de l'Algérie contemporaine*, 118.
56 Brubaker, *Citizenship and Nationhood*, 91.

therefore be surrounded, in all places, by solid guarantees.'[57] Dain was, of course, factually wrong. The *sénatus-consulte* of 1865 had defined precisely a colonial nationality that granted its holders only very limited rights. But the concern he expressed was shared by many. While Dain remained vague, the discussions, legislation bills, and court rulings of the 1880s and 1890s produced a series of practices aimed at assuring that the suggested change would not apply to Algerian Muslims.

The main object of French concerns over the *péril étranger* in Algeria were the large Spanish 'agglomerations' in the western *département* of Oran. In 1884, Governor Tirman warned that the Spanish were already the majority of the settler population in this *département*, adding: 'It is necessary that the foreigners be more easily stripped of their citizenship and brought closer to us.'[58] A few months later, Tirman told the Minister of Justice that there was a 'necessity of a prompt Francization of foreign groups already in the majority in several places in Algeria.'[59] In 1885, legal adviser Alfred Dain, in a study commissioned by the governor general, flagged not only the growing numbers of foreigners in Algeria but above all their geographic concentrations. Qualifying such enclaves as 'colonies', he argued that demographic studies have shown that ethnic groups concentrated in one area tend to be particularly reluctant to integrate in the majority society ('désagglomérer').[60] The *Conseil supérieur* of the Algerian administration clearly followed this logic when drafting a legislation bill aimed at naturalizing the Spanish and Italians, arguing that 'the presence on French soil of increasingly dense foreign agglomerations which are, as a consequence, less and less susceptible to disbanding constitutes a real danger.'[61] Deputy for Oran Eugène Etienne went as far as warning against the naturalization of the Spanish due to danger of secession: 'In constant contact with their coreligionists [*sic*! Note the elision between nationality and religion], these newcomers would retain their mores, their tendencies, their tastes, their hopes. They would accept being French only for the goal of morally preparing the annexation of the *départment* of Oran by Spain, a goal which many Spaniards have in mind.'[62] Alfred Dain saw it differently. 'Born in Algeria, they [the Spanish] live with the illusion that, by merit of this fact, they are "Algerians", that is, French; the

---

57 Dain, *Étude sur la naturalisation des étrangers*, 15.
58 ANOM, F80/2043: Extrait des procès-verbaux du Conseil du Gouvernement général de l'Algérie, 8 August 1884.
59 ANOM, F80/2043: Gouverneur général au président du conseil, 23 May 1885.
60 Dain, *Étude sur la naturalisation des étrangers*, 3–4 (note 1), 8, 11.
61 ANOM, F80/2043: Projet de loi relatif à la naturalisation des étrangers en Algérie: Exposé des motifs, evidently March 1885.
62 Cited in Ageron, *Histoire de l'Algérie conmtemporaine*, 122.

majority are convinced of the idea . . . that the nationality is attached to birth in the [state's] territory.'[63] To this confusion added a treaty from 1862, according to which Spanish nationals born in France or Algeria were enlisted to the French rather than the Spanish army.

Another source of concern was the Italian 'colonies' in the *département* of Constantine. Flows of Italian seasonal labourers seeking employment in Algerian agriculture and public works during the winter months had already been recorded in the first decades of French occupation, but it was not until the 1870s that a pattern of permanent residency emerged.[64] By the 1880s, the Italian population outnumbered the French in the coastal cities of Calle, Philippeville and Bône. Bône was particularly important for the discourse of 'colonies' and 'agglomerations', with 6,000 Italian residents not only geographically concentrated in certain parts of the city but also markedly present in the building sector and daily labour in agriculture, as David Prochaska has shown.[65] A further and particular challenge to colonial hierarchies and categories was the small Maltese population in the *département* of Constantine. Like the Italians, they were mostly employed in the construction sector or as shopkeepers, while those worst off earned their living as porters on the quaysides of port cities and as pedlars.[66] Though by 1876 they constituted no more than 4 per cent of the settler population, the Maltese defied the linguistic and ethnographic categorizations so crucial to the colonial order. As Andrea L. Smith shows, a particular anti-Maltese sentiment permeated colonial discourses in the nineteenth century, revolving around a notion of Malta as situated both geographically and culturally between Europe and Africa. It was above all the Maltese language, a variety of Maghribi Arabic, which troubled many French commentators. As late as the 1880s, travellers and ethnographers described the Maltese as markedly different from other European communities in Algeria, stressing their 'wild appearance' and speculating on the origin of their 'race'.[67] The Maltese were still present enough in the public memory and imagination of the European community in the 1950s for Albert Camus to identify a muscular gallant attracting the attention of the protagonist's mother in *The First Man* as '*Maltais d'origine*'.[68]

---

63 Dain, *Étude sur la naturalisation des étrangers*, 10.
64 Prochaska, *Making Algeria French*, 150–1; Gaston Loth, *Le peuplement italien en Tunisie et en Algérie* (Paris: A. Colin, 1905), 136–7, 158–9.
65 Prochaska, *Making Algeria French*, 165–70.
66 Andrea L. Smith, *Colonial Memory and Postcolonial Europe: Maltese Settlers in Algeria and France* (Bloomington: Indiana University Press, 2006), 70–1.
67 Smith, *Colonial Memory*, 85–9, 93–4.
68 Albert Camus, *Le premier homme* (Paris: Gallimard, 1994), 115.

If Oran and Constantine were depicted as the hotbeds of menace and secessionism, Algiers was often portrayed as the birthplace of a new 'Algerian' – that is, common European – society to emerge from the *fusion des races* of various Mediterranean populations. The most ambitious attempt to coin a local, 'Algerian' folklore were the stories of the fictional figure of Cagayous, created in Algiers in 1895 by a local administrator writing under the pseudonym of Musette. Of a mixed European origin, the foul-mouthed Cagayous, speaking the local *pataouète* dialect, was a popular embodiment of a new collective identity, most famously through his proud, even spiteful statement '*Algériens nous sommes!*' ('Algerians we are!').[69] However, by 1914, the stories of Cagayous had already become an object of cultural nostalgia, as James McDougall notes.[70] *Pataouète*, for its part, never became an autonomous creole. Spoken mainly in Algeria's port cities, it included numerous loanwords from Spanish, Italian and southern French dialects, as well as Arabic, with a clear preference for curses.[71] It did not, however, develop distinct grammatical patterns and remained, as Paul Siblot observes, an Algerian dialect of French.[72]

Outside settler popular culture, the idea of a new, 'Algerian' society was followed with some ambivalence by French politicians and commentators. Liberal economist and colonial reformer Paul Leroy-Beaulieu, for instance, argued that the '*fusion des races*' would strengthen French presence in Algeria: 'In blending with the Spanish, the Italians, the Maltese, the French race, though it may lose its purity, augments it capacity in enduring the [local] climate. Mixed marriages should be recommended simply from a physiologic perspective. . . . Marriages between the French and the more meridional races will render their definitive acclimatization easier and quicker.'[73] At the same time, this development posed a threat of secessionism, which France, as Leroy-Beaulieu argued, had to avert: 'Different modes of naturalization, mixed marriages, schools of course, but also religion should make sure that our efforts do not lead to such lamentable result.'[74] Colonial policies followed precisely this reasoning. After the mandatory education law of 1883 and with 84 per cent of Europeans in Algeria attending

---

69 Paul Siblot, '« Cagayous antijuif ». Un discours colonial en proie à la racisation', *Mots* 15 (October 1987): 61.
70 McDougall, *A History of Algeria*, 112.
71 Prochaska, *Making Algeria French*, 224.
72 Siblot, 'Cagayous antijuif'. See also on pataouète and settler literature: Dunwoodie, *Writing French Algeria*, esp. 117–20.
73 Leroy-Beaulieu, *L'Algérie et la Tunisie*, 43.
74 Ibid., 42.

French schools by 1901, *pataouète* was being rapidly replaced by standardized French amongst the Europeans in Algeria.[75]

Debates on citizenship reform in the 1880s engendered a fascinating attempt to introduce Europeanness and European origin as a legal criterion into French legislation. For 'European' was, of course, a geographical and cultural attribute not a legal category. Even as a geographical term, 'Europe' was deeply ambiguous and the subject of lengthy debates on where Europe began and where it ended.[76] Perhaps more than elsewhere, 'Europe' in the Algerian context was also connoted religiously, implying 'Christian' or even 'Catholic'. For the Maltese in Algeria, a reputation as devout Catholics, and it alone, distinguished them from the Algerian Muslims and associated them with the French, the Italians, and the Spanish.[77] In the Algerian political order, 'European origin' was a powerful marker of inclusion, an intuitive category laden with meaning through the everyday, omnipresent contrast with the categories of 'indigenous' and 'Muslim.' In 1881, the *Conseil supérieur* of the Algerian administration transmitted draft legislation to the Ministry of Justice, seeking the collective naturalization of the colony's European population.[78] An even clearer example of this tendency is a formulation adopted by the *Conseil supérieur* in 1884, suggesting the naturalization of 'every individual of European origin' born in the colony. This phrase was used time and again in deliberations of the *Conseil Supérieur* and was included in its final legislation proposal submitted to the Ministry of Justice for review.[79] Though this formulation was eventually dropped, it reveals the emergence of ethnic categories at the very moment when France was turning to a territory-based citizenship law.

Once debates on citizenship reform began in Paris, the colonial administration sought to convince legislators and Ministry of Justice officials

---

75   McDougall, *A History of Algeria*, 112.
76   Prince Metternich's alleged remark that 'the Balkan begins in Vienna' has gone down in public memory as no more than a gibe, but other contexts yielded lengthy debates, whether it was German liberals othering Poland and Russia in the 1840s or the American scholar William Ripely arguing that 'beyond the Pyrenees begins Africa.' See: Tessa Hofmann, 'Der radikale Wandel: Das deutsche Polenbild zwischen 1772 und 1848', *Zeitschrift für Ostforschung*, no. 42 (1993): 376–7; William Z. Ripley, *The Races of Europe: A sociological study* . . . (London: Kegan & Paul, 1899), 272.
77   According to one report, when Cardinal Lavigerie of Algiers first visited Malta he was received with enthusiasm by the local population, who was made familiar with his figure and undertakings through familial ties to Algeria. See: Francois Renault, *Cardinal Lavigerie: Churchman, Prophet and Missionary*, trans. John O'Donohue (London: Athlone Press, 1994), 274.
78   Dain, *Étude sur la naturalisation des étrangers*, 3–4, note 1.
79   ANOM, F80/2043: Extrait des procès-verbaux du Conseil du Gouvernement général de l'Algérie, 8 August 1884; Projet de loi sur la naturalisation en Algérie, 6 March 1885; Gouverneur général au Président du conseil des ministres, 23 May 1885.

to apply the planned reform to Algeria.[80] This was met with little understanding in the Ministry of Justice, where legal experts, well-aware of the particularities of the Algerian political order, sought to exempt it from the new legislation altogether.[81] Pressure by the colonial administration to apply the 1889 law to Algeria ultimately bore fruit. In 1887, it was agreed that the new citizenship law would apply to Algeria alongside the *sénatus-consulte* of 1865 – which by now applied almost exclusively to Algerian Muslims.[82] The final legislation text thus introduced the *jus soli* in the metropole as well as in Algeria and the small colonies of Guadeloupe, Martinique La Réunion, in conjunction with the *sénatus-consulte* and further, unspecified dispositions applying to Algeria.[83]

Technical though it may seem, the writing of the *sénatus-consulte* of 1865 into the *Code civil* was a crucial moment, creating an ethnically delineated *jus soli* that did not apply to Algerian Muslims. Indeed, it was the result of a wider political and intellectual development, which witnessed the redefinition of such categories as 'religion' and 'origin' to make them valid criteria for political inclusion and exclusion. In 1880, the prolific legal commentator and later deputy Daniel de Folleville published a *Theoretical and Practical Treaty on Naturalization*. His reasoning encapsulated the generalization of measures defined in the *sénatus-consulte* of 1865 and their formulation as fundamental criteria of belonging and exclusion:

> When a conqueror finds himself in the presence of a population with mores and customs essentially contrary to his own, faced with individuals with their own religion, exercising a particular ritual, it is evident that he cannot change from one day to another the character of this territory and promptly make it resemble his vision.[84]

This was a fascinating exercise in excluding Algerian Muslims not only from French citizenship but from the reach of universally framed principles more

---

80 The Algerian administration also sought certain modifications: Whereas the Senate suggested declaring a French citizen upon birth any foreigner born in France to parents born there as well, the Algerian administration sought to naturalise the first generation of foreigners in Algeria. See: ANOM, F80/2043: Extrait des procès-verbaux du Conseil du Gouvernement général de l'Algérie, 8 August 1884.
81 ANOM, F80/2043: Ministère de la Justice – Direction des affaires civiles au Gouverneur général, 6 December 1884.
82 ANOM, F80/2043: Gouverneur général au Ministre de la Justice, 17 March 1887. The one exception was the Jewish population of the Saharan M'zab region, occupied by France in 1882, to whom the Crémieux Decree was not applied. See: Sarah Abrevaya-Stein, *Saharan Jews and the Fate of French Algeria* (Chicago: Chicago University Press, 2014), 42–7.
83 'Loi sur la naturalisation, 27 June 1889', *JO*. Lois et Décrets, 28 June 1889, 2977–8.
84 Daniel de Folleville, *Traité théorique et pratique de la naturalisation: Études de droit international privé* (Paris: A. Marescq aîné, 1880), 210–11.

generally. Though formulated as general observations, de Folleville wrote expressly that he referred above all to native societies in Algeria and the French colonial possessions in India. And while he argued that 'the diversity of races and languages does not prevent the unity of a nation' and that 'for an annexation to be legitimate, it requires the prior consent of the populations that will have to change nationality' (the latter assertion presumably a reference to the German annexation of Alsace-Lorraine in 1871),[85] Folleville nevertheless concluded that amid clear religious and societal difference, 'the regime imposed on the new citizens [citoyens] must differ from that imposed following a voluntary cession.'[86]

This elision of religion and descent, of ethnographic characterizations and legal categories was very present in legislation and jurisprudence. The most important legal concept in this context was the *statut personnel*. What in the 1860s had still denoted a loose ensemble of religious legislation and jurisprudence governing the Muslim population in civil matters of marriage, divorce and inheritance was turned by the legal experts of the late nineteenth and early twentieth centuries into a strict legal category. This codified *statut personnel* was designed to contrast the Islamic civil law with the *Code civil* and underline their alleged incompatibility. Though it was a purely French construct, the *statut personnel* and the alleged attachment of the Muslim population to it were nevertheless regarded by deputies and commentators in the metropole as an insurmountable obstacle hindering the naturalization of the Muslim population.[87]

This codified legal category of indigeneity was introduced into penal law with the systematization of the *Code de l'indigénat* in 1881. Originating in French martial law, the *Code de l'indigénat* consisted of various decrees and orders and was deployed in Algeria following the gradual French occupation during the 1830s and 1840s and remained intact when a civilian regime was established after 1870. French lawmakers, therefore, deemed it necessary to codify it in legislation, as was done in 1881. What emerged was a highly repressive regime, rooted in martial law but executed either by appointed civil administrators with sweeping disciplinary powers (in the *communes mixtes*, where the majority of Algerian Muslims lived) or by elected settler mayors (in the *communes de plein exercice*, where the majority of Europeans resided).[88]

The 1890s saw the emergence of yet another neologism: 'Muslim origin'. For Muslim subjects seeking naturalization, conversion to Catholicism was

---

85 Ibid., 194, 199.
86 Ibid., 211.
87 Blévis, *Sociologie d'un droit colonial*, 107–8.
88 Ageron, *Les Algériens musulmans*, 173–5, 184–92. Guignard, *L'Abus de pouvoir*, 45–60, 282–8.

no guarantee, as their descent remained the crucial factor, and they were often referred to as *chrétiens musulmans*.[89] In 1903, the Appeal Court in Algiers went as far as arguing that the term *musulman* designated not only confession 'but rather refers to the ensemble of individuals of Muslim origin who, not having been naturalized, have necessarily conserved their Muslim *statut personnel*, regardless of whether or not they belong to the Mohammedan religion'.[90] As Patrick Weil notes, this ruling highlighted the 'ethno-political' rather than religious or civil character of the status of indigeneity.[91] While the coinage 'European origin' remained a legal dead letter, the term 'musulman' was redefined by colonial authorities so as to imply descent rather than religion. If the *sénatus-consulte* of 1865 created the legal status of colonial subjecthood and the Crémieux Decree brought about the clear correlation between this status and the Algerian Muslim population, legislation and jurisprudence in the late nineteenth and early twentieth century aimed to make the crossing of these boundaries impossible.

Emerging unease

The legal and intellectual developments discussed here did not remain confined to the colony. Presented to parliament in 1881, the legislation on the *indigénat* was considered so excessive that it was approved as a measure of exception with a sunset clause that required its renewal every seven years. From here on and until its abolition in 1944, this legislation was repeatedly debated – and approved – by the National Assembly.[92] Moreover, colonial legislation and the legal status of colonial subjects were the matter of various studies, articles and scholarly debates. They were taught at the law faculties of the metropole. Most important, as Laure Blévis has pointed out, jurists and parliament members construed colonial legislation 'not as an exception, but as a moral, if marginal, branch of French law'.[93]

The passing of the *Code de l'indigénat* in the French parliament prompted the first calls for substantial reforms in Algeria, most notably with the founding of the *Société de protections des indigènes des colonies*. The society portrayed itself as the intellectual heir of Thomas Ismaÿl Urbain, who in the 1860s had played a

---

89 McDougall, *A History of Algeria*, 107, note 61.
90 Cited in Weil, *Qu'est-ce qu'un Français?*, 354.
91 Ibid., 355.
92 Blévis, 'La situation coloniale', 94.
93 Ibid., 98.

key role in devising the Algerian policies of the Second Empire.⁹⁴ The society's president, Paul Leroy-Beaulieu, who had established himself since the 1870s as a prominent commentator on colonial affairs, described the 'indigenes' in the first issue of the society's bulletin as 'useful instruments, precious auxiliaries' of colonization.⁹⁵ Henri de Lamothe, with whom we have opened this chapter, provided an even more detailed vision for a different political order in Algeria. He proposed to grant political rights to every male resident of Algeria who could prove his proficiency in spoken and written French and – though less explicitly stated – his willingness to 'assimilate'.⁹⁶ He argued that Islam was susceptible to French cultural and intellectual influence, envisioning an Algerian, French-educated elite whose members would 'lead their coreligionists in the path of progress and tolerance'.⁹⁷ Moreover, the society's bulletin offered Algerians one of the first platforms in the metropole for discussing and criticizing the colonial order.⁹⁸ Such ideas and initiatives, however, found little resonance. Counting some 300 members at its peak, the *Société de protections des indigènes* ceased its activity after only a few years, having raised merely limited interest in the French press (and indignation in settler newspapers in Algeria).⁹⁹ Looking back at the society's activity, de Lamothe would write in 1911: 'Whether the sower ill-chose his moment or whether the seeds fell on a soil unsuitable to receive them ... the campaign ... did not achieve all the results for which we had hoped.'¹⁰⁰

Though rare and largely unsuccessful, such voices nevertheless allow us to draw a more complex picture of the political and intellectual landscape of colonial France. It is by studying critical voices and identifying the weaknesses and limitations of their critiques that we can identify the contours of an overriding

---

94 'Ismail Urbain' [unsigned text], *Bulletin de la Société française pour la protection des indigènes des colonies* 2, no. 5–6 (June-September 1883): 334. On the society see also Ageron, *Les Algériens musulmans*, 423–4.
95 Paul Leroy-Beaulieu, 'Lettre aux membres de la société', *Bulletin de la société française pour la protection des indigènes des colonies* 1, no. 1 (March 1882): 2.
96 de Lamothe, 'De la représentation des indigènes', 160.
97 Ibid., 158.
98 See e.g.: Tounsi Ahmed Ben Mohammed Etshalbi, 'Mémoire sur le passé et l'avenir des indigènes en Algérie', *Bulletin de la société française pour la protection des indigènes des colonies* 2, no. 5–6 (June-September 1883): 24–5.
99 Amongst the society's most prominent members were Ferdinand de Lesseps, who had played a major role in the construction of the Suez Canal, as well as figures not immediately related to colonial expansion, such as the chief rabbi of Paris, Zadok Kahn. See: Ageron, *Les Algérins musulmans*, 423–4.
100 Henri de Lamothe, 'Accession aux droits politiques', *La Revue indigene* 6, no. 63–64 (July-August 1911): 412. On reactions to the society in France and Algeria see: 'Revue de la presse parisienne' [unsigned text], *Bulletin de la société française pour la protection des indigènes des colonies*, Deuxième Année no. 5–6, (June-September 1883): 124–36; F.L.B., 'Revue de la presse parisienne', *Bulletin de la Société française pour la protection des indigènes des colonies* 1, no. 3 (September 1882): 230.

political consensus. Indeed, the most radical and in no sense representative critique of the colonial order was articulated by a disillusioned member of the *Société de protection des indigènes*, the celebrated geographer Élisée Reclus. A former *communard*, an anarchist and a member of the First Internationale, Reclus visited Algeria as part of his scholarly work. Originally sympathetic to the association's goals, Reclus wrote to one of its members upon his return from Algeria in 1884:

> I return from Algeria feeling the horror of the conquest more profoundly than before . . . I shall certainly remove my name from the list of those who accept the principle of conquest. [For] protecting the indigenes by French laws implies that they should remain French subjects. If, by virtue of my skin, my language and my mores I belong to the conquerors, I have but one thing to do facing the indigenes: to ask for forgiveness for my participation in the crime. I have nothing to do amongst the 'protectors': we have neither the same sentiments, nor the same wishes nor the same experience.[101]

Such views were confined to the very fringes of the Left, where notions of developed versus backward 'races', of Europe spreading progress to the colonies were widely shared.[102] In France, left-wing politicians supported colonial expansion with varying degrees of enthusiasm, with two main arguments: either that it was the responsibility of French socialism to spread Enlightenment and progress, or that, once the colonies had been conquered, French socialism would betray the colonized by leaving them to the mercy of the bourgeoisie.[103] Socialist and republican legacies informed the first and most radical proposition to naturalize the entire Algerian Muslim population, formulated in 1887 by deputies Henri Michelin of the far left and Alfred Gaulier of the Radicals. Michelin and Gaulier mentioned the shortage in manpower amongst the French army and maintained that sweeping naturalization would allow it to recruit 200,000 soldiers.[104] Moreover, Michelin and Gaulier suggested to abolish all measures of exception and all special regulations in Algeria – an idea which earned the

---

101 Cited in: Federico Ferretti and Philippe Pelletier, 'Sciences impériales et discours hétérodoxes? Élisée Reclus et le colonialisme français', *L'Espace géographique* 42, no. 1 (January 2013): 8.
102 The most famous example is of course Karl Marx's article on British rule in India: Karl Marx, 'The Future Results of British Rule in India', in *The Collected Works of Marx and Engels. Electronic Edition*, vol. 12 (Charlottesville: InteLex Corporation, 2006), 217–22.
103 Manuela Semidei, 'Les socialistes français et le problème colonial entre les deux guerres (1919–1939)', *Revue française de science politique* 18, no. 6 (Autumn 1968): 1118–9.
104 Ouanassa Siari Tengour, 'Constantine 1887: des notables contre la « naturalisation »', in *Histoire de l'Algérie à la période coloniale*, ed. Abderrahmane Bouchène et al. (Paris: La Découverte, 2012), 235–6.

two deputies fierce criticism in the Algerian press.[105] Strong opposition came from Muslim representatives as well: in Constantine, dozens of notables signed a petition to the Chamber of Deputies to protest against any change to their civil status.[106] It was only in the aftermath of the First World War that some Algerians would demand French citizenship.[107]

Unsurprisingly, opposition to reform was particularly strong amongst the colonial administration. When in 1884 a member of the *Conseil supérieur* suggested that naturalization of Europeans should be accompanied by reform to the legal status of Muslims, he was met with strong opposition, above all from Governor Tirman who argued that the *statut personnel* posed a barrier and could not be changed.[108] It was the same Tirman who, after cautiously criticizing the excesses of the *Code de l'indigénat* shortly after his appointment in 1881, quickly retreated when told by other administrators that 'it is important that the indigenes remain completely in the grip of the administration.'[109] Amid calls for reform, Tirman told the Minister of Justice in late 1884 that, for the time being, no modification was possible to the legal status of Muslims.[110] The same reasoning was provided as explanation for the continued exclusion of the Algerian Muslim population in a draft legislation for the naturalization of Europeans prepared by the administration in 1885: 'The main obstacle for the naturalization of the indigenes emerges from their *statut personnel* . . . No efficient reform can be carried out until we can modify that status. However, it seems that the moment for taking such a decision has not arrived yet.'[111] The strong emphasis on time was characteristic. Rather than specifying any concrete social or economic conditions which must be achieved before any reform could be considered, this passage – like much of the colonial thought at the time – postponed any such debate to an undefined future.

What the colonial administration failed to anticipate – as did the French government and colonial reformers – was that the battlefield for struggles over the boundaries of French citizenship was about to shift dramatically. Politically enfranchised, a nascent European community would soon seek to assert its

---

105 Lazard, *L'accession des indigènes algériens à la citoyenneté française*, 49–50; Ageron, *Les Algériens musulmans*, 349.
106 Tengour, 'Constantine 1887', 236–8.
107 See below, chapters 4–5.
108 ANOM, F80/2043: Extrait des procès-verbaux du Conseil du Gouvernement général de l'Algérie, 8 August 1884; Projet de loi sur la naturalisation en Algérie, 27 February 1885.
109 Cited in Ageron, *Les Algériens musulmans*, 175.
110 ANOM, F80/2043: Gouverneur général au Ministre de la Justice, 30 September 1884.
111 ANOM, F80/2043: Projet de loi relatif à la naturalisation des étrangers en Algérie: Exposé des motifs, evidently March 1885.

vision for the demarcation of the *cité française* in Algeria. Pursuing the logic of ethnicity and origin which guided the naturalization law of 1889 and the *Code de l'indigénat*, a wave of violent agitation was soon to erupt in protest against what was seen as an inconceivable, unforgiveable breach of this logic: the naturalization of the Arabic-speaking, 'indigenous' Jewish minority. This powerful assertion of a local, 'Algerian' identity shattered Algeria with its one, simple call: 'Down with the Jews!'

3

'Ta'ish al-République!' – 'À bas les Youdis!'

The twin dichotomies of citizen/subject and European/Muslim that had emerged in the 1860s–80s were disrupted by one case: the Algerian Jewish minority, naturalized in 1870 following a decade of campaigning. To the new generation of settler leaders who emerged in the 1880s and 1890s – many of whom were of Italian and Spanish origin who had been naturalized in 1889 – the political inclusion of the 'indigenous', Arabic-speaking Jewish population represented an inconceivable anomaly that deeply discredited the legal and political institutions of the metropole. Their main demand – the abrogation of the Crémieux Decree – was an attempt to assert a vision of the body politic in Algeria as defined exclusively by ethnicity and descent, in accordance with the legislation and jurisprudence of the previous decades.

While they were shocked by the extreme violence and virulence of anti-Jewish sentiment amongst the European community in Algeria, metropolitan Jewish politicians, scholars, and journalists largely interpreted it as a similar phenomenon to the French one. Portraying Algerian Jewry as a community undergoing a rapid and thorough cultural and political assimilation, they interpreted settler anti-Semitism as an attack on the legacy of 1789, of assimilation and regeneration.[1] Scholarship on settler anti-Jewish politics in the 1880s and 1890s, too, tends to interpret it as an attack on the project of Jewish assimilation, as the 'absolute negation of Algerian Jews' Frenchness', to quote Michel Abitbol.[2] This tendency is of course supported by the fact that outspoken

---

1 Examples of this tendency are abundant. See, for example, Crémieux's response to attacks on the naturalization decree: Adolphe Crémieux, *Réfutation de la pétition de M. du Bouzet* (Paris: Imprimerie Schiller, 1871), 7–14. See also: B.M., 'Choses d'Algérie', *L'Univers israélite*, 5 February 1897, 621–5; B.M. 'Le décret Crémieux', *L'Univers israélite*, 5 March 1897, 749–54.
2 Michel Abitbol, 'L'Affaire Dreyfus et la montée de l'antisémitisme colonial en Algérie', *Archives juives* 31, no. 1 (1998): 78–9. See also: Sophie B. Roberts, *Citizenship and Antisemitism in French Colonial Algeria, 1870–1962* (Cambridge: Cambridge University Press, 2017), 39–40.

settler anti-Semites were propelled to local and national power positions by the upheaval of the Dreyfus Affair in 1898.[3]

Yet, as this chapter shows, settler anti-Jewish politics was fuelled and shaped precisely by the decades-long Algerian Jewish attempt to solicit and later exercise citizenship *without* subscribing to the French idea of citizenship-as-assimilation which emerged since the 1860s. Above and beyond economic factors, fears of the Jewish vote, and the drama of the Dreyfus Affair, settler anti-Semitism was a revolt against the inclusion of difference within the body politic.

Settler leaders certainly adopted and adapted anti-Semitic tropes and patterns that had evolved in Europe over centuries. Algerian Jews were the most visible and menacing 'Other' to the Europeans in Algeria, as both communities were predominantly urban and worked as petty merchants and artisans. Local stereotypes evolved accordingly, bringing together the ethnic hierarchies of French colonial thought with the olden images of European anti-Semitism. Jews were depicted as usurers, as barbarous, uneducated and unhygienic.[4] Anti-Semitism amongst the Europeans in Algeria was also fuelled by a severe economic crisis in the 1890s, making it a widely shared cause that was endorsed in the metropole by the highest ranks of the socialist party, including none other than Jean Jaurès, who would only later become a leading *Dreyfusard*.[5] Most importantly, the Dreyfus Affair brought about a political alliance between anti-Semites on both sides of the Mediterranean. In early 1898, Max Régis, who had been catapulted within months from absolute anonymity into the anti-Semitic pantheon, invited Eduard Drumont, France's most prominent anti-Semitic writer at the time, to stand for parliament as deputy of Algiers in the upcoming elections. Before long, however, the meanwhile mayor-elect of Algiers overshadowed Drumont as the unchallenged leader of the anti-Semitic cause.

It is no coincidence, as Zeev Sternhell observed, that with Régis, 'a [French] political movement for the first time turned to Algeria in search of a leader.'[6] The legal measures of the 1860s–80s – the *sénatus-consulte* of 1865, the Crémieux

---

3   See most notably Pierre Birnbaum, *The Anti-Semitic Moment: A Tour of France in 1898*, trans. Jane Todd (London: University of Chicago Press, 2011), esp. 151–62.
4   Emmanuel Sivan, 'L'antisémitisme comme reflet de la situation coloniale en Algérie', in *Pa'amei Ma'arav. Etudes judeo-maghrébines*, ed. Itzhak Bezalel (Jerusalem: Ben-Zvi Institute, 1983), 58–74. (Hebrew).
5   Michel Abitbol, *From Crémieux to Pétain: Antisemitism in Colonial Algeria 1870–1940* (Jerusalem: Zalman Shazar Centre, 1993) (Hebrew), 43.
6   Zeev Sternhell, *La Droite révolutionnaire, 1885–1914: Les origines françaises du fascisme* (Paris: Fayard, 2000), 242.

Decree of 1870, the *Code de l'indigénat* of 1881 and the new citizenship law of 1889 – made the colony a fertile ground for anti-Jewish sentiment. To many settler leaders, the collective naturalization of the 'indigenous' Jewish population amounted to nothing short of a disruption of the political order in the colony, where the boundaries of within and without were drawn according to ethnicity and descent. In such a societal order and against the backdrop of the Dreyfus Affair, settler anti-Semites launched not only the most lethal anti-Jewish attacks but the most radical vision of the national community as defined by nothing but 'Latin' origin, shorn of republican pretence.

Beyond attacks on the Jewish minority, the anti-Jewish crisis of the late 1890s was a constitutive moment for settler politics in Algeria. Moving back and forth between Algiers and Paris, this chapter explores the coming of a new type of settler leader: young, manly, anti-metropolitan, and often of a non-French origin. The most prominent amongst this emerging generation was Régis, who skilfully cast himself as a local, authentic leader by appealing to his supporters' basest instincts and repeatedly clashing with metropolitan authorities. Though his political career lasted only five years, Régis announced the coming of a new archetype of a settler leader which would dominate Algerian politics for decades to come.

The language of difference

On 15 November 1889, a man by the name of Prosper Saraffe from Oran published the first issue of a new, bilingual newspaper named *Qol Israel / La Voix d'Israël* ('The Voice of [the people of] Israel'). Under the motto 'Ta'ish al-République! Ta'ish Faransa! Ta'ish l'Algérie!' ('Long Live the Republic! Long Live France! Long Live Algeria' [here in its French name]) Saraffe declared his goal to be 'the emancipation and the civilization of our esteemed coreligionists':

> We know that since the day of our entry into the great French family, the Algerian Jews have done a lot; their efforts towards civilization and progress, their strong love of education and their desire to assimilate are incontestable. Contrary to what some of our relentless adversaries think of us, we think that the Jews have justified and justify completely and every day the great honour given to us.[7]

---

7 Prosper S., 'À nos Lecteurs', *Qol Israel / La Voix d'Israël*, 15 November 1889, 1.

Despite this declared confidence, Saraffe's text had an unmistakably apologetic, even defensive, tone. He pledged to explain the rights and duties of citizens to the 'very small number' of his coreligionists who had a 'merely vague, imperfect, or confused' understanding of their political status.

The 1880s and 1890s witnessed a flourishing of Judeo-Arabic press in Algeria, as the 'Arabic print revolution' spread throughout the Middle East and North Africa.[8] The first and short-lived Judeo-Arabic/French newspaper *A-Daziri/ L'Israélite algérien*, discussed in the last chapter, was now followed by various newspapers, particularly in Oran, which became an important centre of Jewish journalism.[9] In Algiers, the rabbi, scholar and publisher Shalom Beccache founded in 1891 the Judeo-Arabic weekly *Bet Yisrael* ('The People of Israel'), which published 107 issues in the next three years.[10] These newspapers were mostly short-lived or appeared irregularly, but they provided a forum for debates on cultural, religious and political matters. Alongside journalism, Judeo-Arabic was widely used in the late nineteenth and early twentieth centuries in liturgy, everyday communication and personal correspondence. It was visibly and audibly present on the streets, at the market, around synagogues and Jewish primary schools and in Jewish shops and businesses.[11]

It was this persistence and indeed renaissance of Judeo-Arabic, this continued demonstration of cultural and linguistic difference that infuriated colonial lobbyists and settler leaders and which Saraffe sought to address in *Qol Israel/La Voix d'Israël*. In 1881, French legislation prohibited non-citizens from printing newspapers. Algerian Jews, naturalized since 1870, were now in the unique position of an 'indigenous' population nevertheless allowed to publish freely in

---

8   Ami Ayalon, T*he Arabic Print Revolution: Cultural Production and Mass Readership* (Cambridge: Cambridge University Press, 2016), 18–28; Yosef Tobi and Tsivia Tobi, *Judeo-Arabic Literature in Tunisia, 1850–1950* (Detroit: Wayne State University Press, 2014), 10–15.
9   These newspapers included *Shomer Israel* ('The Guardian of [the people of] Israel'), *L'Maguid Wahrani* ('The Declarer of Oran', possibly a reference to the famous European Hebrew newspaper *Hamagid*, copies of which were circulated in Algeria), or *Maguid Misharim* ('The Declarer of Justice').
10 Aharon Maman, *Mirqam Leshonot HaYehudim BiTzfon Afriqa* (*The Fabric of Jewish Languages in North Africa*) (Jerusalem: Mossad Bialik, 2014), 19. Yosef Tobi, 'Bekache, Shalom', in *Encyclopedia of Jews in the Islamic World*, Executive Editor Norman A. Stillman. Consulted online on 30 August 2021. On *Hamagid* and other Hebrew newspapers from Europe being read in Algeria see: Efraim Hazan, 'Po'alo HaSifruti shel Rabi Yitzhak Mer'ali VeTochnito LeKhinus HaShira VeHapiyut BeAljiria', ('Isaac Morali's Literary Activity and his Programme of collecting poetry and *Piyutim* in Algeria'), *Pe'amim*, no. 91 (2002): 70. Some Judeo-Arabic newspapers are available through the digitization projects of the French and Israeli national libraries at: www.gallica.bnf.fr and www.nli.org.il/en/newspapers/titles.
11 For liturgy and everyday communication see: Marcel Cohen, *Le parler arabe des Juifs d'Alger* (Paris: H. Champion, 1912). For private correspondence see, for example, documents archived in: Central Archives for the History of the Jewish People, Jerusalem: AL/Al 2, 'Lettres et télégramme pour intervenir en faveur du soldat Henri Sebbah', 1898–1900.

its own language. This, however, did not remain unchallenged. When in 1886 the Judeo-Arabic newspaper *Qol HaTor* ('The Voice of the Turtledove', a Hebrew reference to springtime and renewal, similar to the symbolism of the swallow in European languages) was about to be founded, the local prefect tried to limit the publication by requiring that the editor provide regular French translations.[12] The inclusion of a French text in *Qol Israel/La Voix d'Israël*, then, appears to have been a compromise rather than an ideological statement, a choice made by the publisher amid the difficult position in which Algerian Jews found themselves following the Crémieux Decree. It seems to be no coincidence that the French text of the first issue remained vague when explaining the newspapers bilingualism, referring merely to the 'hybrid, mixed writing, with the advantage of satisfying all classes of our readers', while the Judeo-Arabic version was very concrete: 'You will notice that *Qol Israel* is written in two languages: French and Arabic, so that the Jews will read it each in his language.'[13]

One of the earliest uses of Judeo-Arabic as a marker of otherness in the decades-long campaign against Algerian Jews' citizenship was a passionate petition against the Crémieux Decree, submitted to parliament in 1871 by the former interim governor of Algeria and prefect of Oran Charles du Bouzet. Having failed to win the support of local Jewry in a bid to become Oran's mayor, du Bouzet fell out with the local community – and with Algerian Jews more generally, as his protest clearly revealed:

> The Algerian Jews are not French. *Their native language is Arabic, which they speak poorly and write in Hebrew script.* Their customs are oriental and amongst almost all of them, the habitual attire is that of the Orient. Nil intellectual culture, a sole profession – commerce – a sole passion – that of amassing money ... Strangers to the traditions of the French nation [nationalité française], left outside European civilization, these Orientals have no homeland.[14]

It is no coincidence that du Bouzet made language such a central criterion of political inclusion. As prefect of Oran in late 1870, he would have most probably been aware of the 1869 Judeo-Arabic petition for citizenship and the subsequent consultations in which his predecessor had been involved. His reference to the language of Algerian Jews and its depiction as a distorted version of Arabic express the indignation of a colonial official and aspiring mayor over a request

---

12 The response from the Ministry of the Interior, however, stressed that Algerian Jews were allowed to print freely as per the 1881 law. See: Asseraf, *Electric News*, 42–3, 58–9.
13 Assimilus, 'Ila-Qarayna, *Qol Israel / La Voix d'Israël*', 15 November 1889, 2.
14 Charles du Bouzet, *Les Israélites indigènes de l'Algérie. Pétition à l'Assemblée nationale contre le décret du 24 octobre 1870* (Paris: Imprimerie Schiller, 1871), 4. Emphasis added.

for citizenship made in a language other than French. Du Bouzet's terminology was echoed by the then Minister of the Interior Félix Lambrecht's 1871 bill to abrogate the Crémieux Decree, which claimed that Algerian Jews have 'conserved their customs and their traditional institutions' and alleged that 'generally, they do not consider themselves to belong to the political community [in their place of residence]. The interests preoccupying them allow them to remain strangers to that community and do not attach them to the land on which they reside.'[15]

Such depictions of Algerian Jewry not merely as inherently non-French but as a defective, incomplete version of Arab civilization would soon become a central element of anti-Semitic writing on Algeria. A common and lethal claim in the anti-Jewish campaign of the late nineteenth century was that the Crémieux Decree had ignited Al-Muqrani's major revolt in Kabylia in the early months of 1871. Politicians, officials, and provocateurs construed a narrative of Muslim disregard towards Algerian Jews, claiming that Algerian Muslims couldn't possibly accept their naturalization. In the immediate aftermath of the revolt, a series of high-ranking politicians and administrators claimed that the decree had antagonized Algerian Muslims by elevating the once *dhimmi* (protected, yet inferior Ottoman subjects) Jews to a higher political status. In his bid to repeal the Crémieux Decree in July 1871, Minister of the Interior Lambrecht argued that the Kabylian insurrection 'revealed everything dangerous and impolitic' about it.[16] The governor of Algeria at the time of the revolt Louis-Henri de Gueydon agreed, describing the Crémieux Decree as 'the decisive cause of the insurrection'.[17]

Crémieux and others sought to refute such allegations – in vain. Crémieux's well-documented pamphlet, showing that the revolt was well underway before the news of the decree could have reached Kabylia and reiterating assurances from Muslim leaders that they did not object to the naturalization of the Jews, found little consideration; a further, even better-evidenced refutation from 1897 was similarly ignored.[18] The myth of the Crémieux Decree as the cause of the Kabylian revolt was simply too convenient to be refuted by factual evidence, as it ostensibly proved the Second Empire's tolerance of difference – however

---

15 Assemblée nationale, session de 1871, no. 412, Annexe au procès-verbal de la séance du 21 juillet 1871: Projet de loi ayant pour objet d'abroger le décret du 24 octobre 1870 [. . .], 2.
16 Assemblée nationale, session de 1871, no. 412, Annexe au procès-verbal de la séance du 21 juillet 1871: Projet de loi ayant pour objet d'abroger le décret du 24 octobre 1870 [. . .], 3.
17 Léon de la Sicotière, *Rapport fait au nom de la Commission d'enquête sur les actes du Gouvernement de la défense nationale – Algérie*, vol. 2 (Versailles: Cerf et fils, 1875), 207.
18 Crémieux, *Réfutation de la pétition de M. du Bouzet*; Louis Forest, *La Naturalisation des Juifs algériens et l'insurrection de 1871* (Paris: Société française d'imprimerie et de librairie, 1897). See also on Algerian consistories' response: Roberts, *Citizenship and Anti-Semitism*, 11–12.

temporary and conditional – to be fatally wrong. To those who reiterated and popularized this myth in the following decades, it confirmed the absolute validity of the ethnic hierarchy governing Algeria and the danger in any attempt to alter it.

The person who formulated these claims in the clearest, most violent manner was Edouard Drumont in his 1885 bestselling tale of centuries-old Jewish perfidy *La France juive*. After a first volume dedicated to France's alleged corruption by Jewish influence throughout history, the second volume of *La France juive* turned the reader's attention to Algeria: 'Never has the Jew proved himself to be more brazenly indifferent to anything concerning the homeland, more relentlessly preoccupied with himself and his race than with the decrees issued by Crémieux ordering the emancipation of the Algerian Jews.'[19] Drumont went much further than previous attacks on Crémieux, describing him not merely as one amongst several factors of the 1871 Kabylian uprising but as 'the main perpetrator, the sole person to blame for the Algerian insurrection'.[20] Against this embodiment of treachery and self-interest, Drumont placed Al-Muqrani, whom he portrayed as a 'noble, loyal figure'.[21] The Crémieux Decree was all the more scandalous for him in light of what he saw as the poor military achievements of the Jews and the bravery of Algerian Muslim warriors. If any population group earned the right to participate in political life after 1871, it was the latter. And like many of his contemporaries, Drumont turned to Rome for inspiration:

> We would hardly be surprised if the Government of National Defence had granted some spectacular reward to these heroic Arabs who, after having fought against us for so long, defended us at a time of peril. Rome emancipated the slaves who fought for her during the War of the Allies, and a certain proclamation, honouring with the status of a French citizen those who proved themselves to be worthy of it, would have had a considerable effect in Algeria.[22]

Throughout the 1880s and 1890s, Drumont's ideas set the tone of settler anti-Jewish agitation. Though clearly intended for an aristocratic and high-bourgeois readership, *La France juive* quickly became a commercial success amongst working-class milieus. An abridged, illustrated version from 1887 helped popularize Drumont's ideas in France. In Algeria, a vibrant scene of anti-Semitic literature and press provided a crucial link between the high-brow,

---

19 Édouard Drumont, *La France juive: Essai d'histoire contemporaine* (Paris: C. Marpon & E. Flammarion, 1887), vol. II, 11.
20 Ibid.
21 Ibid., 22.
22 Ibid., 12–13.

conservative Drumont and the lower, urban classes, which were the power base of local anti-Semitism.[23] In 1887, a certain Georges Meynié published a tractate entitled *L'Algérie juive*. The indebtedness of this account to *La France juive* was explicitly acknowledged by the author, who repeated many of Drumont's claims concerning the Jews in Algeria, albeit in a more detailed and less flamboyant manner. Most importantly, Meynié reiterated the claim that the Crémieux Decree was responsible for the 1871 uprising, stressing what he thought was a disproportionate Jewish influence in the Tours delegation.[24]

Drumont saw Algeria as the promised land of liberation from Jewish yoke. With its widely disseminated anti-Semitic press – 'independent', as he called it – the colony provided a fertile ground for his ideas. 'Perhaps in Algeria', Drumont half-hoped, half-predicted, 'will begin the French anti-Semitic campaign.'[25] Indeed, anti-Semitic press and literature flourished in Algeria. Anti-Semitic newspapers were printed in tens of thousands of copies and disseminated even in the merest towns, where few or no Jews lived. Plays, songs, caricatures and merchandise were highly popular in Algeria, and helped disseminate negative images of Jews.[26] A host of *ligues* and committees were founded in the 1880s and provided regular social and leisure activities, particularly for the lower classes, who would remain the power base of the movement. Before long, settler anti-Semitism would make spectacular political gains, and Drumont himself would fulfil his prophecy with a successful bid to represent Algiers in parliament.

The two leitmotifs of the campaign against Jewish citizenship in Algeria – indignation over the inclusion of an 'indigenous', Arabic-speaking minority and anxieties over the maintaining of the colonial hierarchy – came to the fore with renewed ferocity and unprecedented violence in 1897–8, as the Dreyfus Affair propelled this campaign into an urgent cause of metropolitan anti-Semitism. In February 1898, after weeks of anti-Jewish riots following the publication of Emile Zola's *J'accuse . . . !*, prominent anti-Semites from Algeria made their first public appearance in Paris. Alongside Max Régis, who was hailed as hero and made the abrogation of the Crémieux Decree the central demand of his speech, stood his colleague Louis Pradelle, mayor of the town of Mustapha near Algiers, who vividly expressed the humiliation which anti-Semites saw in the naturalization of Algerian Jews: 'Before 1830, every fifteen years the Arabs would distribute

---

23 Édouard Drumont, *La France juive: Edition populaire* (Paris: V. Palmé, 1888); Abitbol, *From Crémieux to Pétain*, 45–6.
24 Georges Meynié, *L'Algérie juive* (Paris: A. Savine, 1887), on dedication and acknowledgement of Drumont see preface, on Crémieux decree and insurrection see esp. 172–4.
25 Drumont, *La France juive*, vol. II, 48. For praise for the settler press see: *La France juive*, vol. II, 51.
26 Abitbol, *From Crémieux to Pétain*, 45–8, 64–7.

amongst themselves the [confiscated] property of the Jews, and now you want them [the Jews] to be equal to the Arabs, equal to us?'[27] A few months earlier, a violent crowd looted the synagogue in the coastal town of Mostaganem to the east of Oran as police stood by. The attackers vandalized the interior, destroyed liturgical objects and tore up the prayer and exegesis books in Hebrew and Judeo-Arabic. Local authorities later photographed a page from one of these books. But the bitter irony of this piece of evidence of settler anti-Jewish violence was most likely lost on both the perpetrators and the authorities. It contained a famous sentence from the Book of Proverbs: *Do not gloat when your enemy falls.*[28]

Origin, violence and the city

Settler anti-Jewish politics had developed its own distinctively colonial character since the early days of the campaign to repeal the Crémieux Decree. In a political order that pivoted around the exclusion of the Algerian Muslim majority, the Jewish population made a significant percentage of the electorate. This was particularly marked in the *département* of Oran, where the Jewish percentage of the electorate reached 15 per cent and in some towns even 50 per cent.[29] Anti-Jewish agitators here claimed a handful of Jewish leaders to be controlling the Jewish vote and dominating local politics, and a number of citizens submitted petitions to the National Assembly demanding the annulment of the Crémieux Decree almost immediately after its promulgation.[30] As Sophie Roberts shows, settler anti-Jewish agitation was very much a local movement, with mayors and councillors consolidating their power by excluding Jews from the public sphere and economic life, thus catering to their own, predominantly lower-class clientele.[31]

But it was in the 1890s that an urban, popular movement emerged, one which displayed its power through demonstrations and violent attacks on Jews and turned the city into a public sphere where various social groups united in shared hostility to the Jews and, not less importantly, the Paris-controlled

---

27 For Régis's speech see: AN, BB/18/6238: Extrait du rapport de M. M. Martin, Commissaire aux délégations judiciaires à Paris: Réunion de la Salle de Chaynes [certified copy made for trial against Régis on 21 March 1898]. For Pradelle's speech see: *Le Figaro*, 21 February 1898 [archived in: AN, F/7/16001/1].
28 ANOM, F80/1685: Mémoire sur les troubles de l'Oranie, 31 May 1897.
29 Ageron, *Les Algériens musulmans*, 584–5.
30 Assan, *Les consistoires israélites*, 339; Geneviève Dermenjian, *La crise anti-juive oranaise: 1895–1905, l'antisémitisme dans l'Algérie coloniale* (Paris: L'Harmattan, 1986), 33–8.
31 Roberts, *Citizenship and Antisemitism*, 80–1.

administration. The significant and unapologetic presence of naturalized Europeans in this movement and their virtuosity in using origin and identity to mobilize supporters made the confrontation with the authorities particularly explosive. What started as a campaign against the Crémieux Decree soon developed into a movement propagating a new vision of citizenship and belonging, one which was exclusively grounded in ethnicity and descent. In the words of the later mayor of Mustapha, near Algiers, Lucien Chaze: 'Here is an entire people [peuple], composed of diverse elements whose cohesion is perhaps not yet perfect . . . Here is an entire people, shouting in unison: "Down with the Jews".'[32]

In the late 1890s, unprecedented anti-Jewish violence engulfed Algeria's towns and cities. In Constantine during the elections of 1896, armed rioters, often helped by the police, physically prevented Jews from voting.[33] The attack on the synagogue and various Jewish shops in Mostaganem in May 1897 soon spread to Oran, where looters were joined by city councillors, while police and military stood by and occasionally joined in. The violence then spread throughout the province. Some twenty people were injured, hundreds of shops were plundered and five synagogues attacked.[34] In Algiers, deadly riots erupted following Zola's *J'accuse. . .!* in January 1898. Rioters attacked the Jewish population as well as the governor general and the *prefect*. Police and military often stood by. Two people were killed, dozens injured and the damage was estimated at half a million francs. The anti-Semitic press ignited riots by calling for violence and boycotts.[35] Violence on the streets and in the press was soon translated into political power: in the parliamentary elections of 1898, anti-Semites won four out of Algeria's six seats. Even before that, anti-Semitic lists conquered various municipalities and mayoralties, including Oran and, most importantly, Algiers.

Algiers soon became the most important centre of the agitation. The main city connecting the colony and the metropole, the seat of the governor general, and the theatre of the Drumont-Régis alliance, Algiers represented like no other site the attempt to foster a common, 'Algerian' and 'Latin' identity. At the peak of the riots in Algiers in 1898, even the popular fictional figure of Cagayous was mobilized for the anti-Semitic cause. As discussed in the previous chapter, Cagayous was a highly popular epitome of the myth of an Algerian melting pot emerging on the streets and quays of Algiers. Anti-Semitism was now made an

---

32 As quoted by Jean Drault in *La libre parole*, 4 September 1898 [archived in: ANOM, F80/1690].
33 Abitbol, *From Crémieux to Pétain*, 55.
34 ANOM, F80/1685: Mémoire sur les troubles de l'Oranie, 31 May 1897.
35 Abitbol, *From Crémieux to Pétain*, 58–67.

inseparable part of that myth with the publication of a special edition entitled *Cagayous antijuif*.[36] Fiction aside, the most important and instructive political figure in Algiers of those days was Max Régis, who rose from the anonymity of a young law student in early 1897 to local and national fame the following year. Born to an Italian family, Régis became a French citizen in the late 1880s – a biographical detail which his opponents sought to use against him. But as we shall see, Régis skilfully turned his and many of his supporters' foreign origin into a source of pride, asserting a new collective identity and a new conception of being French.

Origin, history and the sense of a shared Latin identity were at the core of what triggered anti-Semitic agitation in Algiers in 1897. In January, a Jewish jurist by the name of Emmanuel Lévy was nominated as professor of Roman law at the Algiers law faculty, sparking immediate protests. Lévy's first lecture in early February was disrupted by some 200 protesting students who forcibly made their way into the lecture theatre, shouting 'Down with the Jews! Down with Lévy!' and forcing the professor out of the room.[37] The protests only ended after two weeks, following a promise by none other than the Minister of Education that Lévy would return to France at the end of the academic year. A report to the governor general revealed the priorities – and, as we know in hindsight, misjudgement – of the Algerian administration in its attempt to restore order with minimum confrontation, including asking the victim to cooperate with the agitators: 'Order has been restored and it can be expected that the agitation of the last days . . . will soon make way to a sounder assessment of the situation. Mr. Lévy seems to be willing to do all that he can in order not to be the matter of troubles any longer.'[38] The students' success in ousting a professor soon became a pattern of anti-Semitic confrontation with the metropole. In June 1898, governor Lépine and several other functionaries were called back to Paris by the government, in an attempt to appease the anti-Semitic movement.[39] Ever since then, settler leaders pledged to oust any metropolitan official standing in their way.

This minor incident reveals the interplay of religion, origin and politics in 1890s Algeria. In a settler population composed of French, Maltese, Italians and Spaniards and undergoing rapid homogenization through the institutions of

---

36 On the anti-Semitic twist of Cagayous and its wider social context see: Prochaska, 'History as Literature', 694–9.
37 ANOM, GGA 7 G 10: Commissaire spécial au Gouverneur général, 3 February 1897.
38 ANOM, GGA 7 G 10: Secrétaire générale du Gouvernement général de l'Algérie, Rapport pour le Gouverneur général, 15 February 1897.
39 Abitbol, *From Crémieux to Pétain*, 69.

citizenship, schooling, military service and higher education, being 'Latin' was a crucial marker of belonging. References to the historical Roman presence in North Africa served to portray this emerging 'Latin' community as pioneering a veritable Reconquista on the southern Mediterranean shore. The appointment of a Jewish professor to teach Roman law could easily be depicted as an assault by an arrogant, decaying metropole on the sweat and tears of the nascent, dynamic society. As the Parisian Jewish weekly *l'Univers israélite* commented: 'They [the protesters] were appalled by that name, Lévy. A Jew teaching Roman law in Algeria – that was a scandal they couldn't tolerate.'[40]

It was in these protests at the Algiers law faculty that Max Régis first emerged as a prominent figure of the anti-Semitic scene. His opponents were quick to point out his foreign origin. In March 1898, the French newspaper *Siècle* mocked him – and Algerian anti-Semites more generally – by stressing his Italian origin in an article entitled with the famous anti-Semitic slogan '*La France aux Français*'.[41] The Parisian daily *Le Radical* was less subtle when informing its readers that Régis's father had only been naturalized in 1888 and that his full surname was Régis-Milano. Max Régis, reported the article, omitted the second part of his surname, 'which doesn't have a French allure.'[42] The newspaper *Droit de l'Homme* did not only mention Régis's Italian origin but reported on his father's convictions: 'Long before his naturalization, this Italian gave clear evidence of his love for France ... On 18 February 1875, he was sentenced for a month in prison and a fine of two hundred francs for having sold gunpowder to the Arabs.'[43] More than anything else, this passage demonstrates what a central criterion origin and ethnicity had become: A *Dreyfusard* newspaper, struggling against anti-Semitism in the name of universal rights, subscribed to the colonial view of transactions with 'the Arabs' as an act of betrayal.

For the authorities, too, there was no doubt that foreigners were the main problem, if not the very source of the crisis. 'The population of Bab el Oued, the Lalahoum quarter and the Prefecture quarter is predominantly Spanish, and it is particularly in these areas that one finds the most uncompromising anti-Semites.'[44] Such was the concern about the foreign populations that a prominent member of the Algiers departmental council called for the Spanish, Italian and German consuls in Algiers to be warned that their nationals could be deported

---

40 B.M., 'Les incidents d'Alger', *L'Univers israélite* 52-(1), no. 21 (12 February 1897): 653.
41 'La France aux Français', *Le Siècle*, 4 March 1898 [archived in: AN, F/7/16001/1].
42 'Arrestation de M. Max Régis', *Le Radical*, 23 March 1898 [archived in: AN, F/7/16001/1].
43 'La famille Régis', *Droit de l'homme*, 23 June 1898 [archived in: AN, F/7/16001/1].
44 ANOM, GGA 7G 17: Commissaire central d'Alger au Gouverneur général, 1 April 1898.

if involved in riots.⁴⁵ In Oran, the Spanish consul published placards warning Spaniards to stay away from any form of anti-Semitic riots.⁴⁶

Besides foreigners, the anti-Jewish movement in Algiers also saw the participation of women on a scale not known before. As the movement gained momentum in 1898, police agents repeatedly noted the large numbers of women in anti-Semitic political meetings and during the gatherings on the streets and quays of Algiers whenever Régis, and later Drumont, arrived from mainland France.⁴⁷ Régis explicitly addressed women, and sometimes only them, in the crowds listening to his speeches, and women were also much present in his well-staged public appearances.⁴⁸ Leaflets distributed by anti-Semitic groups often made an explicit appeal to women, appealing to 'Antijuives! Antijuifs!' (note the order).⁴⁹ Drumont, for his part, in an article bidding farewell to Algiers after losing his parliamentary seat in 1902, praised Algeria for leading the way to French anti-Semitism and acknowledged the active role of women as a unique, inspiring development: 'In other countries, women are afraid of political battles . . . Our valiant women of Algiers are not as spineless, they are always at the forefront, and one sees the energy in the charming eyes.'⁵⁰

Anti-Jewish leaders also sought to mobilize the Algerian Muslim population, but this remained a very limited attempt with limited success. Agitators in the *département* of Oran occasionally hired young male Muslims to participate in demonstrations and riots and even provided them with arms.⁵¹ However, there was no real effort to address propaganda at the Muslim population or to appeal to its grievances. Anti-Jewish agitation in Algeria was and remained a movement of the European population, born out of the quest to preserve political monopoly and articulated as the collective voice of an emerging 'Algerian' and 'Latin' society. Anti-Jewish demonstrations and meetings were at times attended by Muslims, but numbers never exceeded a few dozens.⁵² Of all anti-Semitic leaders, Drumont was the most serious in these efforts and held several meetings

---

45 Charles Marchal, *Les troubles d'Alger: Opinion d'un témoin* (Algiers: Imprimerie Charles Zamith & Cie, 1898), 6.
46 ANOM, F80/1684: Spanish consul in Oran: 'A los Españoles', 21 May 1897.
47 See for instance: ANOM, GGA 7G 10: Commissaire central d'Alger, Rapport, 8 March 1898; ANOM, GGA 7G 17: Commissaire central d'Alger au Gouverneur général, 1 April 1898.
48 Abitbol, *From Crémieux to Pétain*, 74.
49 ANOM, GGA 7G 17: Leaflet inviting for punch for Drumont, organised by comités antijuifs of Algiers, Mustapha and St. Eugène, 1902 (no specific date mentioned).
50 Édouard Drumont, 'Merci à Alger!', *L'Antijuif algérien*, 16 January 1902 [archived in: ANOM, GGA 7G 17].
51 Ageron, *Les Algériens musulmans*, 602–3.
52 See for instance: ANOM, GGA 7G 17: Commissaire central d'Alger au Gouverneur général, April 1898 (no specific date mentioned).

with Algerian Muslim notables.[53] But for all of his admiration for 'the Arabs' as expressed in *La France juive*, such meetings remained rare, and the actual power relations underlying his encounter with Muslim society – and with women – were those which were at work in his brothel visits in the Casbah of Algiers. It was here that the devout Catholic and his allies from the anti-Semitic mouthpiece *La Libre parole*, watching nude dancers, staged for themselves local society as they were taught to imagine it by exoticist, sensual representations such as Delacroix's *Femmes d'Alger* or later by Jean Geiser's *danseues* photographs.[54]

By mobilizing foreigners, women, and to a limited extent Algerian Muslims, Régis and his fellow agitators succeeded in initiating a movement that challenged traditional hierarchies and was galvanized in its opposition to a common enemy around a simple language of slogans, symbols and gestures. At a political rally in the town of St. Eugène near Algiers in June 1897, attended, according to the local police commissaire, by an equal number of foreigners and 'real French', Régis declared: 'We shall fight with all our forces and all our energy against the Jew; We shall gather around one and the same flag in order to push back this invasive mass and our motto must be: "Algeria to the Algerians!"'[55]

The separatist subtext in Régis's rhetoric alarmed the metropolitan authorities more than the riot or provocation he sought to instigate. Settler anti-Semites indeed flirted with separatism occasionally. But it was above all by asserting a local, shared identity rather than outright secessionism that anti-Semites built their movement, as Régis skilfully did in this speech. The reassuring sign, police agents believed, was the fact that the majority of the audience in such rallies were all but illiterate and thus incapable of understanding any political message. Such rhetoric, they argued when Régis emerged as a prominent local leader in the early months of 1897, was unlikely to have any lasting impact.[56] That, of course, was a fatal misjudgement. Régis's mastery was in mobilizing precisely those parts of the population ignored by the administration. In this sense, Algeria was no novelty. Here as in Europe, the mythical, elusive figure of 'the Jew' appealed

---

53 ANOM, GGA 7G 17: Commissaire de Police de Mustapha au contrôleur général des services de police et de sûreté, 15 May 1898.
54 ANOM, GGA 7G 17: Cabinet du Commissaire central d'Alger, Rapport pour le commissaire central, 29 April 1899. On the influence of Delacroix on contemporary perceptions of Muslim women and sexuality see: Judith Surkis, 'Propriété, polygamie et statut personnel en Algérie coloniale, 1830–1873', *Revue d'histoire du XIXe siècle* 41, no. 2 (Spring 2010): 29–30. On Jean Geiser's photographs see McDougall, *A History of Algeria*, 92.
55 ANOM, GGA 7 G 10: Commissaire spécial de Saint-Eugène, Rapport au préfet d'Alger, 21 June 1897.
56 ANOM, GGA 7 G 10: Préfet d'Alger au Gouverneur général, 22 and 23 June 1897.

to the darkest fears and envies of the dispossessed. In the heterogenous settler society of Algeria, this mythical enemy served as a powerful call for unity.

The leaders of the Algiers movement were innovative above all in their use of urban space. The close police surveillance of Régis allows us to trace this in detail. In the months preceding his election as mayor, Régis spent much of his days on the streets of Algiers, meeting fellow activists and agitators in cafés and leading spontaneous gatherings of supporters. These were quickly turned into improvised demonstrations, with Régis addressing the crowds with the same short, simple slogans repeated time and again – above all 'À bas les Juifs!'[57] The audience at Régis's appearances grew rapidly in 1898, and crowds greeting him upon his returns from journeys to Paris easily reached several thousands – composed, according to police, mainly of Europeans and Muslims, and to a far lesser extent by French people.[58]

It was the combination of vulgar propaganda and a masterly use of the streets and cafés of Algiers that helped Régis into the town hall in November 1898. Drumont's *La Libre parole* cheered at this victory of the popular movement, saying: 'This is Algiers's response to the *Dreyfusards* who had the outrageous intension of presenting Max Régis… as a professional rioter.'[59] In fact, 'professional rioter' was an apt description: Clashes with the law and its representatives were not by-products of anti-Jewish agitation, but their very essence. It was through them and their consequences – above all his suspension as mayor – that Régis portrayed himself as a victim, an authentic representative of the popular will oppressed by the institutions of the metropole. Régis continued to write in his newspaper *l'Antijuif algérien* after his election and used it to publish not only anti-Semitic propaganda and municipal orders restricting Jewish rituals but also fierce articles against metropolitan authorities.

Indeed, Régis's most dramatic public appearances was made upon his return from Paris in January 1899, two months after his election success. Suspended by the governor general soon after his election due to repeated breaches of law and attacks on the republican institutions, Régis, now more than ever before, portrayed himself as representing a popular 'Algerian' sentiment oppressed by unelected authorities controlled by the metropole. In defiance of his suspension, he made his way from the harbour to the town hall through a crowd of a

---

57 See for instance routine police report: ANOM, GGA 7 G 10: Commissaire central d'Alger au contrôleur général des services de police et de sûreté, 1 December 1897.
58 See for instance: ANOM, GGA 7 G 10: Commissaire spécial de sûreté (Alger), 10 July 1898; Commissaire spécial de sûreté (Alger): Rapport pour le Gouverneur général, 10 July 1898.
59 'Le nouveau maire d'Alger', *La Libre parole*, 21 November 1898 [archived in: AN, F/7/16001/1].

thousand-strong chanting 'Vive Régis! À bas les Juifs!' and, surrounded by female supporters, climbed to the town hall balcony. In a highly symbolic gesture, a woman standing beside him detached a tricolour flag from the railing and handed it to Régis who, waving the flag, said to the crowd:

> This flag is better placed at the hands of naturalised foreigners than entrusted to such people of French origin as [governor general] Lafarrière. Instead of hiding in the Summer Palace or at the Place Soult-Berg [seats of the governor general and the prefecture, respectively], Lafarrière and [Algiers prefect] Lutaud should join this crowd in order to understand its demands.[60]

In a society founded on violence, where rights and laws were always secondary to ethnic divisions as imagined by the state, anti-Semitism appeared in its pristine form, declaring ethnicity as the highest, indeed the sole criteria of belonging to the national community. By defying the metropole's authorities, Régis masterly cast himself as the loyal, authentic representative of the true, popular will, embodying the emergence of a new, once diverse, now unified crowd. Waving the tricolour from the town hall's balcony and condemning unelected authorities in front of a cheering crowd, the suspended mayor staged the clearest, most radical version of the anti-Dreyfusard cause: the idea of popular sentiment and national pride as the highest moral authority.

Clashing with the metropole

Settler leaders did little to hide their scorn towards metropolitan France. Though they repeatedly denied allegations of separatism, their anti-establishment tone and growing confidence in asserting their own, local identity eventually led to a conflict with the state authorities and the political mainstream in Paris.[61] While the myth of Jewish conspiracy was by no means new to European thought, settler anti-Semites were unique in turning the allegation towards France itself. While Drumont depicted France as suffering under a Jewish yoke, he never claimed it to be morally or culturally contaminated by it. A pessimist view of society and history was certainly present in *fin de siècle* France, but Jews were rarely seen

---

60   ANOM, GGA 7G 10: Commissaire spécial adjoint des ports et des chemins de fer (Alger), Rapport, 8 January 1899.
61   See for instance Régis's speech in January 1899 as recorded in: ANOM, GGA 7G 10: Commissariat spécial de sûreté (Alger), Rapport, 11 January 1899. See also a leaflet written by Régis's successor as mayor of Algiers: ANOM, GGA 7G 17: Maire d'Alger, Appel aux citoyens (evidently from 19 April 1899).

as the source of cultural decadence and decay. This was where old French and new Algerian anti-Semitism parted. Régis and his allies repeatedly described France not only as manipulated by the Jews but as willing to obey their rule. This can be seen in the closing sentence of Régis's aforementioned speech delivered from the Algiers town hall in January 1899: 'No one can halt the anti-Jewish idea from advancing and, should it face any obstacles, be it Lutaud or Lafarrière, they shall be swept away like all other obstacles.'[62] While they never seriously considered declaring independence, settler anti-Semites did evoke a sense of moral superiority by contrasting their 'Latin' and 'Algerian' identity with a weak, servile metropole.

This subtle yet significant change of tone regarding the metropole was never explicitly articulated. Rather, it can be inferred from the ensemble of slogans, metaphors and symbols of local anti-Semitic propaganda, from leaflets, newspapers and ephemera that circulated in 1890s Algiers and from chants and speeches recorded in thousands of police reports. In June 1899, as Régis was set to return to Algeria after yet another arrest and trial, an anti-Semitic committee in Algiers called on the population to greet this 'prisoner of the Jews' upon his arrival in Algiers.[63] Three months later, Régis's newspaper *l'Antijuif* printed the following leaflet after the pardoning of Dreyfus by the President of the Republic Emile Loubet: 'Since by pardoning Dreyfus the government provokes both our army and our patriotic population, we appeal to all our fellow citizens to support us in our rebellion against those who only hold power in order to violate our dearest sentiments. We must not allow the Jews to triumph today.'[64]

The message of such leaflets was clear. While Régis was arrested, Dreyfus was pardoned, and local anti-Semites in Algeria skilfully portrayed this as evidence that the government in Paris was willingly collaborating with Jewish conspiracy. Following this logic, resistance and rebellion were the only option, and it was for the Algerian anti-Semites to lead the rebellion with all their energy and fearlessness – much in line with Drumont's prophecy in *La France juive*. Against this backdrop, the slogan 'Vive l'Algérie! À bas les Juifs!', printed, for instance, on pins distributed to Drumont's supporters during his visit to Algiers in April 1901, seems as composed not of two separate sentences but of a juxtaposition, in which

---

62 ANOM, GGA 7G 10: Commissaire spécial adjoint des ports et des chemins de fer (Alger), Rapport, 8 January 1899.
63 ANOM, GGA 7G 10: Leaflet: 'Appel à la population', signé par Le comité central, imprimérie spéciale de *L'Express* [no date in document itself, but marked 6 June 1899 in handwriting – evidently by an administration member].
64 ANOM, GGA 7G 10: Leaflet: 'A nos Amis', imprimerie de L'Antijuif [no date on leaflet, but archived in folder covering September 1899].

Algeria stands for the opposite of anything Jewish.[65] Another expression of the same idea was a popular chant amongst protesters: 'Vive la République honnête!' ('Long live the honest Republic').[66] *République honnête* must clearly be understood as a demand or indeed a pledge rather than a description of a given reality, implying that the current republic was dishonest and corrupt.

A key feature of settler anti-Semitic rhetoric was the adaptation and rewriting of republican and revolutionary imagery. Concluding his speech in Paris in February 1898, Régis said: 'What we need is either the expulsion of the Jews or their extermination ... If necessary, we will water with Jewish blood the tree of our liberties.'[67] This image, which was popular amongst Régis and his allies, evoked the reinvigoration of the Republic using a well-known allegory of freedom in nineteenth century France – the tree of liberty. It presumably also implied a far more concrete threat to the Jewish community of Algiers: In October 1870, republican settlers had planted a Tree of Liberty at the *Place du gouvernement* to celebrate the newly declared Third Republic. It is not unthinkable that it was to this specific site in Algiers that Régis referred.[68] Another symbol of the revolutionary legacy appropriated by anti-Jewish leaders in Algeria to rewrite the Republic was the national anthem: Several versions of the *Marseillaise antijuive* circulated in Algiers around the turn of the twentieth century. One of them, from the neighbourhood of Bab el-Oued, read: 'Dans la ville d'Alger / Il n'y a plus qu'un cri / Patrie, fraternité / À bas les youdis' ('In the city of Algiers there's but one shout: Homeland, Fraternity, and Down with the Jews').[69]

The rapid radicalization of settler anti-Jewish politics and the high percentage of naturalized Europeans sparked a controversy regarding the sweeping naturalization law of 1889. Such was the threat to public order that even some outspoken anti-Semites of French origin feared they were about to lose control over the situation. One of them was Charles Marchal, a member of the departmental council of Algiers who wrote in February 1898: 'The legislator must urgently consider the status of both the Jews and the Foreigners, whose

---

65 Archived in: ANOM, GGA 7G 17.
66 See, for instance, a report on a political meeting in Algiers presided by Régis: ANOM, GGA 7G 10: Commissariat spécial des chemins de fer et des ports (Alger), Procès-verbal administrative, 11 January 1899.
67 AN, BB/18/6238: Extrait du rapport de M.M. Martin, Commissaire aux délégations judiciaires à Paris: Réunion de la Salle de Chaynes [certified copy made for process against Régis on 21 March 1898]. Emphasis added. 'Watering the tree of liberty with Jewish blood' recurred as a motif, for instance in a speech by Mustapha mayor Pradelle as recorded in: *Le Figaro*, 21 February 1898 [archived in: AN, F/7/16001/1].
68 On the Tree of Liberty planted in Algiers in 1870 see: L.-C. Dominique, *Un Gouverneur général de l'Algérie: L'Amiral de Guyedon* (Algiers: Typ. Adolphe Jourdan, 1908), 13.
69 Sivan, 'L'antisémitisme comme reflet', 72.

premature admission into the French electoral body, with no conditions and no reserves, will soon cause considerable disturbances.'[70] Marchal was not alone. Alarmed by the interplay of riots, anti-republicanism, and the emerging 'Algerianism' of recently naturalized Italians and Spaniards, French politicians and administrators throughout Algeria called for the collective naturalization of 1889 to be revised – either through the outright annulment of citizenship or by suspending the right of vote amongst the first generation of the new citizens.[71]

Though none of these proposals was implemented, they reveal just how immediate the threat to the entire colonial order seemed at the peak of the anti-Semitic crisis. What began as a demand to strip 'indigenous' Jews off their citizenship quickly developed into a political movement that sought to pursue the ethnic idea of citizenship in full and threatened the fragile equilibrium between the Republic and its colony. Amid escalating anti-metropolitan rhetoric, French officials finally acted. Alongside various concessions to settler demands – in 1898, the colony gained budgetary autonomy from the metropole, and Europeans gained greater influence upon its administration – the metropole eventually moved to curb the anti-Semitic movement. In the Chamber, a growing number of deputies denounced the anti-Semitic movement, and in 1900, a parliamentary inquiry commission refuted all claims about the absence of integration of the Jewish minority and the necessity to abrogate the Crémieux Decree. When Régis was re-elected as mayor of Algiers in 1901, the governor general convinced the government to limit the mayor's authorities and give sweeping powers to the prefect, thus impeding Régis's ability to ignite riots and disorder.

In the parliamentary elections of 1902, the anti-Semites suffered a bitter defeat. An election placard by Drumont's rival Maurice Colin warned: 'Voting for Drumont is voting against the Republic.'[72] Drumont lost his seat, as did two other deputies of the anti-Semitic movement, whose political careers ended after this election. As for Régis, he failed to win a parliamentary seat for the 11th arrondissement in Paris and vanished from the public eye as spectacularly as he had made his appearance only five years earlier, publishing one last pamphlet to announce his departure from the political stage.[73] The only anti-Semitic deputy to be re-elected was Emile Morinaud of Constantine, who would spend the following years fighting with the same energy against any form of political

70 Marchal, *Les troubles d'Alger*, 25.
71 Dermenjian, *La crise anti-juive oranaise*, 101.
72 ANOM, GGA 7G 17: Election banner for and approved by candidate Maurice Colin, Mustapha: Imprimerie algérienne, evidently 1902.
73 Max Régis, *Pourquoi je me reitre de la lutte politique* (Algiers: Imprimerie P. Crescenzo, no publication date specified). Archived in: ANOM, 91 1F 14.

inclusion of Algerian Muslims, now once again seen by Europeans in Algeria as their main, most menacing enemy.

A key event in the decline of the anti-Semitic movement in Algeria was the so-called Margueritte Affair in April 1901, when a group of Algerian Muslims attacked a colonial settlement. The attackers killed six settlers and took dozens of hostages, forcing them to pronounce the *Shahada* – the sentence by which a person recognizes Allah and the Prophet Mohammed in order to convert to Islam. These events shocked public opinion amongst Europeans in Algeria and in the metropole and opened a public debate on the political, legal and economic situation in the colony. During this debate, severe allegations were made against the anti-Semitic movement. In the Chamber, deputy Gaston Thomson of Constantine accused Drumont and Morinaud of having undermined the French authority in the eyes of the Algerian Muslim population and of having trained Algerian Muslims and provided them with arms.[74] The prefect of Algiers Charles Lutaud claimed in a letter to Prime Minister Waldeck-Rousseau that the chaos and agitation of the anti-Semitic crisis were responsible for the Margueritte attack, since the Francophone press, including anti-Semitic newspapers, was widely read by Algerian Muslims.[75] The newly appointed governor general Charles Jonnart made similar allegations against Drumont, accusing him and the anti-Semitic movement more generally of having distracted the colonial administration from the policing and surveillance of the Muslim population.[76] The anti-Semites in turn blamed Margueritte on the 'Jewish-controlled' administration which, as they claimed, had neglected the interests of the settlers.[77]

While the main impact of the Margueritte Affair was the reappearance of *les indgiènes* or *les Arabes* as the arch-enemy of settler and mainstream French public opinion, it nevertheless re-opened a debate on the political order in the colony. In some circles on the Left, amongst colonial reformers and in parts of the liberal press, the Affair raised with renewed urgency the question of the economic situation, the rights and the legal status of the Algerian Muslim population. Deputy Albin Rozet, a prominent opponent of the *Code de l'indigénat* since the 1890s, delivered a long speech at the Chamber denouncing it as one of the causes of the Margueritte attack.[78] Rozet would go on to become an important ally of the Young Algerians in their struggle for penal and legal reform in the colony

---

74 JO, 24 May 1901, 1148–9.
75 ANOM, F80/1691: Préfet d'Alger au Président du conseil des ministres, 10 May 1901.
76 Abitbol, *From Crémieux to Pétain*, 114–16; Ageron, *Les Algériens musulmans*, 606–8.
77 See for instance: Max Régis, 'Les vrais assassins de Margueritte', *L'Antijuif algérien*, 30 April 1901 [archived in: ANOM, F80/1691].
78 JO, 31 May 1901, 1193–7.

until 1914, as we shall see in the next chapter. The Parisian daily *Le Temps* went even further, reminding its readers of the broader context: The settlement of Margueritte was founded on lands confiscated from the local population and its extension was funded by their taxes. Neither the anti-Semites nor their opponents, the article claimed, seemed to be concerned by such injustices.[79] An even more militant attack on the anti-Semites and their approach to the Muslim population was launched by Jean Jaurès in an article published in *Le Petit Républicain* in late April 1901. Jaurès, who had meanwhile abandoned his anti-Jewish approach from the mid-1890s and had become a leading *Dreyfusard*, mocked the anti-Semites' purported allegiance with the Algerian Muslim population: 'When we demanded that the body politic [la cité politique] be finally opened to the Arabs, when we protested against their complete exclusion from the right to vote and showed by which measures and adaptations one could prepare them for universal suffrage, the Algerian anti-Semites and indeed Drumont himself accused us of seeking to hand over Algeria to the indigenes.'[80]

This was a new tone. Though the French mainstream did not consider any major political change in the colony, there was nevertheless a growing realization of just how little control the metropole could exercise in Algeria. Ever since the 1890s, an increasing number of French politicians grew critical of the political system in Algeria and the settler exigences it engendered. In 1894, an inquiry commission presided by Jules Ferry, a prominent advocate of French expansionism, submitted a damning report on the consequences of colonization and settlement in Algeria.[81] By the end of the anti-Semitic crisis in the early 1900s, settlers in Algeria had lost much of their earlier prestige in metropolitan public opinion. What had started as a local campaign against the Crémieux Decree developed in the 1890s into an all-out crisis that threatened the very foundations of the colonial order and the power balance between the metropole and the colony. In the following years, as officials and politicians would promote a vision of imperial governance relying on the labour and military manpower of the empire's colonized populations, Algerian settlers would become the *enfants terribles* of the French empire.

---

79 'L'Algérie à la Chambre', *Le Temps*, 26 May 1901 [archived in: ANOM, F80/1690].
80 Jean Jaurès, 'Antisémites et Indigènes', *Le Petit républicain*, 27 April 1901 [archived in: ANOM, F80/1690].
81 Henri Pensa, *L'Algérie: organisation politique et administrative, justice, sécurité, instruction publique, travaux publics . . . Voyage de la délégation de la commission sénatoriale d'études des questions algériennes présidée par Jules Ferry* (Paris, 1894), esp. 335–408.

4

The levy of blood

In early September 1909, the Radical-Socialist deputy for the Seine Adolphe Messimy published a combative piece in the Parisian daily *Le Matin*. Under the title 'Let Us Call Africa to Our Help', Messimy wrote: 'Africa has cost us piles of gold, thousands of soldiers and streams of blood. We do not dream of reclaiming the gold from her. But the men and the blood, she ought to pay them back to us with usury, now that we have lifted her from barbary, have given her order and wealth.'[1] This was not the first time that Messimy turned to Africa in search of manpower. A former general and colonial administrator in Niger, he had served in parliament as *rapporteur* of the defence, marine and colonies budget. As *rapporteur* of the war budget in 1907, Messimy pointed out that conscription had been introduced amongst colonial subjects in Tunisia since the first days of the French protectorate in 1881, thus yielding for France more soldiers (in relative numbers) than Algeria – a French possession since 1830.[2] All in all, Messimy was convinced: 'Evidently, the protectorate regime offers all kinds of advantages compared with that of colonization.'[3]

The prelude, course and aftermath of the First World War set in motion a wave of new thinking on empire and Algeria's position within it. By the turn of the twentieth century, the unease and scorn of metropolitan commentators concerning settler mentalities since the 1880s turned into outright shock following the anti-Jewish crisis of the 1890s, its secessionist or at least autonomist undertones and its defiance of French authorities. Meanwhile in Morocco, under partial French military occupation since 1906 and a French protectorate since 1912, the first resident-general Hubert Lyautey advanced a model of colonial rule based on maintaining a degree of autonomy by local elites and ruling classes – most notably the sultan – casting the protectorate as the 'modern' and efficient

---

1 Adolphe Messimy, 'Appelons l'Afrique à notre secours!', *Le Matin,* 3 September 1909, 1, A-C.
2 AN, 509AP/5 – dossier 2: Lettre adressée par le rapporteur du budget au ministre de la guerre au sujet de l'organisation des réserves algériennes, annexe XXI, 30 September 1907.
3 Messimy, 'Les effectifs de l'armée et le service militaire des indigènes algériens (suite)', 802.

counter-model to abuse-ridden Algeria.⁴ Amid conflicts on the seams of the Russian, Ottoman and Austro-Hungarian empires and escalating tensions with Germany, statesmen and officials were seeking to exploit the full potential of the empire's manpower in the event of war, shifting their focus from settlers to colonial subjects.⁵

How radical was this new thinking on empire in terms of citizenship and participation? Gary Wilder has argued that the discourse and concept of Greater France (*la plus grande France*), promoted by various colonial reformers in the 1920s, was an attempt to transcend the binary of metropole versus colonies and to accommodate difference in a way that marked a significant departure from the republican quest for cultural-religious uniformity.⁶ Beyond the French empire, Erez Manela and Susan Pedersen have each explored the politics of participation and rights in the new imperial order after 1918. Manela has argued that President Wilson's rhetoric of self-determination was the main factor behind a wave of political demands from across the colonized world.⁷ Pedersen contends that the League of Nations – in particular the Permanent Mandates Commission – though unable to hold France and Britain accountable to the promise of gradual movement towards self-determination in the mandated territories as defined in Versailles in 1919, nevertheless provided representatives from these territories with important communication channels, platforms and forums in which to press Paris and London on colonial matters and the question of independence.⁸

Yet, as this chapter argues, the years around the First World War showed above all the limitations of new imperial politics. At the level of official policymaking, the early twentieth century witnessed the attempt to enhance and systematize French sovereignty in the overseas territories. As Mary Dewhurst-Lewis has shown drawing on the example of the protectorate of Tunisia, the politics of indirect rule, though widely celebrated by French colonial reformers as a counter-model to settler-dominated Algeria, came to a crisis in the early twentieth century, as both colonial officials and French settlers sought to consolidate French

---

4   Paul Rabinow, *French Modern: Norms and Forms of the Social Environment* (Chicago: The University of Chicago Press, 2014), 290–6.
5   The origins of the First World War are of course a huge topic. For the most recent, capacious (and controversial) analysis see: Christopher Clark, *The Sleepwalkers: How Europe Went to War in 1914* (London: Penguin 2013), esp. 28–47, 132–5, 155–7, 204–14, 314–66.
6   Wilder, *The French Imperial Nation-State*, 25–35.
7   Erez Manela, *The Wilsonian Moment: Self Determination and the International Origins of Anticolonial Nationalism* (New York: Oxford University Press, 2007).
8   Susan Pedersen, *The Guardians: The League of Nations and the Crisis of Empire* (Oxford: Oxford University Press, 2015), 4–8, 77–8.

'preponderance'.⁹ By the time Messimy was praising the protectorate, this very model was already coming under pressure from officials and colonial lobbyists. For intellectuals and political leaders in Algeria, the reimagining of empire was of limited interest. As studies by Arthur Asseraf and Cemil Aydin show, we must look 'beyond Wilson and Lenin' to understand the political horizon in which activists and writers thought and operated during and after the war.¹⁰ Whether it was the half-mythical figure of 'hadj Guillaume' (Kaiser Wilhelm) who would redeem Algerians from French yoke or a new interest taken by Algerian Arabic press in the legislation and institutions of the new Turkish Republic, the promise of change was being sought not in the corridors of European centres of power but in the rapid rise of mass politics.¹¹

New thinking on imperial governance and reform, this chapter argues, was deeply apolitical or indeed anti-political. It was characterized by the avoidance of the demand that now resonated throughout the colonized world: that of participating in the running of one's country. Minister of the Colonies Albert Sarraut's rhetoric in a major 'valorization' programme for the French empire from 1921 is a case in point. This ambitious programme, designed to invigorate France after four years of war, focused on economic, agricultural and administrative reforms. As for political participation, Sarraut argued that unlike Britain, France rewarded its colonial subjects not with rights but with its 'tenderness': 'Paternally against our breast, we softly press the humble face of our black or yellow brother, who hears our hearts beating in unison with his.'¹²

This apolitical trend was particularly glaring in Algeria. After a temporary suspension of the *Code de l'indigénat* during the war and a brief period of mainstream openness to the idea of enfranchising Algerians, much of the status quo was reasserted after 1918. A limited reform in 1919, which extended the Algerian electorate in municipal elections and slightly simplified the procedure of individual naturalization, fell short of even the elementary demands for political participation formulated by Algerian representatives since 1908. Instead, it was above all in the realm of symbolic gestures that colonial officials and experts sought to imagine and stage France as a 'Muslim power'.

---

9   Mary Dewhurst-Lewis, *Divided Rule: Sovereignty and Empire in French Tunisia, 1881–1938* (Berkeley: University of California Press, 2014), 3–4, 100–3.
10 For 'beyond Wilson and Lenin' see: Aydin, *The Idea of the Muslim World*, 122–3.
11 On the figure of 'Hadj Guillaume' see Asseraf, *Electric News in Colonial Algeria*, 118–24. For report on legislation in Turkey see e.g.: 'Al-Qanun al-muduni al-turki', *Al-Najah*, 21 July 1926, 1.
12 I use here Gary Wilder's translation in *The French Imperial Nation-State,* 33. For the original quote see: *Projet de loi portant fixation d'un programme général de Mise en valeur des colonies françaises présenté . . . par M. Albert Sarraut* (Paris: Chambre des députés, 1921), 58.

Ultimately, the course and aftermath of the First World War marked the coming of bottom-up citizenship politics. Some 172,000 Algerian colonial subjects were recruited as soldiers and another 120,000 were sent as workers to *usines de défense nationale* in the metropole between 1914 and 1918, marking, alongside soldiers from Morocco and Tunisia, the emergence of a Maghribi community in France after the war.[13] As Gilbert Meynier and James McDougall have shown, the most significant consequence of the military mobilization and the limited reforms of 1919 was the rapid politicization and radicalization of hundreds of thousands of Algerians.[14] This new wave of mass participation rendered more visible than ever before the contradictions and injustices of the Algerian colonial order, leading a new generation of French politicians to propagate the idea of Algerian Muslims participating in significant numbers in the Republic.

Conscription and rights

With his reasoning, his career and his political inclinations, Adolphe Messimy reflected many of the controversies and changes in French public opinion concerning the introduction of conscription amongst Algerians during the 1900s–10s. A staunch advocate of the Jacobin military legacy of a republican, conscription-based army, Messimy, like many others at the time, was concerned by the reduction of mandatory military service from three to two years and statistics showing declining birth rates in France. However, well-aware of grievances amongst settlers and colonial lobbyists, Messimy stressed that he envisaged no *levée en masse* in Algeria and opposed any form of collective naturalization of those Algerians who were to serve under the French flag. The only rewards he was willing to consider were some reforms of the *Code de l'indigénat* and extended Muslim representation in local Algerian councils.[15]

Messimy's calls to introduce conscription amongst Algerian Muslims set in motion an overall strategic shift amongst generals, administrators and commentators who were now hoping to exploit the populations of the new colonies militarily. This was a major change: Of the three armies composing the French military, only the *Armée métropolitaine*, consisting of French citizens,

---

13 Gilbert Meynier, 'Les Algériens et la guerre de 1914–1918', in *Histoire de l'Algérie à la période coloniale*, ed. Abderrahmane Bouchène et al. (Paris: La Découverte, 2012), 230–2.
14 Meynier, *L'Algérie révélée*, 441, 480–4; McDougall, *A History of Algeria*, 185.
15 Messimy, 'Les effectifs de l'armée et le service militaire des indigènes algériens (suite)', 802–3.

relied exclusively on conscription. The other two armies, the *Coloniale*, dating back to the French colonies of the seventeenth century, and the *Armée d'Afrique*, which was founded in Algeria after 1830, recruited soldiers from the local populations as volunteers.[16] But the prospect of escalation in Europe gave rise to new ideas: In 1910, colonel Charles Mangin, a veteran of colonial expeditions in Asia and Africa, published his book *La force noire*, in which he advocated the deployment of troops from the colonies in a future European war.[17] If in 1908 Messimy's estimation that *une grande armée arabe* could be 'the decisive factor of victory' in a future war was still a view confined to colonial and military milieus, it was very quickly popularized.[18] In 1911, Maurice Barrès wrote: 'I love Morocco because it gives us men . . . Thirty to forty thousand good soldiers, Kabyles, the old Berber race.'[19]

What turned a debate on military strategy into a contentious political controversy was the question of political rights to be granted to soldiers and veterans after the war. As the members of the Chamber of Agriculture in Oran feared, 'it would be impossible to deny them [Algerian Muslim conscripts] moral and material advantages, among them the exercise of the civil and political rights of French citizens.'[20] Indeed, plans to introduce conscription amongst Algerians resulted almost immediately in a debate on the boundaries of the French body politic. In September 1908, the *Revue indigène*, founded two years earlier by a group of French scholars and colonial officials, dedicated an entire issue to Messimy's plan and the question of political rights under the title '*l'Empire franco-barbaresque*'. An important platform to advocate colonial reforms in the early twentieth century, the *Revue indigène* advanced a more nuanced understanding of Islam amid widespread concerns over 'pan-Islamism' or the territorial ambitions of the Ottoman Empire. Its lengthy studies and scholarly articles were amplified by the daily press, most notably by *Le Temps* – a long-time arena for critical writing on Algeria and the *Code de l'indigénat*. In the opening sentences of the September 1908 issue, the review's editor Paul Bourdarie, a scholar of the history of equatorial Africa who would go on to advise the colonial administrator in Morocco,[21] wrote: 'The Franco-Berber empire is

---

16 Anthony Clayton, *France, Soldiers and Africa* (London: Brassey's Defence, 1988), 6–8, 16. The French citizens residing in Algeria were subjected to conscription – albeit for shorter periods.
17 Girardet, *L'idée coloniale en France*, 99–100.
18 Messimy, 'Les effectifs de l'armée et le service militaire des indigènes algériens', 776.
19 Quoted in: Girardet, *L'idée coloniale en France*, 100.
20 Quoted in: *La Revue indigène* 3, no 29 «L'empire franco-barbaresque» (September 1908), 377.
21 Biographical details from: http://www.academieoutremer.fr/academiciens/fiche.php?aId=302. Accessed: 13 December 2017.

not a project to be founded. It exists. It is sealed with blood.'[22] A detailed study of Messimy's conscription project, the *Revue indigène* issue contended that military service had to be rewarded with political benefits. While rejecting both collective naturalization and any change to the *statut personnel*, the review argued that even a gradual reform of the *Code de l'indigénat* and some limited political rights to soldiers and veterans would be a considerable achievement.

A key role in this process of rethinking exclusion and inclusion was played by the emerging generation of the Young Algerians, who successfully mobilized sections of French public opinion in their struggle for representation and rights. These mostly urban, French-educated, often French-naturalized men were much influenced by political developments in the Ottoman Empire and the Young Turks' demands to restore the 1876 constitution and restrain the power of Sultan Abdul Hamid II. A significant number amongst them were active members of the *Ligue des droits de l'homme* and close to French Freemasonry.[23] In 1904, *Le Temps* published what was probably the first article in the metropolitan press on this emerging generation and called upon the Algerian administration to encourage their political development.[24] In 1908, a delegation of the Young Algerians to Paris submitted a petition against Messimy's ideas. In a meeting with Prime Minister Georges Clemenceau, they stressed that they could only accept mandatory military service in return for civil and political rights. Though Clemenceau refused to commit to the delegation's demand, the Young Algerians did have some success in their advocacy. In 1908, Governor Charles Jonnart wrote to Clemenceau and acknowledged the need for some reforms of the Muslim electorate for local elections.[25] Messimy, however, was unimpressed by the Young Algerians' demands:

> The indigenes demand 'political rights', and French public opinion may ask itself whether we are about to see in parliament sixty deputies wearing burnous [long woollen cloak worn in the Maghrib] soon. That is out of the question. The educated Arabs are very few and the masses of the population are still very backward. They know and believe just what the French administrators, the sheikhs and the marabouts tell them.[26]

Despite vehement opposition, the activity of the Young Algerians set in motion a slow yet significant shift across the French political spectrum, which was now

---

22 'L'empire franco-barbaresque', *La Revue indigène* 3, no 29 (September 1908): 329.
23 Ageron, *Les Algériens musulmans*, 1040–52.
24 Ibid., 1032–3, 1040.
25 Ageron, *Les Algériens musulmans*, 1037–8, 1056.
26 Messimy, 'Les effectifs de l'armée et le service militaire des indigènes algériens (suite)', 802.

more open to the idea of tolerating difference within the French body politic. The organ which led this change was the *Revue indigène*. In an issue dedicated to the question of naturalization in 1911, the editors and contributors suggested allowing for naturalization without demanding that Muslims renounce Islamic legislation. Of course, such proposals had been drafted already in the 1880s, as we have seen. But the 1911 publication of the *Revue indigène* exerted a far more significant influence on French public opinion. Gathering a group of renowned jurists and colonial administrators at the crucial moment of introducing conscription amongst Algeria's Muslim population, the *Revue indigène* effectively broke a decade-long taboo in openly calling for practising Muslims to be let into the *cité française*. This call would be taken up by prominent political figures and would preoccupy the Chamber on several occasions during the war.

Articulating their ideas through the language of assimilation and the 'civilizing mission', most contributors to the 1911 publication of the *Revue indigène* viewed citizenship instrumentally: it was to be granted to certain colonial subjects not as a natural right but as a reward used selectively by the French state. Editor Bourdarie, for instance, though declaring the ultimate objective of his reform agenda to be the 'complete and definite fusion of the Arabo-Berber people [peuple] within the French nationality', made it clear that political rights ought to be granted selectively.[27] Criticizing the indiscriminate application of the *Code de l'indigénat*, he argued that the Algerian Muslim population should be divided into two major categories: 'One composed of everything notable and honourable in the indigenous population; the other including everything that is the subject of caution in the same population ... If the *indigénat* is justified vis-à-vis the second, it is absolutely impolitic vis-à-vis the first.'[28] The same principle was to apply to the question of citizenship, and the Algerian administration was encouraged to adopt the 'American principle' of distinguishing between 'desirable' and 'undesirable' immigrants when considering which Algerians should be admitted into the French body politic.[29] This last remark highlights a key element of French colonial thought: Though it was France which occupied Algeria, Algerians were perceived as immigrants to the *cité française*.

A particularly interesting view was provided by Henri de Lamothe, who had been active in colonial reform campaigns since the 1880s as discussed in Chapter 2. Then as now, de Lamothe insisted that the right to vote had to be granted to parts of Algerian society. Most crucially, he provided an unusual

---

27 Paul Bourdarie, 'Avant-propos', *La Revue indigène* 6, no. 63–64 (July-August 1911): 401.
28 Ibid., 402.
29 Ibid., 406.

view of the *statut personnel* – the simplified French codification of Islamic civil legislation to which Algerians were subjected. 'The personal and familial status of the Muslim inhabitants of North Africa is as worthy of the legislator's respect as the Gallic-Roman customs sanctioned by the codes of the metropole.'[30] Abandoning the common view of French civil legislation as the highest accomplishment of modernity and standardization, de Lamothe portrayed it as equally respectable as Islamic legislation. Rather than presented as an objective, infallible canon, the *Code civil* was historicized and portrayed as stemming from a specific constellation. As such, the 'Gallic-Roman' legislation was of equal merit as Islamic legislation.

Though various contributors to the *Revue indigène* agreed that Islamic legislation posed no real obstacle to naturalization, they all vehemently rejected the option of collectively granting citizenship to Algerian Muslims. 'The experience with the so-called Crémieux Decree', Bourdarie wrote, 'prohibits us from repeating a similar mistake in the future.'[31] Bourdarie and the other contributors who viewed the Crémieux Decree as a 'counter-model' of colonial policy were clearly still under the impression of the anti-Jewish crisis which had paralysed Algerian politics and administration in the late 1890s. Tellingly, they attributed this crisis not to the sweeping European naturalization of 1889 but to the naturalization of some 34,000 Algerian Jews in 1870. With their critique of the Crémieux Decree, the contributors to the *Revue indigène* showed how well-cemented the colonial division between 'European' and 'indigenous' had become and how successful the anti-Semites had been in contesting the very idea that an 'indigenous' population could be made French. Ten years after Régis, Drumont and their allies had thrown Algeria into chaos, a series of colonial reformers identified the source of the troubles in the naturalization of the anti-Semites' victims.

The campaign launched by the *Revue indigène* successfully broke the silence concerning Islamic legislation and French citizenship. But this scholarly debate also reiterated and indeed sharpened various tropes of contemporary colonial thought. If supporters of the new approach were to have their way, the scholarly distinction between 'developed' and less developed or 'desirable' and 'undesirable' subjects was to be made a legal category. Furthermore, the various contributors to the *Revue indigène* viewed citizenship not as a right but rather as a tool in the hands of the state in its attempt to promote its own interests – whether it

30 Ibid., 411.
31 Ibid., 428.

was countering Ottoman influence amongst Algerians in the run-up to the war, guaranteeing 'the future of our domination', or encouraging 'the spreading of our language and education in North Africa'.[32]

But none of these commentators equalled the cynicism of one of the most unequivocal opponents of Algerian participation in the republic, the influential colonial thinker Arthur Girault, author of the widely read and oft-reprinted book *Principes de la domination coloniale*. In his contribution to the 1911 issue of the *Revue indigène*, Girault rejected any reform to the legal regime in Algeria. Commenting on the plan to introduce conscription amongst Algerians Girault dismissed the idea that this should be recompensed with civil rights. Concluding his argument, Girault wrote with astonishing sangfroid: 'The fact that the Muslims are not French citizens does not currently prevent them from being subjected to taxes. The same condition does not suffice to prevent them from being subjected to the levy of blood.'[33]

Chilling as such cynicism may be, this was exactly the outcome. In February 1912, Messimy, now serving as Minister of War, introduced conscription amongst colonial subjects in Algeria without any form of political representation in return, ignoring protests by Algerians. However, this initially remained of limited practical consequence. Opposition to Algerians' mobilization from settlers and the Algerian administration led to actual recruitment being limited to 5 per cent of the overall potential contingent.[34] Though the main consideration behind such opposition was clearly the anxiety that military training and access to arms might lead to uprisings, opponents to the conscription of Algerians were also concerned that it might lead to political representation.

Indeed, the introduction of conscription under such conditions was met with vehement rejection amongst Algerians. Already during the debates of 1908, petitions from across Algeria were sent to the governor in protest over the intention to introduce conscription. In numerous demonstrations, the recurring slogan 'You will not get our children' was shouted.[35] In June 1912, a delegation of the 'Committee for the Defence of Muslim Interests' in Algeria submitted to Prime Minister Raymond Poincaré a petition demanding substantial political

---

32 'Position de la question au point de vue juridique', *La Revue indigene* 6, no. 63–64 (July-August 1911): 447 (opinion expressed by jurist Charles de Bœck), 422 (opinion expressed by jurist André Weiss), 421 (introduction by editorial board, most probably written by Bourdarie) – respectively.
33 'Position de la question au point de vue juridique', opinion expressed by Arthur Girault (mistakenly spelled 'Girauld' in the issue), 426.
34 AN, 509AP/5 – dossier 2: Note sur le service militaire des indigènes musulmans de l'Algérie (neither signature nor date. Document doubtless from early 1916, as can be inferred from its content).
35 Meynier, *L'Algérie révélée*, 91.

reforms in return for military service. 'The indigenes of Algeria', they wrote, 'are prepared to fulfil all their duties vis-a-vis the motherland, but they believe that this new duty [conscription] should have as reward an amelioration of their situation.'[36] They demanded that military service for Algerian Muslims have the same duration as that of French citizens and that conscripts be recruited from a minimum age of twenty rather than eighteen. More substantially, they demanded 'a reform to the repressive regime', 'a serious and sufficient representation in all assemblies in Algeria and the metropole', 'a just distribution of taxes' and 'equitable designation of budget resources for the different elements of the Algerian population'. Concerning political representation, the petitioners demanded:

> that the electoral college be extended to assure the efficiency and fairness [*sincerité*] of the vote . . . that the number of indigenous representatives in the Algerian assemblies be extended to two fifths . . . that the electoral college be composed in the same way for the elections to all Algerian assemblies . . . that indigenous municipal councillors have the rights to partake in the election of mayors and their deputies . . . that the indigenes be represented in the French parliament or that a council be created in Paris were the Algerian Muslims be represented by deputies elected by them . . . that those who will satisfy the obligation of military service by way of conscription or voluntarily have the right to opt for the quality of French citizens without being subjected to the current formalities and by a simple declaration.[37]

These demands, which would have meant a considerable change to the balance of power in Algeria, were vehemently rejected. Governor of Algeria Charles Lutaud in a 1913 letter to the prefects of Algeria warned of any initiative of accepting them. The anxieties and pathos of the colonial cadre of an empire in crisis can be read in this dramatic warning on the eve of war: 'I do not forget the lesson of history; It was by conferring too early and too quickly the entirety of electoral rights to the Africans . . . that Rome precipitated its decline!'[38]

As war loomed nearer, attempts to implement certain reforms in order to gain Algerians' support for the war effort intensified. Throughout 1914, Messimy, once again serving as Minister of War, abandoned his past scorn and expressed support for the Young Algerians' demands that military service be rewarded with

36 'Le « Manifeste jeune algérien » (juin 1912)', in *Le Mouvement national algérien: textes 1912–1954*, ed. Claude Collot and Jean-Robert Henry (Algiers: Office des publication universitaires, 1978), 23–4.
37 Ibid., 24.
38 ANOM, GGA 12H 6: Gouverneur général au préfet d'Oran, 20 May 1913 (the same letter was evidently sent to the other prefects as well).

certain rights and liberties. In July 1914, as war seemed inevitable, the Chamber exempted serving Muslim soldiers from the *Code de l'indigénat*.

Once the war started, French authorities were particularly concerned about German-Ottoman propaganda and calls upon the Muslim populations in the colonies to join the Central Powers in a sacred effort (*jihad*) and liberate themselves from British and French yoke. The French government appealed to Algerians to join the 'sacred union' of the 'civilized peoples' against the 'barbarism' of the Central Powers. Such measures and messages did have some resonance amongst Algerians in the early phase of the war. As Gilbert Meynier has argued, 'finding oneself all of a sudden among the camp of the "civilized" after having been treated as barbarian for so long may explain unusual attitudes: It was the first time that Algerians were approached by the colonial power in such a way.'[39] However, conscription was met with significant protests and even armed resistance, most notably in Batna, south of Constantine, in November 1916, where insurgents killed the *sous-préfet* and burned his official records.[40] For Messimy, this proved the need for urgent reforms in taxation and the *Code de l'indigénat*, as well as the need for a pay raise for conscripts.[41]

In 1915, former prime minister Georges Clemenceau called for the naturalization of Muslim soldiers without requiring them to renounce Islamic jurisprudence in matters of marriage, divorce and inheritance. With Clemenceau's endorsement, the acceptance of naturalization of Muslims still subjected to the *statut personnel* entered the French mainstream. Naturalization *dans le statut*, as this principle came to be known, became a credible, acceptable political stance. Serving as chairman of the Senate's Commission of Foreign Affairs, Clemenceau, together with his counterpart in the Chamber Georges Leygues (who would later come to serve as prime minister as well), wrote to the Minister of Foreign Affairs to demand on behalf of the two commissions a new policy in Algeria. Clemenceau and Leygues expressed one key demand: the gradual accession of the indigenes to the quality and political rights of French citizens without demanding them to renounce the *statut personnel*.[42] What in 1911 was still an opinion confined to the Young Algerians and a limited number of colonial reformers in the metropole now became a demand raised by some of

---

39 Meynier, 'Les Algériens et la guerre de 1914–1918', 231.
40 Meynier, *L'Algérie révélée*, 588–98.
41 AN – Fonds Messimy, 509AP/5 – dossier 2: Quelques mots sur les événements d'Ain Touta, January 1917.
42 ANOM, GGA 12H 6: Leygues, président de la commission des affaires extérieures de la Chambre des Députés au Ministre des affaires étrangères, 3 December 1915.

France's most prominent politicians and approved by two of the Assembly's most important commissions.

But the most important turning point regarding conscription came in 1916. In September, amid continuing battles and no end to the conflict in sight, previous decrees limiting the use of conscription were annulled and tens of thousands of Algerian Muslims were mobilized. Despite the Batna insurrection in November 1916, the mass mobilization of Algerians continued. The units that proved to be the most crucial for the war effort were those of the *Tirailleurs algériens* – Muslim-only infantry regiments with French officers and an interface of Muslim NCOs. Amongst the oldest units of the *Armée d'Afrique*, the *tirallieurs algériens* had previously taken part in the repression of the Kabylian uprising of 1871 and later in occupation campaigns throughout Algeria and Morocco.[43] After the war, the *Armée d'Afrique* would come to be seen by generals as a crucial factor in the French victory, and its deployment would be considered necessary in all war strategies developed in the 1920s.[44] Muslim Algerians were now an indispensable part of the French war effort. Providing them with incentives to fight for France was no longer the caprice of a limited reformist milieu but a concern of a national order.

Taboos questioned and reaffirmed

The mass mobilization of Algerians and the need to counter protests and resistance made conceivable what until the 1910s had been an almost uncontested taboo: Algerian Muslims becoming French citizens without renouncing Islamic civil legislation. It was in this context that two prominent colonial reformers emerged: Maurice Viollette and Joseph Lagrosillière. In 1915, when still a rather anonymous deputy, Viollette proposed to allow for the naturalization *dans le statut* of Muslim colonial subjects in Algeria and throughout the French empire. Seeking to respond to the usual critique directed at such proposals, Viollette suggested to annul marriages in cases of polygamy so as not to create contradictions with the *Code civil*.[45] These intrusive suggestions were harshly criticized by the Chamber's Commission of Foreign Affairs which, in 1918,

---

43 Clayton, *France, Soldiers and Africa*, 246–8.
44 Ibid., 37.
45 Assemblée nationale, onzième législature, session de 1918, no. 4383, annexe au procès-verbal de la séance du 1ᵉʳ mars 1918: Rapport fait au nom de la commission [. . .] chargée d'examiner les propositions de loi concernant l'accession des indigènes aux droits civils et politiques par M. Marius Moutet (Paris: Imprimerie de la Chambre des Députés, 1918), 147–51.

published a report on the various proposals regarding Algerians' legal and political status. Attacking the attempt to apply the *Code civil* to Algerian Muslims, the report argued that Viollette's proposal contained 'dangerous assimilationist tendencies' and affirmed 'the quasi-mystical belief in the universal value of the *Code civil*, in the possibility of one legislation for the entirety of human beings'.[46] Even more worrying for the commission was the prospect of the French losing their majority and predominance in local and above all national assemblies should colonial subjects be given the vote.[47] Indeed, with this mixture of limited tolerance towards religious difference and intrusive policies in matrimonial matters, Viollette showed his unorthodox mode of thinking early on. He would go on to systematize and advocate a significant reform of French jurisdictional politics in Algeria as governor, senator, and finally state secretary in the 1920s and 1930s.

Beside Viollette, the war years saw the emergence of Joseph Lagrosillière as a prominent colonial reformer. Founder of the socialist movement in Martinique and the island's deputy to the National Assembly, Lagrosillière was a voice of unique creativity in seeking to reconcile the principles of the French *cité* with social structures of the Muslim society in Algeria. He proposed to grant French citizenship upon individual request not only to veterans but to any male subject whose son or sons had served in the French army, thus respecting family structures and paternal authority in Algeria as Lagrosillière understood them.[48] Lagrosillière did not suggest granting citizenship to Algerians *dans le statut* and viewed proficiency in French as a binding precondition for naturalization. But his proposal was, nevertheless, radical: seeking to accommodate difference and account for the various social and familial structures across the French empire, it showed unusual pragmatism. Lagrosillière stripped French citizenship of the ideological value with which it had been loaded by French legislation, jurisprudence and commentary since the 1860s, viewing it instead as a tool in the hands of the empire-state. Moreover, his proposal understood citizenship as functioning within a given social context. Rather than shaping society according to the *Code civil*, as was the implicit demand in many debates, citizenship ought to be adapted to surrounding social conditions. Lagrosillière would come to be an important advocate of the Blum-Viollette reform project under the first Popular Front government in 1936–7.

---

46   Ibid., 148.
47   Ibid., 150.
48   Ibid., 152.

It was no coincidence that a proposal so radical in its willingness to accept difference within the *cité française* originated in the periphery of the French empire. Lagrosillière, who would later refer explicitly to his mixed origin as a motivation for his quest for reforms, was part of a broader pattern of mutual alliance and solidarity between colonized populations across the French empire.[49] A prominent example of such alliance would soon emerge between Algeria and Senegal. In 1916, political rights were given to some 4,000 Muslim *originaires* of the 'Four Communes' of Senegal who had in 1830 obtained the rights of citizens, but whose vote had been heavily restricted since the late nineteenth century.[50] A crucial figure behind this move was the Senegalese deputy Blaise Diagne. A longtime advocate of colonial subjects' political rights, Diagne would in 1927 call for the naturalization *dans le statut* of Algerian Muslims according to the principles applied in Senegal in 1916.[51]

The acceptance of religious or social difference as envisaged by Viollette and Lagrosillière failed to gain sufficient support and was rejected by the Commission of Foreign Affairs, which judged their proposals to be either too assimilationist or too liberal in granting French citizenship. Certainly, the campaign for reform successfully challenged the view of the *statut personnel* as an insurmountable obstacle to naturalization. In 1918, the Commission of Foreign Affairs accepted that 'though Muslims' *statut personnel* runs counter to our sentiments, our moral conceptions, our judicial idea of public order, one cannot really contend that it is an obstacle to the bestowal of political rights or the quality of citizen.'[52] Yet in the end, the commission chose not to legislate for the naturalization *dans le statut*. Instead, it argued that French citizenship was to be viewed as a right to be granted to any Muslim willing to adopt French civil jurisdiction and satisfy further criteria. Furthermore, it suggested extending the civil and political rights of those Algerians who were not willing to adopt French civil jurisprudence. The term used in the report to refer to this latter group is telling: *indigènes restés musulmans*.[53] In the end, then, the view of French citizenship and Islam as irreconcilable was even further cemented, and colonial subjects were given the

---

49 For Lagrossilière's remark see: ANOM, GGA 12H 13: Sûreté départementale d'Oran, Rapprt: Union Socialiste républicaine – Apéritif offert à M. Lagrosillière, 9 June 1937.
50 Coquery-Vidrovitch, 'Nationalité et citoyenneté en Afrique occidentale française', 288–92.
51 For Diagne's speech see: *Journal officiel de la République française*, 11 July 1927, 2526.
52 Assemblée nationale, onzième législature, session de 1918, no. 4383, annexe au procès-verbal de la séance du 1ᵉʳ mars 1918: Rapport fait au nom de la commission [. . .] chargée d'examiner les propositions de loi concernant l'accession des indigènes aux droits civils et politiques par M. Marius Moutet (Paris: Imprimerie de la Chambre des Députés, 1918), 85.
53 Ibid., 171.

choice between two diverging paths: accept the *Code civil* and become citizens, or else 'remain Muslims'.

The Commission of Foreign Affairs finally endorsed a proposition which was prepared by Socialist deputy Marius Moutet on behalf of the government, and which remained loyal to the orthodoxy of French colonial thought. An emerging authority on colonial questions who would serve as the Minister of the Colonies under the Popular Front, Moutet reapproved the fundamental principle of French rule in Algeria: in order to become French citizens, Muslims would have to accept French civil legislation. The only reform in this respect was the idea that for those colonial subjects willing to do so, naturalization would be recognized as a right (*droit*) rather than a privilege (*faveur*) and could thus only be refused under exceptional circumstances. A second, more substantial suggested reform was Moutet's proposal to guarantee Algerian Muslims representation in all local councils in Algeria and to participate in the election of mayors – though not on a proportionate basis.[54]

These two principles – the recognition of naturalization as right rather than privilege and the increase of Algerians' representation in local councils – were the main elements of the 1919 Jonnart law. In June 1918, Charles Jonnart, then governor of Algeria, sought to convince the *Délégation financières* – especially their European members – of the urgent need for legal and political reforms in the colony. Alongside abolishing special taxes that applied to the Algerian population only (the *impôt arabe*) and allowing Algerians to reach higher ranks in the French military, Jonnart made a case for some reforms in the Algerian electoral system. He argued that Algerians ought to participate in electing mayors and suggested introducing 'partial naturalization' – an 'intermediary status between that of French subject and French citizen, of which will benefit all those indigenes who by virtue of their personal situation, their degree of evolution or the services they have done are capable of usefully participating in public life and to cooperate, either directly or via their elected representatives in the administration of the community's interests'.[55] The holders of this intermediary

---

54 ANOM, GGA 12H 5: Commission interministérielle des affaires musulmanes – séance du 11 octobre 1917, annexe 1: Rapport concernant l'accession des indigènes algériens aux droits politiques: Exposé du projet de la commission.
55 ANOM GGA 12 H 5: Les réformes indigènes. Discours prononcé par GG Jonnart à la séance plénière des délégations financières algériennes du 23 juin 1918, Alger: Imprimerie orientale Fontana Frères, 1918, 7–8. Jonnart repeated his speech in the Chamber in November of the same year. See: FR ANOM GGA 12 H 11: Discours prononcé par M. Jonnart, Gouverneur général de l'Algérie sur le projet de loi relatif à l'accession des indigènes de l'Algérie aux droits politiques. Première séance de la Chambre des Députés, du 7 novembre 1918, Alger: Imprimerie orientale Fontana Frères 1918.

status, Jonnart stressed, would constitute a separate electoral college, thus ensuring the continued disproportionate representations of the European minority in all councils and assemblies.

Settler representatives, for their part, reacted furiously to the reform bill, which was described by newspapers in Algeria as a grave mistake which would jeopardize French sovereignty in the colony.[56] The main point of controversy was to do with the question of Algerian Muslims' representation – however limited – in local councils. A report from 1917, almost certainly prepared by the governor general's office, argued that local representation should be exclusively reserved for full citizens, arguing that 'there is, in the functions of mayor, a reflection of the nation's sovereignty.'[57] Mayors in Algeria exercised considerable political power and controlled economic resources on a much wider scale than in the metropole. In a colony drawing its riches from heavy taxation of the Algerian population and its disproportionate distribution for the Europeans' benefit, admitting more Algerians into local councils would have meant a considerable change of economic and political order.[58] It is thus not surprising that mayors were always at the front of settler agitation. This pattern, which emerged during the anti-Semitic crisis of the late 1890s, now recurred with similar determination. Emile Morinaud, for instance, anti-Semitic deputy in the 1890s and now mayor of Constantine, warned that any attempt to grant political rights collectively to certain social groups within the Muslim population would irreversibly shift the political balance in Algeria.[59]

With their vehement rejection of the Jonnart law, politicians like Morinaud only deepened the rift with the metropole. Modest though it was, this reform was viewed by many – most importantly, by Jonnart himself – as a powerful propaganda tool and a crucial way to secure Algerians' support for the French war effort. In October 1918, the Ministry of War was sent a hundred copies of Jonnart's speech, translated into Arabic. 'It seemed to me', Jonnart wrote, 'that this document could be used with benefit for our propaganda amongst the Muslim militants and soldiers currently serving in the metropole.'[60] Further copies in

---

56 Vincent Confer, *France and Algeria: The Problem of Civil and Political Reform, 1870–1920* (Syracuse: Syracuse University Press, 1966), 109–12; Ageron, *Les Algériens musulmans*, 1208–11.
57 ANOM, GGA 12H 11: Gouvernement général de l'Algérie: Evaluation de la proposition de loi du député de Lyon Maurice Moutet [neither date nor signautre].
58 Guignard, *L'Abus de pouvoir*, 144–6, 152–3.
59 Assemblée nationale, onzième législature, session de 1918, no. 4383, annexe au procès-verbal de la séance du 1er mars 1918: Rapport fait au nom de la commission [. . .] chargée d'examiner les propositions de loi concernant l'accession des indigènes aux droits civils et politiques par M. Marius Moutet (Paris: Imprimerie de la Chambre des Députés, 1918), 313–16.
60 ANOM, GGA 12H 11: Gouverneur général au Ministre de la Guerre, 8 October 1918.

French and Arabic were sent with a similar explanation to the Foreign Ministry, the French resident generals in Morocco and Tunisia, as well as the British consul in Algiers, who was asked to forward these to the British 'propaganda service' at the Foreign Office.[61] Four years of bloodshed in Europe had left their imprint. France's force had been exhausted and new manpower was urgently needed. By rejecting the modest reform of 1919, settlers positioned themselves against what was seen by many as the national interest: an urgent and thorough rethink of the French empire.

A mosque in Paris

What remained of the colonial order and what changed after the war? The collapse of the Ottoman Empire, the creation of the mandates system and the rhetoric of liberal self-determination and revolutionary anti-Imperialism emanating from President Wilson in the United States and Lenin in the Soviet Union resonated worldwide. Like elsewhere in the colonized world, emerging Algerian leaders sought to use the Versailles conference as a forum for their cause. In 1919, the emir Khaled, grandson of Abd al-Qadir who had served in the French army during the war, wrote to President Wilson to demand that Algerians be represented at the Versailles conference. At the same time, a group of notables from Algeria and Tunisia sent from their Swiss exile a similar letter to the Versailles conference and later to President Wilson himself.[62]

The rhetoric of self-determination and the politics of indirect colonial rule certainly had a strong impact on French perceptions of the Algerian colonial order. In an expanding empire, now consisting of new protectorates and mandates – from the Moroccan protectorate to the mandates in Syria and Lebanon – direct colonial governance was increasingly viewed as dated and inefficient. Already in 1912, deputy Albin Rozet, a prominent advocate of reforms in Algeria, spoke at the Chamber against the suggested prolongation of sweeping penal powers given to administrators in the colony. Praising the establishment of the protectorate in Morocco, Rozet argued that France's nascent 'Arabo-Berber empire', whose local

---

61 ANOM, GGA 12H 11: Gouverneur général au Consul général britannique à Alger, 8 October 1918; Gouverneur général au Ministre des affaires étrangères, 10 October 1918; Gouverneur général aux résidents généraux de France au Maroc et à Tunis, 10 October 1918.
62 'Mémoire adressé au congrès de la paix par le comité algéro-tunisien en Janvier 1919', in Collot and Henry, *Le Mouvement national algérien*, 25–30; McDougall, *History and Culture of Nationalism*, 44–5; Ageron, *Les Algériens musulmans*, 1052.

population was predicted to reach 30 million within twenty-five years, required new modes of governance:

> Amid such a situation, we cannot dream of administrating our possessions in North Africa as did, in the wake of our landing at Sidi Ferruch, the adjutant major who, sitting at the entrance of his camp . . . judged the felons, thieves, and prostitutes . . . You will find yourself confronted with a considerable empire, an enormous aggregation of people augmenting incessantly, which deserve to be treated like every human society deserves, which we cannot think of administering solely by police and by force.[63]

Algeria was now portrayed as an old-fashioned, inefficiently administered colony. This view was buttressed by contrasting Algeria with the new protectorate of Morocco, where the resident-general, Hubert Lyautey, quickly established himself as a champion of modern, efficient colonial rule, and where Europeans were kept in small numbers and in separation from the local population.[64] The changes in the French empire were even clearer in the new mandates. Conceived by the League of Nations – at least in principle – as a temporary step on the way towards independence, the mandates required France and Britain to maintain at least the façade of autonomy and of preparing these territories for self-determination.[65]

The language and institutions of indirect imperial governance also signalled a decisive turn away from settlers as key agents of the colonial state. Celebrated in 1848 and again in 1870–1 as patriotic pioneers, settlers were now increasingly portrayed as obstacle to the modernization of the French empire. Already in 1908, Messimy dismissed settler opposition to the introduction of conscription in Algeria as 'chimeric anxieties'.[66] Lyautey, for his part, frustrated like many others at settler rejection of the merest reforms in Algeria in 1918–19, ascribed to them the mentality of 'pure *boche* (derogatory term for Germans, particularly during and after the First World War), with the same theories of inferior races destined to be exploited without mercy. There is neither humanism nor intelligence among them.'[67] A clear evidence of the turn away from colonial settlement came in 1921, when a senator from the recently

---

63 *Journal officiel de la République française. Débats parlementaires*, 21 June 1912, 1535.
64 Rabinow, *French Modern*, 290–6; Jean-Louis Cohen, 'Casablanca: De la cité de l'énergie à la ville fonctionnelle', in *Architecture française Outre-mer*, ed. Maurice Culot and Jean-Maurice Thiveaud (Liège: Margada 1992), 108–20.
65 Richard S. Fogarty, 'The French Empire', in *Empires at War 1911–1923*, ed. Robert Gerwath and Erez Manela (Oxford: Oxford University Press, 2014), 126–9.
66 Messimy, 'Les effectifs de l'armée et le service militaire des indigènes algériens', 776.
67 Ageron, *Les Algériens musulmans*, 1208.

retaken and reconstituted *département* of Moselle suggested launching a new version of the Alsace-Lorraine settlement project of the early 1870s. By now, even to the Algerian administration, colonial settlement clearly lost its appeal: classified by the governor's office without any further note, the initiative remained a dead letter.[68]

Yet, little changed in the life of the colonial state's Algerian subjects. With its new 'intermediary status', the Jonnart law all but cemented the exclusion of Algerians from French citizenship and the notion of Islamic legislation as irreconcilable with the Republic. In 1920, the National Assembly reintroduced the *Code de l'indigénat*, the most direct and oppressive tool of colonial domination. Settler leaders and colonial lobbyists had successfully fended off the most serious challenge to the Algerian political order in decades.

Perhaps the most palpable expression of the attempt to reimagine the French empire and its relations with its colonial subjects without reforming its political regime was the Mosque of Paris, constructed in the 5th arrondissement of the capital in the early 1920s. As Naomi Davidson has argued, the Mosque of Paris and the adjacent *Institut musulman*, propagated by French journalists, officials and experts, reflected a vision of an Islam rejuvenated under French aegis, one that was reconcilable with French social and cultural life yet had to be clearly and carefully marked.[69]

Proposals for founding a mosque in the capital had been formulated as early as 1895 by a *Comité d'Afrique française*, consisting of prominent figures from the aristocracy and the colonial administration. Yet, it was only in the aftermath of the war, with French officials and politicians seeing their vision of France as an imperial 'Muslim power' closer to realization than ever before that these plans were made concrete. The initiative was revived in the 1910s by the milieu around the *Revue indigène*. When the Algerian delegation visited Paris in 1912 to discuss the government's plans to introduce conscription, a meeting in the review's editorial offices was convoked to discuss the idea. Drafts for the design of the mosque were prepared in 1916 and were viewed and commented on by various Algerian political figures, including Dr Benthami and the emir Khaled when on leave from the front.[70] As the review's editor Paul Bourdarie put it, his vision was for the mosque 'to create in Paris a site for Franco-Muslim

---

68   ANOM, GGA 32L 11: Colonel Stuhl, Sénateur de la Moselle, au gouverneur général, 22 October 1921.
69   Davidson, *Only Muslim*, 47–53.
70   Paul Bourdarie, 'L'Institut musulman et la Mosquée de Paris', *La Revue indigène*, October-December 1919, 177–80.

high culture by introducing to the most cultivated young elements of Islam the flower of French science and society'.⁷¹ The mosque was also to fulfil a diplomatic and representative function by providing a site 'with Islamic character' for receptions, exhibitions and congresses and to serve as a site of liturgy and prayer for Muslims living in Paris. Moreover, the mosque and its affiliated academic institute were to serve the overall goals of colonial administration in the colonies, placing those who had graduated from the institute in key administrative positions in the colonies. 'It is now for our friends in Algeria, Tunisia, and Morocco', Boudarie concluded, 'to show through the concrete and decisive act of personal subscription [souscription] that they understand the great importance of a foundation which should give Islam its place in Paris.'⁷²

On 1 March 1922, the terrain designated for the Mosque by the government was officially allocated to the *Société des habous des lieux-saints de l'Islam*, which was to implement the project on behalf of the government. The ceremony on that day was staged a celebration of France as a nascent internationally recognized 'Muslim power'. Alongside the society's president and representative (*chancelier*) of the Moroccan sultan Si Kaddour ben Gharbit, the guest list included Minister of the Colonies Albert Sarraut, Paul Bourdarie, who was member of the society, representatives of the Moroccan sultan and the Tunisian bey, alongside representatives from Turkey, Persia, Afghanistan and Russia. French Algeria was represented by deputies Thomson, Cuttoli and Morinaud, as well as by the president of the *Délégations financières*.⁷³ Describing France as 'protect[ing] twenty-five million Muslim subjects', state secretary Maurice Colrat, on behalf of the prime minister, portrayed the construction of the mosque as a manifestation of French policies 'not of subjugation and hatred, but of contact and attraction'. Concluding his speech, Colrat declared:

> Towering over the roofs of the city, the minaret ... shall direct at the beautiful blue sky of Ile de France but one more prayer, for which the Catholic towers of Notre Dame shall have no jealousy. But all the French ... shall remember the sombre days and the fields of carnage where, side by side, all French religions fought for the triumph of justice and liberty ... Thus they shall salute this monument

---

71 Ibid., 182.
72 Ibid., 187, emphasis in original.
73 'Fondation de l'Institut musulman et de la Mosquée de Paris', *La Revue indigène*, January–March 1922, 1–6. A law from 1920 allocated a budget of half a million francs to the *Société des habous des lieux-saints de l'Islam*, to be administered by the Ministry of Foreign Affairs. See: 'Projet de loi portant affection d'une subvention de 500,000 francs à la Société des habous des Lieux Saints de l'Islam', *La Revue indigène*, January–March 1920, 35–7.

with piety and gratitude as the testimony of an indissoluble friendship between France and Islam.[74]

Indeed, beyond a new vision of empire, the Paris mosque was an occasion for some French politicians and officials to propagate a rethink of France's state secularism as defined by the 1905 law on the separation of church and state. In his speech at the ceremony marking the beginning of construction works in October 1922, resident-general of Morocco Lyautey said:

> 'What we must internalize is that, if we really wish to serve France as a country of Islam, it is not enough to respect *their* religion, but also the other ones, beginning with that in which was born and grew our country . . . Our force and prestige would only benefit from practising such respect, from understanding the depth and grandeur of the religious spirit.'[75]

This was about restoring at least celebrating the resilience of religiosity in the secularist republic:

> Last summer, when a group of young men from the French-Muslim colleges of Fez and Rabat came to visit France . . . I saw that one of their strongest [impressions] was the one they felt in Marseilles at [the Basilica of] Notre Dame de la Garde, seeing the steady flow and the fervour of believers of all social conditions. They did not think that such a religious force still remained in France.[76]

For Lyautey, the allocation of budget for the *Société des habous* to construct a 'Muslim Institute and Mosque' was not only an attempt to cater to the growing needs of Muslims in France in the new legal situation created by the 1905 law's ban on state funding for religious institutions but an opportune moment to challenge the very principle of state secularism.

The 'liberal gesture', as Ben Gharbit referred to the mosque, this 'leave for Islam to reside in France', was therefore, in the end, a French project of reimagining empire and the metropole.[77] Despite consultations with some Algerian representatives and cooperation with several notables in the Maghrib, and despite the Maghribi style of its architecture, this was a project planned, financed

---

74 'Fondation de l'Institut musulman et de la Mosquée de Paris', *La Revue indigène*, January-March 1922, 19.
75 'L'Institut musulman et la Mosquée de Paris', *La Revue indigène,* September-October 1922, 236–7. Emphasis in original.
76 Ibid.
77 'Fondation de l'Institut musulman et de la Mosquée de Paris', *La Revue indigène*, January-March 1922, 7.

and celebrated above all by French advocates of a new, reformed empire.[78] As Bourdarie and others stated, the mosque was conceived not as a site for Maghribi Islam to be practised in France but as a project towards the shaping of Islam as a French religion subjected to state oversight and its followers subjected to close surveillance.[79]

Though the Paris mosque did receive some attention from the Arabophone Algerian press – the reform-oriented, Constantine-based *Al-Najah*, for instance, called it 'A Message [bushra] to the Islamic World' – it played a merely minor role in the communal, political and religious life of migrant Maghribi communities.[80] In 1926, the year when the president of the Republic and the Sultan of Morocco inaugurated the mosque with great pomp, the *Étoile nord-africaine* ('North African Star' – hereafter: ENA) was founded – the first mass platform advocating the cause of Algerian independence. Like other movements of migrants from across the colonized world that made interwar Paris a vibrant hub of anti-colonial resistance, the ENA was born out of the social and political conditions brought about by the war.[81] As Gilbert Meynier stresses, the war years were a formative time for the nearly 300,000 Algerian soldiers and industrial workers in the metropole, exposing soldiers to a military system experienced by many as less arbitrary than the *Code de l'indigénat* and introducing workers to the institutions and practices of trade unions, demonstrations and strikes first hand.[82] Though numbers dropped sharply after the demobilization, demand for labour force meant that there were c. 20,000 Algerian workers in the metropole in 1920, 60,000 in 1923 and 70,000 in 1924.[83] It was amongst these milieus that the ENA recruited most of its supporters and activists. The ENA was joined by other Maghribi associations such the *Association des étudiants musulmans d'Afrique du Nord* ('Association of North African Students') or the 'Educational Club', operated by the *Association des 'ulama musulmans algériens* ('Association

---

78 On the Mosque's architecture see: Moustafa Bayoumi, 'Shadows and Light: Colonial Modernity and the Grand Mosquee of Paris', *The Yale Journal of Criticism* 13, no. 2 (2000): 272–5.
79 See on this issue: Naomi Davidson, 'La mosquée de Paris. Construire l'islam français et l'islam en France, 1926–1947', *Revue des mondes musulmans et de la Méditerranée*, no. 125 (2009): 197–215. On surveillance of Maghribi migrants in interwar Paris see: Clifford Rosenberg, *Policing Paris: The Origins of Modern Immigration Control between the Wars* (Ithaca: Cornell University Press, 2006), esp. chapters 4–5.
80 'Bushra l-il-'alam il-islami', *Al-Najah*, 23 March 1926, 1. On the (limited) significance of the Paris Mosque to Algerians see: James McDougall, 'The Secular State's Islamic Empire: Muslim Spaces and Subjects of Jurisdiction in Paris and Algiers, 1905–1957', *Comparative Studies in Society and History* 52, no. 3 (2010): 572–3.
81 See most notably: Michael Goebel, *Anti-Imperial Metropolis: Interwar Paris and the Seeds of Third World Nationalism* (Cambridge: Cambridge University Press, 2015).
82 Meynier, *L'Algérie révélée*, 441, 480–4.
83 McDougall, *History and the Culture of Nationalism*, 34, note 22.

of Algerian Muslim 'ulama – hereafter: AUMA) founded in Algiers in 1931.[84] Another post-1918 factor that made the ENA possible was the *Parti communiste français* (French Communist Party – hereafter: PCF). Founded in 1920, the PCF was the first French political party to adopt a decidedly anti-colonial agenda and played a key role in the founding and organization of the ENA.[85]

Formulating radically new demands, this increasingly vibrant Algerian political life – in the metropole as in the colony – was a key factor in the re-emergence of a French colonial reform movement in the 1930s. For colonial reformers, Algerian nationalism represented a real threat that could only be curtailed by significant changes to the political order in the colony. That was the message implied by a brochure published in 1931 by Maurice Viollette who, after being ousted from the post of governor general under settler pressure, was now emerging as the leading figure of the colonial reform movement. It was in this brochure that Viollette first presented the reform ideas which he would later advance as minister of the first Popular Front government and which would become known as the Blum-Viollette plan. Seeking to convey the utmost urgency, Viollette titled his brochure with a question hitherto only hinted at behind closed doors: *Will Algeria Live?*

---

84 Ibid., 35.
85 Ibid., 46.

5

A road not taken? The struggle for reform

By 1939, Ferhat Abbas was a disillusioned man. An eminent writer and political leader who would go on to become the president of the Provisional Government of the Algerian Republic, Abbas began his political career as an advocate of political rights and participation in the French state. During the 1920s and 1930s, he fought for education and equal political rights of Algerians, culminating in a heated campaign for legal and political reform under the governments of the Popular Front (1936–8). Alongside his activity in the Constantine municipal and regional councils in these years, he edited the weekly *l'Entente franco-musulmane* – a key platform in the campaign for reform. Looking back at the Popular Front period, Abbas concluded:

> One found the time to discuss and pass legislation on the paid leave, the forty-hours working week, the pensions of retired workers. One found the time for discussions on wheat, wine, oranges, artichokes and potatoes. One did not find a single week, two days, twenty-four hours to examine the only question that interests us, the political status of Algeria.[1]

Beyond sarcasm and offence, this was a belated realization of just how insignificant and distant an issue the Algerian question had been for most Popular Front politicians and parties. What had been the single most important question in Algerian politics for two turbulent years, the object of intense, at times violent, confrontations between Algerians and Europeans, was but little more than a footnote in the political agenda of Léon Blum's government.[2] State

---

1   Ferhat Abbas, 'Les Paroles et les actes', *L'Entente franco-musulmane*, 13 April 1939, 1.
2   Julian Jackson, *The Popular Front in France: Defending democracy 1934-1938* (Cambridge: Cambridge University Press, 1990), 154–6; William B. Cohen, 'The Colonial Policy of the Popular Front', *French Historical Studies* 7, no. 3 (Spring 1972): 369–76; Semidei, 'Les socialistes français et le problème colonial', 1145–51; Thomas Adrian Schweitzer, 'Le Parti communiste français, le Comintern et l'Algérie dans les années 1930', *Le Mouvement sociale*, no. 78 (March 1972); Ethan Katz, 'Crémieux's Children: Joseph Reinach, Léon Blum, and René Cassin as Jews of French Empire', in *Colonialism and the Jews*, ed. Ethan Katz, Lisa Moses Leff and Maud S. Mandel (Bloomington: Indiana University Press, 2017), 141–5.

secretary Maurice Viollette, the driving force behind the proposal to grant political rights to some 25,000 Algerians *dans le statut*, was well-aware of this. Even before introducing his legislation bill in December 1936, Viollette saw how administrators in Algeria were acting to block any reform and warned of his own government's inaction. In a letter to the like-minded official and later celebrated historian Charles-André Julien, Viollette asked with frustration: 'What is the government doing? Is it the governor [general of Algeria] who governs the government or the opposite?'[3]

Indeed, Viollette's bill was seen by the vast majority of the Europeans' political leadership in Algeria as an imminent political threat and an inconceivable intellectual iconoclasm. 'The Blum-Viollette plan will cause us to lose Algeria. 40,000 indigenous electors becoming French, having in average three children, will make a total of 360,000 electors in forty years', a delegation of Algerian mayors told the National Assembly's *Commission du suffrage universel* in 1938. 'At that moment, the indigenes will have the destiny of our beautiful colony in their hands.'[4] Prejudice and far-right agitation aside – the 1930s witnessed a resurgence of anti-Semitism and anti-republicanism in settler politics – opponents of reform recognized what Viollette did not: that the inherent repression of the Algerian order could not be reformed within the colonial system, and that his plan represented a far more significant concession to the Algerians than he was willing to admit.[5] For Viollette's proposals broke with the legal criteria that had been developed since the 1880s and had constituted a pillar of French political thought.

Historians have long tended to discuss the Blum-Viollette project within the frame of a 'missed opportunity' versus a 'structural impossibility' to reform the Algerian colonial order, often overlooking the vehemence with which this scheme was debated and fought over during two long years.[6] But as Abbas himself put it in 1949, the 'immense failure' of the Blum-Viollette project was a crucial, constitutive moment, 'pulling us away from a mirage and turning us towards ourselves'.[7] To

---

3 Quoted in: Julien, 'Léon Blum et les pays d'outre-mer', 381–2.
4 ANOM, GGA: 3CAB 85: Commissaire de police de la ville de Boufarik, Rapport journalier de 25 au 26 février 1938.
5 For a detailed account of far-right politics in Algeria see: Kalman, *French Colonial Fascism*. See also Joshua Cole, *Lethal Provocation: The Constantine Murders and the Politics of French Algeria* (Ithaca: Cornell University Press, 2019); Roberts, *Citizenship and Antisemitism*.
6 McDougall, *A History of Algeria*, 177; Charles-André Julien, *L'Afrique du nord en marche: nationalismes musulmans et souveraineté française* (Paris: Julliard, 1952), 343–53.
7 Ferhat Abbas, 'Lettre ouverte à monsieur le Président de la République', *La République algérienne*, 27 May 1949, 1. Abbas's role in the struggle around the Blum-Viollette project is mentioned in passing by most historians, see e.g. Charles-Robert Ageron, 'Ferhat Abbas et l'évolution politique de l'Algérie musulmane pendant la Seconde Guerre mondiale', in *Genèse de l'Algéria algérienne*, vol. II (Saint-Denis: Èditons Bouchène, 2005), 259. See also more recently: Malika Rahal, 'Ferhat

capture the intellectual and political significance of this historical moment, we must turn our attention to the nuance and details of the struggle around it. As studies by Claire Marynower and Pierre-Jean Le Foll-Luciani have demonstrated, the Popular Front was a crucial and central movement around which left-wing politics revolved in 1930s Algeria.[8] But as the following pages argue, the origins of the Blum-Viollette project and the political clash that it brought about can only be partly understood in the context of French left-wing politics.

Rather, this is the story of an Algerian political current which, during the 1920s and 1930s, forced significant parts of French public opinion to adopt a more complex view of Algerian society and reconsider some of the most well-established orthodoxies on difference, uniformity and citizenship. Compelling the French government to present a reform plan, Algerian men and women of various classes, occupations and political inclinations endorsed the Blum-Viollette project as a first step towards full political and legal equality and, more importantly, a renaissance of Algerian society. An emerging civil society and flourishing press in Algeria now defied the mechanisms of control, echoing, discussing and advocating the revolutionary ideas that had swept the Arab and Islamic world since the turn of the century.[9] Most importantly, Algerian men and women now contested French notions of female oppression under Islam with increasing confidence, making full use of the feminist congresses, associations and mouthpieces that emerged throughout the Mediterranean in the 1920s and 1930s. By challenging the French view of Islam as stagnant and oppressive, this intellectual movement contested the received wisdom of Islam as irreconcilable with the Republic – and with modern, civic participation more broadly.

Contesting orthodoxies

In late October 1926, the Constantine-based Arabic-language newspaper *Al-Najah* printed the text of a speech held in Paris a few months earlier:

Abbas, de l'assimilationisme au nationalisme', in *Histoire de l'Algérie à la période coloniale (1930–1962)*, ed. A. Bouchène et al. (Paris: La Découverte, 2012), 443–6.

8   Claire Marynower, *L'Algérie à gauche (1900-1962): socialistes à l'époque coloniale* (Paris: PUF, 2018), 48–61; Jean-Pierre Le Foll-Luciani, 'Les Actions judéo-musulmanes pour une réforme de la citoyenneté en Algérie', in *La fabrique coloniale du citoyen: Algérie, Nouvelle-Calédonie*, ed. Eric Savarese and Eric de Mari (Paris: Karthala, 2019).

9   On politicization see Omar Carlier, 'Le café maure: Sociabilité masculine et effervescence citoyenne (Algérie XVIIE-XXe siècles)', *Annales. Economies, sociétes, civilisations*, no. 4 (1990): 975–1003; Omar Carlier, 'Les Traminots algérios des années 1930: un groupe social médiateur et novateur', *Le Mouvement social*, no. 146 (1989): 61–89; Carlier, 'Medina and Modernity'. On defying mechanisms of control see Asseraf, *Electric News*.

'Mrs Huda Sha'arawi's Speech at the International Women's Congress', read the title. Clearly, the editor saw no need to introduce Sha'arawi any further. Born to an affluent family in Upper Egypt in 1879, Sha'arawi had by the 1920s become a prominent advocate of Arab women's rights. As founder and president of the Egyptian Feminist Union, she represented her movement at various congresses throughout Europe and the Arab world.[10] The printing of Sha'arawi's speech by an Algerian newspaper was a prime example of a public debate that grew increasingly reconnected with the wider Arab world and added a prominent voice to a vibrant discussion on education, family structures, and women's participation and visibility in the public sphere. As Judith Surkis shows, polygamy, child marriage and seclusion were central tropes in French and European discourse on Islamic societies and served as justification for the political exclusion of Algerian Muslims.[11] By the 1920s, such discourse was contested by a dense network of activists, journalists and scholars – women and men alike – in Algeria and throughout the Mediterranean.

Sha'arawi's appearances in Europe were an effort to challenge received wisdoms on women and Islam. In her speech in Paris, Sha'arawi turned against some of the most prevalent clichés of European thought. 'I would like to describe to you the situation of the Egyptian woman accurately, unlike how she is portrayed by the wild imagination of certain writers', she opened with dry sarcasm.[12] She went on to dispute the idea that Islam was oppressive towards women, saying that Islamic law had given women the highest level of esteem and opened to them the path to participation in the social and intellectual life of their community. The 'seclusion' ('*azlah*) of women was not an inherent feature of Islam but the legacy of specific ruling dynasties who had brought with them the veil and, as Sha'arawi emphasized, introduced it amongst women of all religions in Egypt – Muslims, Jews and Copts. It was only with the rise of the 'great' ruler Muhammad 'Ali in the early nineteenth century that the situation of Egyptian women began to improve again, Sha'arawi argued – mainly due to the establishment of schools for girls.

Sha'arawi's focus on modern Egypt as a cradle of women's progress and a model to follow fitted well into an Algerian discourse in the 1920s and echoed a long tradition of imagining the east as 'a place of . . . morality and improvement,

10 Huda Shaarawi, *Harem Years: The Memoirs of an Egyptian Feminist (1879-1924)*, trans. and ed. Margot Badran (New York: The Feminist Press, 1993), 3–6.
11 Surkis, *Sex, Law and Sovereignty in French Algeria*, 55–63.
12 'Hitab a-sayidah Huda Hanim Sha'arawi fi ijtima'a al-itihad a-nisaa'i a-duwali b-Jinif', *Al-Najah*, 22 October 1926, 1–2. In fact, the congress was held in Paris.

of purity and purification'.[13] Ever since the late nineteenth century, Egypt had been the centre of intensive debates on women, modernity, and Islam. The 1890s saw a remarkable flourishing of press and literature focusing on these issues and in some cases clearly intended for a female readership.[14] In 1899, Qasim Amin sparked controversy with his work *Tahrir al-Mar'a* (*The Liberation of Women*). Though his calls to facilitate education for girls and his criticism of seclusion and the veil were not new, his depiction of Egyptian society as oppressive and retrograde led to intensive discussions in the meanwhile vibrant literary and press scene.[15] When Huda Sha'arawi led women's demonstrations against British occupation in 1919 and removed her veil in 1923, Egypt had already become a source of inspiration and focus of controversy throughout the Middle East and North Africa.

In this vibrant intellectual climate, the interwar period saw the emergence of the Islamic renewal and reform movement (*islah*) as a social and political force in Algeria. In the 1910s and 1920s, some of the Algerian *'ulama* who would soon rise to prominence returned to their country after years of studies in Egypt and the Hijaz, where they had encountered the impulses of religious renewal and return to Islamic sources (*salafiyyah*). The two most prominent amongst them, sheikhs Abd al-Hamid Ben Badis and Tayeb al-'Uqbi, would go on to found the *Association des 'ulama musulmans algériens* (AUMA) in 1931, a movement that promoted the teaching of classical Arabic and advocated a thorough reform of religious life in Algeria to 'purify' it from saint-worship and local customs.

Alongside sermons in some of Algeria's most important mosques, the main platform of the AUMA was the Arabic-language press.[16] Mouthpieces such as Ben Badis's *Al-Muntaqid*, al-Uqbi's *Al-Islah* and the association's *Al-Shihab* became important forums for discussions on social, political and religious issues. Stressing the significance of Islam, of Islamic history and of classical Arabic in the quest for social betterment and cultural renewal, these newspapers offered a powerful alternative to the language of 'evolution' through French culture

---

13 McDougall, *History and the Culture of Nationalism*, 57.
14 Marylin Booth, 'Before Qasim Amin: Writing women's History in 1890s Egypt', in *The Long 1890s in Egypt: Colonial Quiescence, Subterranean Resistance*, ed. Marylin Booth (Edinburgh: Edinburgh University Press, 2014), 365.
15 For an English translation see e.g.: Qasim Amin, *The Liberation of Women. The New Woman. Two documents in the history of Egyptian feminism*, trans. Samiha Sidhom Peterson (Cairo: The American University in Cairo Press, 2000). For a critical discussion see e.g.: Leila Ahmed, *Women and Gender in Islam: Historical roots of a modern debate* (New Haven: Yale University Press, 1992), 144–68.
16 On sermons see Pessah Shinar, 'A Controversial Exponent of the Algerian Salafiyya: The Kabyle 'Alim, Imam and Sharıf Abu Ya'la Sa'id b. Muhammad al-Zawawı', in *Studies in Islamic History and Civilization in Honour of David Ayalon*, ed. M. Sharon (Leiden: Brill, 1986), 280.

and assimilation, which were advocated in the interwar period by francophone mouthpieces such as *La Voix des humbles*, as discussed by Jonathan Gosnell.[17] One of the most important subjects of these debates was the status of women in Algeria: education for girls, polygamy, women's rights in their relations with their husbands – particularly in matters of divorce and inheritance – and not least the question of the *hijab*.[18] These debates constituted a twofold effort to thoroughly reform religious life in Algeria and to challenge French axioms on the backwardness of Islam and its incompatibility with modernity. As James McDougall shows, by so doing, the *'ulama* laid the cultural and intellectual foundations of what would later emerge as Algerian nationalism.[19]

When contesting French views of Islam, reformist *'ulama* contrasted the original, 'pure' Islamic thought with local traditions and habits which, so the argument went, had little to do with the Quran or the Shari'a or, even worse, distorted the original message of the Prophet.[20] 'We all know what harsh, wild [wahshia] treatment is experienced by the Kabylian woman, and we all know that the woman in that part of Algeria has no rights but those granted to her by her rude, hard-hearted, "master"', wrote the *'alim* Muhammad al-Amin al-'Amudi in late 1929 in *Al-Islah*. But his judgement of Arab men was equally harsh as that of Kabylians: 'Instead of the "customs" that deny the Kabylian woman with unapologising violence of her traditional rights . . . the Arab man unjustly and shamelessly invented what now deprives the Arab woman of these rights.'[21] The key word here was of course 'invented', contesting the religious legitimacy and validity of any treatment depriving women of their rights as defined by the Sharia. Another reformist *'alim*, the Kabylian sheikh Zouwawi, declared in *Al-Shihab* some of the veiling habits in Kabylia to be 'contradicting the spirit of Islamic law'.[22]

While most of the *'ulama* directed their advocacy for reform at their Algerian readers, the charismatic sheikh Tayeb al-'Uqbi made significant efforts to explain and communicate this movement to French public opinion. Though he wrote only in Arabic, al-'Uqbi gave several interviews to French magazines in the 1930s with the help of al-Amin al-'Amudi as his interpreter. Featuring flattering

---

17   Jonathan K. Gosnell, *The Politics of Frenchness in Colonial Algeria, 1930–1954* (Rochester: University of Rochester Press, 2002), 112–15.
18   Sara Rahnama, 'Hijabs and Hats in Interwar Algeria', *Gender & History* 32, no. 2 (2020): 429–46.
19   McDougall, *History and the Culture of Nationalism*, 16–17.
20   This continued a tendency begun by Islamic reformers in the late nineteenth century, as Cemil Aydin notes: *The Idea of the Muslim World*, 9–10.
21   Muhammad al-Amin al-'Amudi, 'Al-Mara' 'l-muslimah 'l-jazai'iriah', *Al-Islah*, 27 November 1929, 1.
22   ANOM, 93/B3/169: Translation of *Al-Shihab*, October 1929. On Zawawi see Shinar, 'A Controversial Exponent of the Algerian Salafiyya', 276–9.

photographs of al-'Uqbi and in one case a translation of some of his verses, these interviews depicted him very favourably, quoting at length his condemnations of the 'superstition' of Maghribi saint-worshipping and his praise for 'pure', rational Islam.[23] Beyond press interviews, al-'Uqbi maintained ties with key figures in French society and even the colonial administration, including the notorious surveillance agency, the *Service des affaires indigènes*.[24] In 1933, the Algiers branch of the *Ligue des droits de l'homme* ('League of Rights of Man' – hereafter: LDH) interviewed al-'Uqbi on his positions regarding Islam, education, and the political future of Algeria.[25] This represented a broader pattern: bringing together Algerian representatives and scholars, colonial reformers, socialists and some members of France's emerging feminist movement, the LDH facilitated exchange of ideas and created some of the most important networks that connected Algeria with the metropole.[26] Through such channels of communication, al-'Uqbi and other intellectuals and political leaders were able to promote a more nuanced understanding of Islam in certain segments of French public opinion.

Whereas the *'ulama* highlighted the 'original', 'pure' essence of Islam, the left-leaning and reform-oriented Francophone press in Algeria advanced a slightly different – though related – argument: that change, 'progress', and the emancipation of women would emerge from within Algerian society as a result of social changes that could not be accelerated or controlled by France. It was around this argument that the most effective critique of colonial thought was formulated. Requiring little knowledge of Arab history and Islamic law and appropriating the language of progress and emancipation, this argument was more accessible for most French readers and could convince French public opinion more easily. As the editors of the Constantine-based newspaper *La Voix indigène* wrote in 1932: 'Unless one is called Peter the Great or Mustapha Kemal [Ataturk], one does not modify social mores with one ordinance.... The only immediate remedy for the situation of the Algerian Muslim woman is the creation of schools for young indigenous girls.'[27]

---

23 See e.g.: Robert Randau, 'Un entretien avec Taieb el Okbi', *L'Afrique du Nord illustrée*, 17 June 1933, 3.
24 As stated by al-'Uqbi in an interview: 'Cheikh Thaieb el-Okbi', *Errihala*, March-April 1933, 142. Other *'ulama* maintained similar ties, see: Shinar, 'A Controversial Exponent of the Algerian Salafiyya', 171.
25 Archives de la Contemporaine, F delta res 798 167: Questions posées au Cheikh Taieb el Okbi par la section d'Alger de la Ligue des Droit de l'Homme (no date, evidently August 1933).
26 See e.g.: Archives de la Contemporaine, F delta res 798 167: Mme. Malterre-Sellier, Présidente du groupe de Paris de UFSF au secrétaire de la LDH M. Guernut, 3 January 1924; Union Française pour le Suffrage des Femme et Ligue des Droits de l'Homme: Grande réunion publique, le 27 January 1924.
27 'La Femme musulmane. Lettre ouverte aux dames françaises du Congrès de Constantine', *La voix indigène*, 10 March 1932, 1.

The power of this argument became evident during the Congress of Mediterranean Women in Constantine in March 1932. Presided by Germaine Malaterre-Sellier, vice-president of the *Union française pour le suffrage des femmes* ('French Union for Women's Suffrage' – hereafter: UFSF), this congress attracted considerable interest from Algeria's Francophone press, as well as some attention in the metropole.[28] Several reports were presented to the delegates by Algerian women and men, focusing above all on the need for education for girls and the question of the veil. 'We are missing just one thing: education – the magic stick of emancipation of the human being, men and women alike', stated Mrs Seghir Hacene from Kabylia. 'As for the veil that we wear, it will disappear with the spread of education.'[29] A statement by a certain Larguehce Hamed from Bône praised early Islam for granting women important liberties, while deploring the alleged stagnation of more recent times: 'After a centuries-long slumber, Islam awakens. A movement of progress can be seen everywhere – in Turkey, Persia, Afghanistan, Egypt, India. Only Muslim Algeria, preceded by her younger sister Tunisia, has yet to make this step. It is for France, who has taken upon herself the mission of civilising us, to complete this work of renovation in the Islamic countries subjected to her laws.'[30] Articulating the call for political change through the framework of the 'civilizing mission' was a common feature of Algerian politics. It was a powerful reminder that the 'backwardness' of Algerian women, mentioned so often by colonial lobbyists as proof that Islam was incompatible with the Republic, was the result of specific historical circumstances and had been caused in no small part by colonial rule itself.

There was by no means a consensus amongst French feminists concerning Algeria. Maria Vérone (1874–1938), chairwoman of the UFSF, viewed Islam as a hindrance to Algerian women's emancipation and saw it as France's historical duty to liberate them. The Algerian branch of the UFSF portrayed itself as an agent of the 'civilizing mission', thus justifying its demand for greater rights and participation for French women in the colony.[31] The branch's chairwoman, Lucienne Jean-Darrouy, demanded that French female suffrage come before any change to Algerian men's political status to allow French women to fulfil their educational mission in the colony: 'The [French] man cannot penetrate

---

28 See e.g.: 'Congrès international des femmes méditerranéennes', *L'Echo d'Alger*, 10 March 1932, 5; 'Un Congrès international des femmes méditerranéennes', *Le Temps*, 7 April 1932, 6; 'Les Femmes méditerranéennes à Constantine', *Le Matin*, 31 March 1932, 2.
29 'Le Congrès des femmes méditerranéennes et la femme musulmane', *La voix indigène*, 21 April 1932, 2.
30 Hamed Larguèche, 'La Femme musulmane II', *La voix indigène*, 12 Mai 1932, 2.
31 Sara L. Kimble, 'Emancipation through Secularisation: French Feminist Views of Muslim Women's Condition in Interwar Algeria', *French Colonial History* 7, no. 1 (2006): 119–24.

the indigenous family. The [French] woman can. Clearly, should she be in a disadvantaged position, her role and action will not be as useful for the colonisation effort.'[32]

And yet, voices in growing numbers and increasing prominence pleaded for a more nuanced view of the situation in Algeria. One of the most important amongst them was that of Marie Bugéja, an author who wrote extensively on Algerian women and gained significant renown, including a prize awarded to her during the 1930 centenary celebrations of the conquest of Algeria.[33] Bugéja was herself a product of the colonial system. The daughter of a colonial administrator, she encountered Algerian women while travelling with her father and formulated her ideas within the framework of colonial amelioration – and often with the most outworn clichés.[34] Yet, flimsy though her observations were, Bugéja's most famous book, *Nos soeurs musulmanes* (*Our Muslim Sisters*) from 1921, was ultimately an appeal to her readers in France to accept, or at least tolerate, difference: 'Do not assume that she [the Algerian woman] wishes to frequent our streets and our grand shops with the same liberty as us. And do not assume that all [Algerian women] wish to immediately abandon the veil.'[35] Even more importantly, her book was one of the earliest publications in the French language to portray Algeria as a society in motion. Bugéja stressed the need for education for girls, reminded her readers of the recent emancipation of women in republican Turkey, and concluded by saying: 'Let us not appear too hasty. Let time and society do their work . . . It is for Muslim society to evolve according to its own habits.'[36] One of the most enthusiastic readers of these passages was none other than Maurice Viollette.[37]

Deeply influenced by Bugéja and by reformist Algerian intellectuals over the previous decades, Viollette's views of Algerian women were far more nuanced than those of most of his French contemporaries and were crucial for his reform agenda. In his 1931 brochure *L'Algérie vivra-t-elle?*, he characterized the common French view of Algerian women as that of 'objects of curiosity'.[38] In a chapter dedicated entirely to the situation of Algerian women, Viollette claimed French

---

32 ANOM, GGA 12H 13: Commission parlementaire d'enquête, séance du 16 avril 1937.
33 Marie Bugéja, *Nos sœurs musulmanes* (Algiers: Éditions France-Afrique, 1931), cover page.
34 See for instance: Bugéja, *Nos sœurs musulmanes*, 191. On Bugéja see: Patricia Lorcin, 'Mediating Gender, Mediating Race: Women Writers in Colonial Algeria', *Culture, Theory and Critique* 45, no. 1 (2004): 54–6.
35 Bugéja, *Nos sœurs musulmanes*, 191.
36 Ibid., 192.
37 Viollette, *L'Algérie vivra-e-elle?* 417–18. Viollette mistakenly named another French writer, but he clearly meant to honour Bugéja. See the "Avertissement par l'éditeur" in the 1931 edition of Bugéja's book.
38 Viollette, *L'Algérie vivra-e-elle?* 417.

public opinion to be fatally misguided and lamented the ignorance amongst French women concerning the conditions and aspirations of their Algerian counterparts. A crucial link in this regard was the activity of Thérèse Viollette (née Mathon) who, during her spouse's time as governor general, sought to bring together European and Algerian women in common meetings and charity projects.[39] Her activism was not confined to private meetings. When the Viollettes visited Algeria in July 1937, they were photographed together upon arrival at the port of Algiers by the left-leaning daily *L'Echo d'Alger*. 'Mrs and Mr. Viollette are the guests of Algiers' read the title. 'A group of Muslim women come to welcome Mr. Violette', the article reported.[40]

Viollette rejected the idea that it was France's role to promote the secularization of Algeria, arguing that such processes should be left to unfold at their own pace. Most important, he contended that conditions in Algeria were rapidly changing, pointing out to the first female Muslim students, the decrease in polygamy and the first Muslim women not wearing the veil – now a shibboleth of 'assimilation' in French colonial writing.[41] Moreover, he stressed the protections given to women by Islamic law and the active role of women in Muslim societies: 'The woman in Arab countries is undoubtedly respected by her husband and has a real influence upon him.'[42] Where most French commentators saw a stagnant populace yet to enter history, Viollette saw rapidly changing society. And, once Islam was not seen as hindering social developments, it logically followed that the *statut personnel* no longer constituted an obstacle to political participation.

The continued effort of Algerian men and women to challenge received wisdoms on Islam had a considerable impact on French public opinion. Much like the dynamics between Egyptian intellectuals and European orientalists in the 1890s, Algerian writing and activism in the 1920s and 1930s did bring about some awareness in France of the dramatic changes taking place in the colony and throughout the Arab and Muslim World.[43] Though only few administrators, politicians or journalists in France had the knowledge or interest to understand the nuances of debates on women, civil status and modernity in the Arab world, some arguments did trickle down. A small yet not insignificant number of officials and commentators came to realize their society's own misconceptions concerning Algeria and the enormity of the societal and political forces that

39 Viollette, *L'Algérie vivra-e-elle?* 417–18.
40 'Mme et M. Maurice Viollette sont les hôtes d'Alger', *L'Echo d'Alger*, 6 July 1937.
41 Viollette, *L'Algérie vivra-e-elle?* 412–16.
42 Ibid., 413.
43 On Egypt see: Booth, 'Before Qasim Amin', 366.

were challenging the colonial system. This emerging, more nuanced view of women and family structures in Algeria made new reform plans and a new idea of Algerians' participation in the Republic possible.

The radicalism and radicalization of reform

For all his innovation, the reform plan so closely associated with Viollette was in fact the result of an intensive campaign by Algerian scholars, writers and representatives. Shortly after the formation of the first Popular Front government under Léon Blum and the appointment of Viollette as state secretary, a newly constituted *Congrès musulman* published a political agenda that amounted to nothing short of the dismantling of the colonial order. Founded in June 1936, the *Congrès musulman* brought together the French-educated elite of representatives and intellectuals, such as Ferhat Abbas and the *'ulama* around al-'Uqbi and Ben Badis and launched an intensive campaign that soon engulfed large sectors of Algerian society. Though eventually unsuccessful, this campaign was decisive in the development of new views of citizenship and participation.

The demands presented by the *Congrès musulman* in June 1936 were a radical challenge to the system that had been established in Algeria during a century of colonial rule. They included the abolition of the colonial administration, the *Délégations financières* and the *communes mixtes*, a halt to expropriation and the restitution of previously expropriated land, as well as unlimited access to Algeria's forestry areas. Furthermore, the *Congrès musulman* demanded mandatory education for both sexes and the abolition of separation between French and 'indigenous' schools. Classical Arabic was to be taught at schools alongside French and restrictions on Arabic press were to be lifted. Arabic was also pivotal for religious practice, for which the document demanded freedom of preaching and the restitution of religious property. In social and economic matters, the *Congrès musulman* demanded proportionate budget expenditure amongst Muslims and Europeans, equal pay for equal work and equal access to military and public posts.[44]

But the most explosive issue concerned the suffrage. The *Congrès musulman* demanded universal male suffrage for the elections of all local, regional and national assemblies – including the French parliament. This was to be done through a single Algerian electorate, unlike the separate Muslim electorate

---

44 ANOM, GGA 12H 13: Charte revendicative du peuple algérien musulman, June 1936.

suggested by various French deputies and legal experts since the First World War. At the same time, it demanded that the *statut personnel* be maintained, save for marginal modifications.[45] Viollette could not agree to such radical demands. Scornful and disapproving of the 'ignorant masses', he contended that the ballot had 'nil value' for most Algerians.[46] Rather than universal suffrage, Viollette suggested granting the vote to c. 25,000 Algerians of certain groups and occupations: officers and NCOs, graduates of French institutions, industrialists, merchants and proprietaries, members of local councils, and certain functionaries of the public service.[47] Crucially, Viollette did not propose full citizenship but an intermediate status that would not be automatically transmissible from one generation to another.[48] By so doing, he aimed to guarantee the state's control over the boundaries and composition of the Algerian electorate.[49]

Pressure on the government to act swiftly was mounting, as the *Congrès musulman* gained ground in Algeria. Some 5,000 participants attended its first rally in Algiers in June 1936. It was endorsed by dozens of unions, associations and ad-hoc initiatives that were set up to promote its cause and expressed their support in telegrams to the prime minister's office.[50] Viollette clearly felt the pressure. In July 1936, he urged Blum to announce reforms as soon as possible so as not to appear to have been pressured by the *Congrès musulman*, whose leadership was soon due in Paris. Given opposition from the Europeans in Algeria, he conceded that political reforms could be postponed but insisted that social measures had to be taken urgently in order to minimize the influence of 'communist propaganda' and of 'nationalists' and 'pan-Islamists' such as Ben Badis.[51] Campaigning in Algeria, then, was now more effective than ever before. Raising its demands in rallies, demonstrations, articles and delegations, the *Congrès musulman* was a movement to reckon with. On 20 December 1936, its

---

45 Ibid.
46 AN, F/60/729: Maurice Viollette, Note pour le président du conseil (no date, evidently mid-1936).
47 Chambre des députés, seizième législature, 2ème session extraordinaire de 1936, no. 1596, annexe au procès-verbal de la séance du 30 décembre 1936: Projet de loi relatif à l'exercice des droits politiques par certaines catégories de sujets français en Algérie.
48 As pointed out in: Joseph Lagrosillière, *Rapport présenté à la Commission de l'Algérie, des Colonies et Pays de Protectorat [. . .] sur les résultats des investigations de la Sous-Commission d'Enquête parlementaire en Algérie [. . .], mars-avril 1937* (Paris: Imprimerie E.P., 1937), 77–9. This was a similar status to the one granted to c. 4,000 Senegalese in 1916. See: AN, F/60/729: Maurice Viollette, Note sur le décret relatif à l'exercice des droits politiques . . . [neither signature nor date]
49 Viollette also hoped that such intermediary status could be decreed without requiring parliamentary approval, but this was rejected by legal experts: AN, F/60/729: Secrétariat général de la présidence du Conseil, Note sur le projet de décret relatif à l'exercice des droits politiques [. . .], 16 June 1936; Note pour le président du Conseil, 8 October 1936 [no signature]; Note sur le projet de décret relatif à l'exercice des droits politiques [. . .], 10 October 1936, [no signature].
50 AN, F/60/728: Dossier 'Congrès musulman'.
51 AN, F/60/729: Maurice Viollette à Léon Blum, 15 July 1936.

general secretary addressed a letter to Prime Minister Blum, reminding him of the movement's allegiance to the Popular Front and expressing disappointment that nothing had been done yet: 'Six months have passed since our first rally. While in France you have transformed in a positive and profound manner the conditions of the workers, in Algeria, your energetic and clearsighted action is yet to be felt.'[52] Ten days later, Viollette's reform bill was presented to parliament.

Though the Viollette bill fell short of the demands expressed by the *Congrès musulman*, it was widely endorsed by Algerian public opinion as a step in the right direction. No fewer than 195 telegrams were received by the prime minister's office from late December 1936 throughout January 1937. They emanated from individuals and associations throughout Algeria, representing a wide range of movements and social groups: local branches of the *Congrès musulman* and its youth organization; branches of the French Socialist and Communist parties; Muslim veterans' associations; civic and mutual aid societies; and telegrams from Muslim councillors.[53] When a parliamentary inquiry commission arrived in Algeria in early 1937 to study the situation and make further recommendations concerning the Viollette bill, the *Congrès musulman* welcomed the delegates with numerous banquets and demonstrations. Presided by socialist deputy for Martinique Joseph Lagrossilière, a supporter of colonial reform since the 1910s inspired, by his own words, by his background as a man of colour, the commission was clearly viewed as a useful forum for the Algerian cause.[54] The campaign was supported by a broad political spectrum, including, most strikingly, Messali Hadj, leader of the nationalist *Parti du peuple algérien* ('Algerian People's Party' – successor of the meanwhile dissolved ENA, hereafter: PPA) and otherwise a vocal critic of the *Congrès musulman*'s reformist agenda.[55] Colonial officials and police agents recorded numerous rallies and 'an extraordinary animation' throughout the country, including the remote southern territories.[56]

A key figure in this popular mobilization was the journalist, activist and later Senator Muhammad al-Aziz Kessous. A disciple and ally of Ferhat Abbas, Kessous joined the French socialist party (formally the *Section française de*

---

52 AN, F/60/728: Secrétaire général du Congrès musulman au Président du conseil, 20 December 1936.
53 A detailed list is kept alongside the telegrams themselves in: AN F/60/730.
54 For Lagrossilière's remark see: ANOM, GGA 12H 13: Sûreté départementale d'Oran, Rapprt: Union Socialiste républicaine – Apéritif offert à M. Lagrosillière, 9 June 1937.
55 On Messali Hadj see: ANOM, GGA 12H 13: Service des affaires indigènes nord-africaines, 29 May 1937. On further banquets and receptions see e.g.: ANOM, GGA 12H 13: Sûreté départementale d'Alger, Rapport, 12 June 1937.
56 See e.g.: ANOM, GGA 12H 13: Département de Constantine, arrondissement de Sétif, Rapport Mensuel, March 1937; Autour du voyage du docteur Bendjeloul au Mzab à l'occasion du passage de la commission parlementaire d'enquête, 18 May 1937.

l'Internationale ouvrière 'French Section of the Workers' International' – SFIO) in 1931 and worked as a journalist for several reformist and left-leaning mouthpieces in Algeria. Politically situated between the French left and the Algerian national movement, he became close with Albert Camus during the Algerian War, during which Camus addressed him in his famous essay 'Letter to an Algerian Militant'.[57] In a series of articles for the left-leaning *Oran républicain* in 1937, Kessous interviewed dozens of representatives, trade unionists, activists and intellectuals who explained the motives behind their endorsement of the Viollette bill. Published during the visit of the parliamentary inquiry committee studying the situation in Algeria, this was a most ambitious effort to advocate the cause of reform by providing a panoramic view of Algerian public opinion.

The central theme of this campaign for reform was the conditional endorsement of the Viollette bill, portrayed as a positive step towards an overall political change in Algeria. Particularly telling were the statements by several Algerian women who demanded the immediate implementation of the Viollette bill and fiercely attacked its opponents – including leading French feminists. Madame el-Boudali Safir, for instance, a teacher from Mascara and a *dévoilée*, as Kessous cared to mention, criticized UFSF president Maria Vérone's opposition to the bill, saying one might only hope to find amongst European electors in Algeria 'the culture, discernment, and liberalism of those Muslims ... to [whom] the Blum-Viollette bill seeks to grant legitimate rights'.[58] Similar arguments were made by Mademoiselle Benabed, a *licenciée ès lettres*, daughter of an employee at the court of Rabat originating from Oran. A *dévoilée* as well, Benabed was one of the few Algerian women to have received French education and possibly the only Algerian woman to hold a French degree at the time. Benabed rejected any notion of her religion as oppressive. Acknowledging a disadvantaged social position of women, she argued that female emancipation would follow that of men once the Viollette bill was implemented: 'Look what has happened in Egypt, in Albania, in Russia, in Turkey. It was first the man who lifted up his head and then reached his hand to his partner ... Polygamy, that convenient pretext which colonialists often invoke, has become obsolete, if not outlawed altogether.'[59]

---

57 Abdellali Merdaci, 'Kessous, Mohamed-Aziz', in *Auteurs algériens de langue française de la période coloniale: dictionnaire biographique* (Paris: L'Harmattan, 2010), Albert Camus, 'Lettre à un militant algérien', in *Essais* (Paris: Gallimard, 1965), 961–6.
58 Mohammed el-Aziz Kessous, 'Une grande enquête sur le Projet Blum-Viollette', *Oran républicain*, 6 May 1937.
59 Mohammed el-Aziz Kessous, 'Une grande enquête sur le Projet Blum-Viollette', *Oran républicain*, 11 May 1937.

Alongside rallies and the press, an important forum for the Algerian campaign for reform was Joseph Lagrosillière's inquiry commission. Hearing dozens of representatives of the European, the Algerian Muslim and the Jewish populations, some of the commission's most fascinating proceedings amounted to negotiations on participation in the Republic. The protocol of al-'Uqbi's hearing, for instance, is testimony to the attempt to bring together Muslim religious and French political reforms. As a prominent reformist 'alim, al-'Uqbi was heard separately from the official 'ulama delegation and emphasized that he was merely presenting his own views. Though the protocol is not available in Arabic, al-'Uqbi was accompanied by his long-time ally and interpreter Al-Amin al-'Amudi, and the final transcript was to be sent for his approval.[60] Describing his intellectual and religious training in Medina in the 1910s as formative for his efforts to reform Maghribi Islam, al-'Uqbi stated: 'I want to purify this Algerian Islam, which is an amalgam of prejudices and superstition. Islam is one! Islam stands for science and for logic!'[61] Al-'Uqbi was in agreement with the mainstream of French public opinion on one crucial issue: polygamy. As we have seen in Chapter 2, polygamy had long been seen as aberration by French jurists and politicians. And while most Algerian advocates of reform responded to this objection by arguing that polygamy would disappear once reforms were implemented, al-'Uqbi took a different approach. When asked by the commission members about naturalization, he replied that he supported citizenship *dans le statut*, but signalled willingness to tolerate certain changes to Islamic law imposed by France, above all the abolition of polygamy.[62]

On all these issues, al-'Uqbi expressed views that differed substantially from those of Ben Badis, who opposed any attempt to modify Islamic legislation. Ben Badis insisted that polygamy was an integral part of the indivisible Quranic law and, therefore, could not be abolished. Furthermore, he argued that Algerian Muslims' compliance with conscription should not be interpreted as a renunciation of the *statut personnel*. Most importantly, he and al-'Uqbi presented different visions of the relation between Algerian Muslims and France. Whereas al-'Uqbi spoke of France as the *peuple protecteur*, Ben Badis described his vision for a future political arrangement in less harmonious terms: 'We are Algerians and we are of Arab blood. We are Muslims in every sense of the word, but we all seek fraternity with the French people. We do not wish to live as French slaves, but as free men under French authority . . . When we say that we do not want to

---

60 ANOM, GGA 12H 13: Entretien à la Commission parlementaire d'enquête, 6 March 1937.
61 Ibid.
62 ANOM, GGA 12H 13: Entretien à la commission parlementaire d'enquête, 6 March 1937.

be French, we mean that we do not want to renounce our descent [*race*] and our religion. *We do not want naturalisation.*'⁶³

Indeed, 1937 witnessed not only the campaign for the Viollette bill but the centenary celebrations for the conquest of Constantine, where Ben Badis resided and preached. In a brochure published shortly before the celebrations, Ben Badis criticized the failure of the French to recognize the sacrifice and heroism of Algerians during a century of French rule, to pay them tribute, 'turn the page' after decades of war and expropriations and open a new chapter in the history of Algeria. As James McDougall observes, this text expressed 'a desire for recognition, a continuing effort to live with the fact of French rule, and to find a workable partnership with the colonial state through which its apparently invincible domination might be negotiated.'⁶⁴ It was in this political climate and as part of this effort that Algerians debated, criticized and conditionally supported the Viollette bill in the radical period of 1936–7.

In these months of upheaval and despite furious opposition from a large part of the European population in Algeria, the *Congrès musulman*'s campaign successfully won the support of Lagrosillière's inquiry commission. In its report, the commission argued that Algerians were almost unanimous in their support for the Viollette bill, stressing that the proposals were widely seen as a first step towards a major political reform.⁶⁵ By so doing, the commission rejected the portrayal of Algerians by the colonial lobby and administration as indifferent to politics and acknowledged the demands of the *Congrès musulman* as representing the will of the Muslim population.⁶⁶ Echoing the extensive debates on Muslim women in Algeria in the mid-1930s, the commission's report described their legal status and social position in very favourable terms. Reiterating the assertion that polygamy was disappearing from Algeria, the report described the position of Muslim women in certain aspects as better than that of French women. More generally, the report argued that the *statut personnel* was not essentially incompatible with the *Code civil* and acknowledged the centrality of Islamic legislation to religious and communal life in Algeria. Warning that any attempt

---

63 ANOM, GGA 12H 13: Entretien à la commission parlementaire d'enquête, 16 April 1937. Emphasis added.
64 McDougall, *History and the Culture of Nationalism*, 64.
65 Lagrosillière, *Rapport présenté à la Commission de l'Algérie*, 37–8.
66 A report written at the prefecture of the Oran department, for instance, claimed eighty per cent of the Muslim population to be indifferent to the Viollette plan: ANOM, GGA 12H/14: Préfecture d'Oran, Centre d'informations et d'études: Note sur le projet Violette et ses répercussions dans le département, 23 March 1938.

to abolish it would cause furious reactions and thus fail, it concluded that the *statut personnel* constituted an 'unassailable bastion'.[67]

But the most important argument in the report concerned the boundaries of political participation in the age of empire. In a significant break with the republican maxim of French legislation as 'one and indivisible', the report stated: 'One has to admit that the existence of such a vast colonial empire as ours will engender new situations, and it would be a sign of extraordinary narrow-mindedness to seek to adapt these under all circumstances to the judicial parameters devised for the metropole.'[68] This broad statement was followed by concrete proposals to extend and improve political reforms in Algeria. While the Viollette bill foresaw an intermediary status that would not to be transmissible from one generation to the next, Lagrosillière's report recommended granting full, transmissible citizenship. This was a significant modification: it would have meant giving up state control over the composition of the Algerian electorate from the second generation of naturalization onwards – as demanded by the *Congrès musulman*.

After decades of Algerian campaigns for reform, accepting religious difference in the French body politic was no longer a taboo. A governmental legislation bill suggested granting the vote – though with numerous caveats – to practising Muslims. A parliamentary commission urged the government to go even further and bestow full citizenship on the Algerian elite. For a brief historical moment, the prospect of a modest yet potentially consequential reform seemed realistic. Even as progress stalled in 1938, Ferhat Abbas promised: 'The Daladier government will not forget us.'[69] To the Europeans in Algeria, too, the scenario of reform seemed closer than ever. Their leadership was up in arms.

Faces of the status quo

To its opponents, the Viollette bill represented a political threat and an intellectual aberration that had to be blocked at almost any price. The prospect of sharing political power with Algerian Muslims was a serious menace to the institutionalized privileges of the Europeans: the unequal distribution of tax revenues and the exclusive access to generously endowed administrative and

---

67 Lagrosillière, *Rapport présenté à la Commission de l'Algérie*, 64.
68 Ibid., 70.
69 Ferhat Abbas, 'Le Gouvernement Daladier ne nous oubliera pas', *L'Entente Franco-Musulmane*, 28 April 1938.

political posts in the colony.⁷⁰ For politicians in the metropole, tolerating Islamic legislation within the Republic was a radical break with the established principles of colonial thought and practice. With the *Congrès musulman* representing with great confidence, the aspirations of a resurgent civil society and the colonial lobby determined to block reform, the late 1930s witnessed an unprecedented clash in Algeria over the nature and boundaries of French citizenship.

In many ways, the campaign against the Viollette bill resembled the clash with the metropole during the anti-Semitic crisis of the late 1890s. A myriad of anti-Republican, anti-Islamic and anti-Semitic tropes was used to demonize Blum and Viollette and discredit a bill that soon became inseparably associated with their names. Even the Crémieux Decree reappeared as the original sin of the metropole, as a government led by a Jewish prime minister suggested extending the vote to an 'indigenous' population. In a Drumont-like – though eventually unsuccessful – bid to represent Algiers in parliament, the Nazi sympathizer Henry Coston urged Europeans in Algeria in August 1936 to resist the 'Jewish plan' that had allegedly begun with the founding of the *Alliance israélite universelle* in 1860 and reached a historical climax with the 'infamous decree granting to Algerian Jews the right that was refused to the indigenes'.⁷¹ Once the Blum government was sworn in, graffitied swastikas appeared across Algeria alongside slogans such as 'Death to the Jews! Foreigners (*métèques*) to Palestine! Blum to the gallows!'⁷²

The slogans and symbols of this campaign reflected the deep changes taking place in French and Algerian politics. In France, the far right was coming to the fore, most prominently through the success of the *Parti Social Français* led by Colonel de la Rocque, and the newly founded *Parti Populaire Français* headed by the former Communist, Jacques Doriot. In Spain, the fragile Second Republic was attacked by an alliance of fascist, Catholic and conservative forces in a planned coup d'état that became a brutal civil war and embodied for many the political divide of the time. Right-wing leaders of the Europeans in Algeria, many of them of Spanish descent, openly sided with the Spanish insurgents and organized in various anti-republican parties and leagues.⁷³ Meanwhile, references to Palestine in the campaign against Blum and Viollette echoed the growing presence of the Jewish immigration and settlement movement and the resulting Arab-Jewish

70 Guignard, *L'Abus de pouvoir*, 168.
71 Archives de la Contemporaine, F delta res 798 (168): Henry Coston, "Le Plan juif" (leaflet, evidently August 1936).
72 Julien, 'Léon Blum et les pays d'outre-mer', 380.
73 Kalman, *French Colonial Fascism*, 105–7.

conflict in Palestine in the Algerian press. The outbreak of communal violence in Jerusalem, Jaffa, Hebron, and Safed in 1929 was reported in great detail by both Francophone and Arabophone newspapers.[74] In 1934, deadly riots between Algerian Jews and Arabs erupted in Constantine, leaving thirty-four dead.[75] As Charles-Robert Ageron has noted, news reports from Palestine were a factor in the escalation.[76]

This aggressive campaign was led by a network of right-wing mayors, who now reappeared as a highly effective political force in Algeria. Their opposition to the Viollette bill culminated in February 1938, when the newly appointed minister of the interior Albert Sarraut – a veteran of colonial administration and surveillance and an ardent anti-Communist – publicly endorsed Viollette's reform plan at the Chamber's *Commission du suffrage universel*.[77] Days later, hundreds of mayors, municipal and departmental councillors, members of the *Délégations financières* and the elected members of the Algerian administration's *Conseil supérieur* met in Algiers to launch a coordinated protest. Attacking 'the spirit of hatred and discord' behind the Viollette bill, the delegates demanded to be heard urgently by the *Commission du suffrage universel*.[78]

As in previous clashes with the metropole, mayors in Algeria now portrayed themselves as the authentic representatives of the popular will, fighting against a naive, detached or indeed perfidious government in Paris. In March 1938, following the adoption of the Viollette plan by the *Commission du suffrage universel*, the quasi-unanimity of them publicly resigned in a most dramatic manner. In a statement broadcasted by *Radio-Alger* on 6 March, the mayors and councillors declared they could no longer serve as Minister of the Interior Sarrault's officials in Algeria. In a clear escalation of tone, they portrayed their resignation as a struggle to maintain national sovereignty, referring to the Viollette plan as 'a grave act imperilling the predominance of French ideas in

---

74 See e.g. ANOM, 93/B3/291: Translations of *Al-Najah*, September-November 1929; ANOM, 93/B3/169: Translations of *Al-Shihab*, September-November 1929; Amin Hussein, 'Les Événements de Paléstine', *La Voix indigènes*, 17 October 1929, 1–2. On the 1929 violence in Palestine as a case of communal strife see: Hillel Cohen, *Year Zero of the Arab-Israeli Conflict 1929* (Waltham: Brandeis University Press, 2015).
75 Ethan Katz, 'Constantine Riots (1934)', in *Encyclopedia of Jews in the Islamic World*, ed. Norman A. Stillman. Consulted online on 01 September 2020. First published online: 2010; Cole, *Lethal Provocation*.
76 Charles-Robert Ageron, 'Une émeute anti-juive à Constantine (août 1934)', *Revue des mondes musulmans et de la Méditerranée* 13, no. 1 (1973): 38.
77 ANOM, GGA 12H 14: Préfecture d'Oran, Centre d'informations et d'études, Note sur le projet Violette et ses répercussions dans le département, 23 March 1938. On Sarraut see: Martin Thomas, 'Albert Sarraut, French Colonial Development, and the Communist Threat, 1919–1930', *The Journal of Modern History* 77, no. 4 (2005): 917–55.
78 Fédération des maires d'Algérie, *Les Droits électoraux des indigènes algériens: Le projet Viollette* (Algiers: Imprimeries la Typo litho et Jules Cabonel, 1938), 5–6.

Algeria and dividing national sovereignty.'[79] Emulating the address of Max Régis to the crowds from atop the Algiers town hall in 1899, the mayors used the new technology of radio to defy the French government with an ultimatum to withdraw its proposed legislation.[80]

The mayors' strategy was successful. Their collective resignation effectively paralysed the work of the Algerian administration. Nearly 92 per cent of the mayors in the *département* of Constantine, 88 per cent in the *département* of Algiers and 58 per cent in the *département* of Oran resigned within ten days.[81] The mayors' continuing pressure achieved its goal in April 1938, when the Daladier government confidentially agreed to cease any activity to advance the Viollette plan. The minister of the interior and the prime minister were to meet in confidence with the leader of the mayors' delegation, Gabriel Abbo, who, in return, was to call upon his colleagues to resume their work.[82] Thus, the last attempt to implement Viollette's proposals was blocked. The mayors' success was complete.

Yet, although they openly challenged the French government and often sided with the Popular Front's ideological enemies in Spain, Italy and Germany, the mayors' campaign cannot be simply described as a form of fascism or even a 'uniquely colonial variant' thereof.[83] Even some of the most outspoken mayors occasionally adopted the terminology of republicanism and 1789. The mayor of Oran, Gabriel Lambert – an outspoken supporter of Mussolini and Hitler and active ally of the Spanish Francoists – presented a more respectable and mainstream image when in the metropole. In a speech in Paris in February 1937, Lambert denied that he or other opponents of reform were fascists, reminding his audience of some leading republican opponents of the Viollette plan – most notably Henri Guernut, former secretary of the LDH.[84] Launching their coordinated protest a year later, the mayors stated that allowing Algerian Muslims to participate in the Republic while retaining their *statut personnel* as suggested by Viollette would give them 'excessive advantages that are incompatible with the equality which the year 1789 has sanctioned with a Revolution that

---

79 AN, F/60/730: Secrétaire général du Gouvernement général de l'Algérie (Alger) au Gouverneur général (Paris), 6 March 1938. Emphasis added.
80 ANOM, GGA: 3CAB 85: Chef-adjoint du cabinet du Gouverneur général au Gouverneur général, 6 March 1938.
81 ANOM, GGA 12H 14: Cabinet du Gouverneur général, 17 March 1938.
82 AN, F/60/730: Gouverneur général au Ministre de l'Intérieur, 11 April 1938.
83 Kalman, *French Colonial Fascism*, 2.
84 Gabriel Lambert, *L'Algérie et le projet Viollette* (Oran: F. Plaza, 1938), 14–16. Guernut later presided a parliamentary commission appointed in 1938 to investigate the situation in the colonies and which recommended to postpone political reforms. On Lambert see: Kalman, *French Colonial Fascism*, 105–7.

eliminated all privileges to proclaim the equality of all citizens before the law, one and indivisible'.[85] What was at stake in Algeria during the turbulent years of the Popular Front was not abolishing parliament, establishing corporate statism or blocking communism but the question of the vote.

In this conflict over the nature and boundaries of the French body politic, Islam played a pivotal role. Compelled to address recent developments in the Arab and Islamic world, reform opponents insisted that Islam – at least as practised in Algeria – was irreconcilable with the Republic. In a brochure from 1938, the mayors' federation sought to cast Algeria as an exception, a stark contrast to the rest of the Arab world. In response to the claim that Islam no longer poses an obstacle to political inclusion and participation, the mayors stated: 'Whilst this might be true in Turkey, Albania and even in Egypt, it is absolutely false in Algeria, where the *statut personnel* has been upheld in all its rigour concerning matters of inheritance, marriage, the situation of women and children and polygamy'.[86] Paul Saurin, mayor of Rivoli in western Algeria, Radical deputy since 1934 and later a supporter of Pétain, was even more damning in his verdict of the Viollette plan and its prospects. For him, the plan jeopardized 'French sovereignty' in Algeria, as it would create a group of voters subjected to a 'religious, anti-democratic law, immutable in its sacred Quranic text and therefore incommensurate with the normal evolution and the progress of human societies'.[87]

Viollette, for his part, responded in early 1939 with a frontal attack on his opponents, reminding them that Catholics, too, had their *statut personnel*, and that this set of rules was itself hardly compatible with the *Code civil*: 'It is no exaggeration to say that for a believer wishing to respect all anathema of the Church, life in the society of 1938 would be far more impossible than for a Muslim attached with no reserve to Quranic principles'.[88] Equating Islam with Catholicism was provocative enough but suggesting that Muslims were in certain aspects closer to the institutions of the French Republic than Catholic Frenchmen was simply scandalous – particularly in Algeria, where the Catholic faith served as a unifying factor for the various Mediterranean communities. Viollette, a colonial administrator well acquainted with Algeria, was surely aware

---

85 ANOM, GGA: 3CAB 85: Fédération des maires d'Algérie: Congrès des maires du 27 janvier 1938, Oran.
86 Fédération des maires d'Algérie, *Les Droits électoraux des indigènes algériens*, 5–6.
87 AN, F/60/729: Amendement au projet de loi relatif à l'exercice des droits politiques par certaines catégories de sujets français en Algérie, présenté par M. Paul Saurin, 22 January 1937.
88 Maurice Viollette, 'La Question indigène', *Alger-Républicain*, 2 February 1939.

of that. More than anything else, his remarks were a sign of his realization that his attempt to accommodate difference within the French Republic was doomed.

For decades, Islam had been portrayed as inherently incompatible with French citizenship. The consolidation of a permanent state of exception in Algeria allowed to exempt Muslim subjects even from the most fundamental principles of the Republic. The mayors' and colonial lobbyists' victory stemmed not only from a deeply asymmetrical power balance but ran much deeper. Reform advocates could invoke 1789 as often as they pleased; in French imagination, this legacy had been configured as irrelevant to any discussion on Algerian Muslims. The shelving of the Viollette plan was much more than a defeat for the school of colonial reforms or a bitter disillusionment for such supporters of reform and inclusion as Abbas. It was the failure of an attempt to envisage an alternative model of political participation. Before long, the horizon of the Algerian struggle would shift dramatically.

6

Shifting horizons

In the spring of 1944, new graffiti appeared on the walls of cities across Algeria: 'French citizens, No, Algerian citizens, Yes'; 'Down with French citizenship'; 'Long live Algerian citizenship for all.' These mottos, which were noted and reported with considerable concern by colonial officials in cities such as Algiers, Constantine or Sétif were a testimony of a rapidly changing public mood. Rather than the colonial administration, the *indigénat* or the European population, what Algerians were now increasingly rejecting was French citizenship itself.[1]

For colonial officials, such graffiti represented an atmosphere which was seen as a key factor in the eruption of violence in the Algerian east in May 1945. On 8 May, the PPA organized a separate demonstration than the one led by other political parties to mark VE Day. PPA members insisted on carrying Algerian green-and-white flags and placards with nationalist messages calling for independence. As police intervened to confiscate these, shots were fired, killing a few demonstrators and spreading panic, anger and confusion in the city. In the following hours and days, Algerian peasants killed 102 Europeans, while dozens more were wounded or endured sexualized violence. Repression and retaliation over the next two weeks were brutal and indiscriminate. Civilian authorities handed policing powers to the military, weapons were distributed to settler militia and villages and towns throughout Kabylia and the Constantine region were bombed by French planes and warships, killing between 6,000 and 8,000 people.[2]

The connection drawn by French officials between the rejection of French citizenship and the explosion of May 1945 is illuminating for the discussion of citizenship as promise – and its demise. For the author of the report cited above (possibly none other than the secretary general of the colonial administration),

---

1   ANOM, GGA 8CAB 180: L'émeute de Constantine (1945) – secret, no author or date mentioned. The formulations in French as cited in the report read: « Citoyens français non, citoyens algériens oui », « A bas la citoyenneté française », « Vive la citoyenneté algérienne pour tous »
2   On the violence and repression of May 1945 see most recently McDougall, *A History of Algeria*, 179–82.

the very prospect of political rights and participation had the power of containing social and political tensions and maintaining order in Algeria.³ Indeed, though the Algerian struggle for citizenship in the 1930s was far more radical than most colonial officials were willing or able to infer, it envisioned a non-violent transformation of the social and political order through the gradual extension of the franchise. By 1945, the belief in the transformative capacity of French citizenship, in its potential as a frame of negotiation had evaporated. The dynamics and implications of this development are discussed in this chapter.

Crucially, the demise of citizenship as promise occurred at the very same time as political rights were extended in Algeria and a flurry of proposals for the reorganization of the French empire was published in the metropole and the colonies. In a speech in Constantine on 12 December 1943, less than a year after the Allied landing that had ended Vichy rule in Algeria, General Charles de Gaulle, head of the new provisional government established in Algiers (officially known as the *Comité français de libération nationale* – 'French Committee of National Liberation – hereafter: CFLN), announced a series of reforms. Paying tribute to the sacrifice of North African soldiers during the war, he declared: 'The *Comité de libération* has decided . . . to grant immediately to tens of thousands of Muslim Frenchmen their full rights as citizens, without allowing the exercise of these rights to be prevented or limited by . . . the *statut personnel*.'⁴ De Gaulle also pledged to extend the representation of Algerians Muslims in the municipal and departmental councils and promised a series of economic reforms. Three months later, the ordinance of 7 March 1944 abrogated the repressive laws of the *indigénat*. It bestowed French citizenship '*au titre personnel*' – that is, as non-transmittable to the next generation – to certain groups, gave all male Algerians aged 21 or older the right to vote for local councils and declared all male Algerians to be eligible for full citizenship.⁵ Further reforms were being discussed throughout the empire. At the conference of colonial officials in Brazzaville in January 1944, in the preparatory debates on the Fourth Republic and its constitutions in 1945–6 and in a host of reviews and mouthpieces, French statesmen and jurists proposed different models for a reorganized empire.

3   The French political activist and chronicler Jacques Jurquet has identified the report's author as Pierre René Gazagne, secretary general of the GGA, who wrote it on 8 October 1945. See: Jacques Jurquet, *La Révolution nationale algérienne et le Parti communiste français*, vol III (Paris: Editions du Centenaire, 1979), 162.
4   Charles de Gaulle, 'Discours prononcé à Constantine', 12 December 1943, in *Charles de Gaulle – Discours et Messages*, vol. I (Paris: Plon, 1970), 352–3. For the decision formulated by the CFLN see: ANOM, GGA 12H 15: Décision, Algiers, 11 December 1943.
5   'Ordonnance du 7 mars 1944 relative au statut des Français musulmans d'Algérie', JO (Édition d'Alger), 18 March 1944, 217–18.

Some envisioned concentric circles of affiliation with France, others spoke of 'federalism', and above all was the new principle of governing different territories with different laws as formulated by De Gaulle in Brazzaville.[6]

These debates were not exclusively led by French statesmen. In 1946, the Senegalese deputy Amadou Lamine-Guèye successfully pursued in the Constituent Assembly of the Fourth Republic legislation that gave French citizenship to all residents of the French empire, regardless of their *statut personnel*. The law of 7 May 1946 stated: 'From 1 June 1946, all residents [ressortissants] of the overseas territories (including Algeria) shall possess the quality of citizens with the same status as the French nationals of the metropole or the overseas territories' (note the special clarification on Algeria).[7] This law was integrated in its entirety into the 1946 Constitution of the Fourth Republic, which redefined the empire as a 'French Union' and created mechanisms and procedures of representation for the colonies – including Algeria.[8] As Frederick Cooper has put it, 'World War II created an opening in French politics that Africans were able to pry wider.'[9] Yet, as Cooper acknowledges, it was above all West African politicians and intellectuals who participated in these consultations, drawing on the historic example of the *originaires* in Senegal exercising political rights. Algerians' participation was on a much more limited scale, with only Bendjelloul taking part in the preparatory debates of the nascent Fourth Republic.[10]

Far more significant was the envisioning of a new, Algerian citizenship. By the mid-1940s, French citizenship no longer seemed to be reformable to figures such as Abbas or Bendjelloul. One reason for this was the small print behind the solemn promises for equality and rights. The 7 March 1944 ordinance set a system of two different electoral colleges for local assemblies, in which Algerians were in the minority (two to five). The Lamine-Guèye Law, while promising citizenship to all subjects of the empire, left it for 'particular laws' to define the conditions and procedures of participation, which allowed to uphold the unequal representation of Algerians and Europeans. More substantially, this chapter argues, the rejection of French citizenship marked a departure from an earlier assumption that though rarely articulated explicitly, underlay the campaign for participation in the 1930s: that one could be an Algerian Muslim and yet a French

6   Cooper, *Citizenship between Nation and Empire,* 28–34, 40–4, 54.
7   'Loi du 7 mai 1946 tendant à proclamer citoyens tous les ressortissants des territoires d'outre-mer', *JO – Lois et décrets,* 8 May 1946, 3888.
8   Constitution de 1946, IVᵉ République, article 80: https://www.conseil-constitutionnel.fr/les-constitutions-dans-l-histoire/constitution-de-1946-ive-republique. Accessed 28 March 2022.
9   Cooper, *Citizenship between Nation and Empire,* 7.
10 Ibid., 6–9, 55, 85. Bendjelloul was the only Algerian member of the *Assemblée consultative provisoire* which prepared the terms and procedures of the nascent republic's Constituent Assembly.

citizen, that cultural and ethnoreligious belonging did not have to correspond with membership in a certain polity. This assumption was now gone. As Ferhat Abbas wrote in his immensely influential *Manifesto of the Algerian People* from 1943: 'The time has passed when an Algerian Muslim could wish to be anything but a Muslim Algerian.'[11]

Envisioning Algerian citizenship

Perhaps nowhere in the French empire were the fall of Vichy and the emerging post-war international order felt so early and so tangibly as in Algeria. The Allied landing of November 1942 did not only make Algiers the capital of Free France, but it also demonstrated the American military and economic might and spread the word of the Atlantic Charter and Roosevelt's rhetoric of self-determination. Ferhat Abbas, who evoked the Atlantic Charter in his *Manifesto of the Algerian People*, discussed the application of the charter to Algeria in several meetings with Roosevelt's representative in North Africa.[12]

The *Manifesto of the Algerian People* was the expression of a rapid shift in political strategies and worldviews that had taken place since the shelving of the Blum-Viollette plan. With Messali under house arrest and the *Parti communiste algérien* (Algerian Communist Party – hereafter: PCA) banned, Abbas had an immense influence on the Algerian political landscape.[13] A former member of the Constantine departmental council and the *Délégations Financières*, Abbas was the author of the 1936 article '*La France c'est moi*', in which he famously questioned the existence of an Algerian nation and as Malika Rahal notes, formulated a dissenting vision for Algerian Muslims' participation in the Republic.[14] But, drawing on the Atlantic Charter, he now demanded a constitution for Algeria that would guarantee 'the absolute equality and liberty of all its inhabitants with no distinction of race or religion' and an 'immediate and effective participation of Algerian Muslims in the government of their country'.[15] 'Algeria of 1830 belonged to the Muslim World', he wrote in 1943. 'It had the same state of civilization as the other provinces of the Turkish empire ... The Algerian people, counting five million, constituted a powerful nation. It defended its soil and

---

11 Ferhat Abbas et al., 'Manifeste du peuple Algérien', in *Le Mouvement national Algérien*, 163.
12 Alistair Horne, *A Savage War of Peace: Algeria, 1954–1962* (New York: The Viking Press, 1977), 42.
13 Ibid, 42–3.
14 Malika Rahal, 'Ferhat Abbas, de l'assimilationisme au nationalisme', 444.
15 Abbas et al., 'Manifeste du peuple Algérien', 163.

its liberty.'[16] At the same time, he quit the *Délégations financières* and later denounced the very foundations of the Algerian administration, demanding that the *Direction des Affaires musulmanes* be abolished and the 'dictatorial' powers of the governor general be limited.[17] Responding to attacks on his writings and activity in the settler press, he stated: 'I prefer to be the last citizen of a free country than the first "indigène" of a colony.'[18]

Abbas's new stance represented a substantial body of Algerian public opinion. In early 1944, Algerian councillors, *'ulama* and other notables collectively formulated a programme that rejected the French administration's proposed reform of citizenship which was modelled after the Blum-Viollette plan and envisaged granting the vote to some 65,000 Algerians.[19] Across the political spectrum, there was a broad agreement that the reform programme of 1936 was no longer adequate. 'Overtaken by recent events' was how Bendjelloul described it in early 1944.[20] 'Simply insignificant' was the verdict of the new president of the AUMA, Rachid al-Ibrahimi.[21] Instead, Algerian leaders and representatives demanded universal suffrage and a new political order that amounted to nothing short of envisaging an Algerian constitution and citizenship.[22]

However, what was at stake was not simply *which* citizenship Algerians should have but the creation of a new body politic, for which Algerian leaders sought to define the boundaries of franchise and participation. The well-established French principle of naturalizing the 'elites' was now rejected more vehemently than ever before. Instead, the Algerian leaders who appeared before the new reform commission in January–February 1944 praised 'the masses' – 'the only issue of interest', as al-Uqbi put it.[23] Representing the socialist party, Muhammad Kessous demanded that the new reform programme take into consideration the

---

16 ANOM, GGA 8CAB 159: Ferhat Abbas, 'Miasmes impériales', 14 July 1943, 1
17 'Un grand débat de politique musulmane aux Délégations financières', *Égalité*, 7 December 1944, 1. (archived in: Archives SciencesPo, Fonds Mécheri, MEC 501). For Abbas's appeal to Pétain see: ANOM, GGA 5CAB 26: Ferhat Abbas, 'L'Algérie de demain', 10 April 1941.
18 ANOM, GGA 8CAB 159: Ferhat Abbas, 'Miasmes impériales', 14 July 1943, 1.
19 The provisional government's reform commission drew on the Blum-Viollette plan and generally adopted its categories of eligibility for the vote. See: ANOM, GGA 12H 15: Sous-commission des réformes musulmanes, séance du 15 janvier 1944. For the number of 65,000 see: ANOM, GGA 12H 15: Deuxième séance de la sous-commission des réformes musulmanes, 17 January 1944.
20 ANOM, GGA 12H 15: Note présentée par le docteur Bendjelloul à la commission des réformes musulmanes, no date, 2.
21 ANOM, GGA 12H 15: Traduction du rapport adressé à la commission des réformes musulmanes par le Cheick Bachir Brahimi, 3 January 1944, 5.
22 For the principle of 'elites' see: ANOM, GGA 12H 15: Sous-commission des réformes musulmanes, séance du 15 janvier 1944.
23 ANOM, GGA 12H 15: Mémoire présentée par cheikh Taieb el Okbi à la commission des réformes musulmanes, 3.

Algerian *fellahin*: 'More than anywhere else, the *fellah* in Algeria is the most vivid, the most genuine [réelle] expression of the country [pays]. He should have his place among the civic elite of tomorrow.'[24] Both men rejected the colonial praxis of granting Algerians a non-hereditary citizenship and demanded that political rights be transmissible – 'an undebatable principle', as Kessous argued.[25] Amar Ouzegane, representing the PCA, criticized the provision that only those Algerian Muslims capable of reading and writing in French should obtain the vote, arguing that command of Arabic enabled one to understand and judge political discussions just as well.[26] Bendjelloul, for his part, while praising the new policy, criticized the ratio of representation proposed by the provisional government (50 per cent Europeans and 50 per cent Algerians, thereby according the Europeans a privileged position). Algerians' goal, he stated, was and remained universal suffrage and one single electorate for all residents of Algeria.[27]

A key issue in the process of imagining a new body politic was the place of Islam in the new political order. For the AUMA president al-Ibrahimi, the answer was clear. The 'Algerian Muslim people [peuple]', as he put it, had to resist any tendency of French assimilation and was to constitute the fundament of the new Algeria.[28] The *statut personnel* was to become the exclusive terrain of Islamic jurisprudence – interpreted and administered by Islamic scholars rather than for the purposes of the colonial administration. This demand was part of a long struggle by the AUMA to restore the autonomy of Islamic teaching and scholarship, long exploited and deformed by the colonial administration, as Charlotte Courreye notes.[29] Moreover, al-Ibrahimi demanded that the authority of qadis and *'ulama* be extended beyond matters of marriage and divorce, and that better training be provided for them. Al-'Uqbi, for his part, demanded that those Algerian Muslims who had been naturalized under the individual principle and had thus renounced their *statut personnel* be allowed to 'recover' it, thus undoing colonial procedures and the boundaries they had drawn across

---

24 ANOM, GGA 12H 15: Exposé fait par M. Kessous ... devant la commission d'Études des réformes musulmanes, 18 January 1944, 2.
25 Ibid., 3. For al-Uqbi on transmissible citizenship see: ANOM, GGA 12H 15: Mémoire présentée par cheikh Taieb el Okbi à la commission des réformes musulmanes, 3.
26 'Audition de M. Amar Ouzegane', in *Le Mouvement national Algérien*, 172.
27 ANOM, GGA 12H 15: Note présentée par le docteur Bendjelloul à la commission des réformes musulmanes, no date.
28 ANOM, GGA 12H 15: Traduction du rapport adressé à la commission des réformes musulmanes par le Cheick Bachir Brahimi, 3 January 1944, 5.
29 Courreye, *L'Algérie des oulémas*, 31–2.

Algerian society.[30] These demands were widely shared across the political spectrum and were later reiterated by Abbas.[31]

At the same time, there was broad agreement that the new political order should allow Europeans – as well as the Jewish minority – to be members of the new Algerian polity. Though the new Algeria was clearly 'Muslim', 'Arab' and 'Berber', leaders across the political spectrum – from Messali to Abbas – envisaged a parliament and a constitution in which all groups would be represented.[32] On 20 October 1944, Kessous published an article in Abbas's newly founded weekly *Égalité* which addressed the issue of Algeria's historical and actual ethnoreligious diversity. He pledged to fight to dissolve the colonial order in Algeria alongside those Europeans who 'understand the sacred legitimacy of our cause.' 'It is with them', he continued, 'that we shall construct tomorrow the Algerian community, the fraternal and humane community, where all those living on this soil will have equal rights and equal duties, regardless of their ethnic origin and their confession'. 'For the new Algeria will be democratic and follow fearlessly socialist solutions . . . It will create a synthesis of the legitimate interests of Muslim, European and Jewish workers destined to live together on a generous soil that will make no distinction between her natural and her adopted sons.'[33] Abbas, for his part, would continue to defend this stance long after 1962 and the mass departure of Europeans and Algerian Jews.[34]

An important impulse in the turn to Algerian citizenship was the abrogation of the Crémieux Decree by the Vichy government in 1940.[35] For Algerian Jews, this was a moment of great distress, one that revealed the precarity of French citizenship, as Jacques Derrida would observe years later.[36] But this precarity was also noted by Algerian Muslims and had repercussions on how they envisaged their future, as Abbas argued in 1943 in the *Manifesto*: 'Since the abrogation

---

30 ANOM, GGA 12H 15: Mémoire présenté par cheikh Taieb el Okbi à la commission des réformes musulmanes, 3.
31 'Il faut restituer à la justice musulmane l'intégralité de sa compétence', *La République algérienne*, 27 May 1949, 3. (Archived in: Archives de Sciences Po, Fonds Mécheri, MEC 501).
32 On Messali see, for example: ANOM, GGA 12H 15: Traduction – extrait du quotidien tunisien « Ez Zohra », numéro 20/01/44.
33 Aziz Kessous, 'La Communauté algérienne accueillera fraternellement tous les Algériens', *Égalité*, 20 October 1944, 1, (archived in: Archives de Sciences Po, Fonds Mécheri, MEC 501).
34 See, for example, Abbas's televised interview on 22 October 1980, archived by the Institut National de l'Audiovisuel and accessible at: https://www.youtube.com/watch?v=soaHAMEewPY (accessed 21 March 2022).
35 Archives de Sciences Po, Fonds Julien, JU 20: Service français d'information: Évolution du statut politique des Français musulmans d'Algérie, 29 July 1947, 9. One of the anomalous results of this saw Algerian Jews who had been French citizens since their birth losing their political rights while foreign Jewish nationals who had been naturalized individually did not.
36 Jacques Derrida, *Le Monolinguisme de l'autre* (Paris: Galilée, 1996), 33–5.

of the Crémieux Decree, the Algerian *nationality* and *citizenship* offer [the Algerian Muslim] greater security and provide a clearer and more logic solution to the problem of his evolution and emancipation.'[37] Abbas's argument that Algerians had little reason to project their hopes on a precarious political status that could be easily abolished by the French government was underscored by the provisional government's decision not to reinstate the Crémieux Decree. Instead, on 14 March 1943, the government published an ordinance abrogating the decree and turning the Algerian Jews into subjects.[38] In the political climate of the mid-1940s, this led Algerian leaders such as Abbas to conclude that they had little reason to throw in their lot with French citizenship.

Algerian Jews, however, still projected their hopes and their expectations for security on French citizenship and campaigned for it to be reinstated.[39] In a letter from April 1943, a group of notables evoked the long history of the Crémieux Decree, 'elaborated by the monarchy, prepared by the [Second] Empire, implemented by the Government of National Defence and ratified by the [Third] Republic.'[40] In a further protest in July, they submitted a selection of documents that bore testimony to their loyalty to France, their sacrifices on the battlefield and the legitimacy of their citizenship: a declaration by Muslim notables and clerics from the Constantine region from 1871, confirming, amid calls to abrogate the then-recent Crémieux Decree, that they did not oppose it; the *Livre d'Or* of Jewish soldiers in the First World War, put together by the Jewish 'Committee for Social Studies' in the 1930s amid resurgent anti-Semitism amongst Europeans in the colony; a 1939 article by Ferhat Abbas confirming that he had no reservations concerning the Crémieux Decree; and a similar statement by Muslim councillors from Oran from April 1943.[41] The protest had international resonance. On 25 April 1943, the French Catholic philosopher Jacques Maritian of the Free School in New York published an article condemning the provisional government for abrogating the Crémieux Decree.[42] Another article was published in *Contemporary Jewish Record* by the aspiring German-Jewish *émigrée* political

---

37 Abbas et al., 'Manifeste du peuple Algérien', 163. Emphasis in original.
38 ANOM, GGA 8CAB 71: Secrétariat à l'Intérieur: Note au sujet de l'abrogation du décret Crémieux, 28 May 1943.
39 On Jewish protests against the Vichy Regime's measure see: ANOM, GGA 8CAB 71: Rapport concernant l'ordonnance du 14 mars 1943, 19 May 1943.
40 ANOM, GGA 8CAB 71: Letter signed by Henri Aboulker, Armand Karsenty, and Simon Tobiana, 5 April 1943.
41 ANOM, GGA 8CAB 71: Lettre du 11 Juillet 1943 du conseiller général Alfred Ghighi (. . .); documents in annexe.
42 Jacques Maritian, 'Cremieux Law Upheld', *The New York Times*, 25 April 1943, 10. Maritian's wife, the poet and philosopher Raïssa Maritian, was of Russian-Jewish heritage. I thank Martin Conway for alerting me to this.

scientist Hannah Arendt, who accused 'the French colonials' who 'took advantage of France's defeat and of their freedom from the control of the mother country in order to introduce into Algeria a measure which they would have never been able to obtain through legal channels.'[43]

French officials were reluctant to reinstate the Crémieux Decree – precisely due to the fear that this might reopen the debate on the political regime in Algeria, as Daniel Schroeter has noted.[44] A government note from August 1943 argued that 'the leaders of the Muslim political parties only wait for the Jewish question to be opened again to address once more the issue of their political demands as formulated in Ferhat Abbas's Manifesto of the Algerian people.'[45] Some officials evoked the argument about 'Muslims' animosity towards the Jews' and the need to 'gain the support of the indigenous [Muslim] masses at a time when they participate in great numbers in the building of the army.'[46] However, there was no agreement within the French government as to how to approach the problem of the Crémieux Decree, and most officials agreed that stripping an entire population of its citizenship posed considerable legal difficulties.[47] The Ministry of Interior suggested reinstating the Crémieux Decree and at the same time offering French citizenship to certain categories of the Algerian society.[48]

Finally, amid pressure in Algeria and abroad, on 21 October 1943, the provisional government decided to reinstate the Crémieux Decree – a decision greeted with gratitude and relief by Jewish representatives.[49] In the following days, police agents reported some 'discontent' amongst Muslim society – but did not provide any specific names or incidents.[50] This was characteristic of a broader phenomenon: a colonial administration that had made the alleged animosity between Jews and Muslims an indispensable working premise and

---

43 Hannah Arendt, 'Why the Crémieux Decree Was Abrogated', in *Contemporary Jewish Record* 1943: 123.
44 Daniel J. Schroeter, 'Between Metropole and French North Africa: Vichy's Anti-Semitic Legislation and Colonialism's Racial Hierarchies', in *The Holocaust in North Africa*, ed. Aomar Boum and Sarah Abrevaya Stein (Stanford: Stanford University Press, 2018), 19–49.
45 ANOM, GGA 8CAB 71: Commissariat à la coordination des affaires musulmanes: Note du Colonel Truchet à l'attention du Général Catroux, 9 August 1943.
46 ANOM, GGA 8CAB 71: Secrétariat à l'Intérieur: Note au sujet de l'abrogation du décret Crémieux, 28 May 1943. See also similar position by Catroux: ANOM, GGA 8CAB 71: Gouverneur général au commissaire à l'intérieur, 29 September 1943.
47 See, for example, ANOM, GGA 8CAB 71: Secrétariat à l'Intérieur: Note au sujet de l'abrogation du décret Crémieux, 28 May 1943.
48 ANOM, GGA 8CAB 71: Rapport concernant l'ordonnance du 14 mars 1943, 19 May 1943.
49 See, for example: ANOM, GGA 8CAB 71: Alfred Ghighi au gouverneur Catroux, 23 October 1943; Société culturelle israélite de Tlemcen au Général de Gaulle, 25 October 1943; 'Conseil général d'Oran – séance du 22 Octobre', in *L'Echo d'Oran*, 23 October 1943, 1.
50 ANOM, GGA 8CAB 71: Police spéciale départementale de Constantine: Au sujet du rétablissement du Décret Crémieux, 26 October 1943.

could hardly see beyond it. This triangular dynamic – a government withholding citizenship from Algerian Jews who had possessed it for decades in order not to antagonize Algerian Muslims who were now rejecting it – encapsulated the erosion of even the idea of French citizenship as a possible, viable or indeed desirable frame of participation.

Carving up

Algerians' rejection of French citizenship was not the only sign of a rapidly changing political climate after the Allied landing. In the aftermath of the bloodshed of Sétif in 1945 – the first eruption of large-scale communal violence in Algeria in decades – leaders of the European population moved away from paying even a lip service of French citizenship as a frame of participation for all. While some figures still used the classical arguments of polygamy and a menace to French sovereignty in an attempt to block Algerians' participation, a growing number of European politicians and journalists in Algeria realized that some political reform was unavoidable and moved to formulate a new programme.[51] Rather than blocking Algerians' participation altogether, they now attempted to create political mechanisms and thresholds that would consolidate their veto on any significant matter and would make Algerians' representation meaningless. Moreover, European leaders moved to draw lines and boundaries between Algerians and Europeans, to formulate plans and strategies of carving up the country and its electoral bodies along ethnoreligious lines.

As deputies and councillors of the new Fourth Republic were discussing in Paris the shape and nature of the new imperial 'French Union', officials, journalists and politicians in Algeria were considering different models for dividing the country into separate administrative units. A report from January 1946 exemplified this ambivalence. While calling for a complete 'fusion' of Algeria and France, the detailed proposals were those of power-sharing arrangements: 'We must turn Algeria into a Corsica rather than an Ireland', the author stated, only to explain later on that 'rather than a Corsica, it is an Alsace that we must create here.'[52] Like Alsace, Algeria ought to become a 'French

---

51 See, for example, the position formulated by André Mallarmé, a Pétaininst and former Radical deputy of Algiers: ANOM, GGA 12H 15: A. Mallarmé, Note sur le projet consistant à adjoindre des indigènes musulmans au corps électoral français en Algérie, 10 January 1944.
52 ANOM, GGA 8CAB 62: Cabinet du Gouverneur général, La Réforme du statut politique et administratif de l'Algérie, 29 January 1946, 9. No author specified.

province with particular status'. This meant citizenship and the right to vote for all but on the basis of 50 per cent Algerians and 50 per cent Europeans in the local councils. The main goal of French policies in Algeria, the report stressed, was 'to cause amongst the Muslim masses such a psychologic shock that would lead them to abandon any notion of separatism or independence'.[53]

In 1947, the French government began preparing a new Organic Law for Algeria, designed to redefine its status within the French Union. The clear goal of the governmental bill was to consolidate Europeans' power in Algeria in the age of universal suffrage by upholding the separation into two electoral colleges – one for Europeans and one for Muslims – which would have an equal number of representatives in different councils.[54] The bill suggested creating an elected 'Algerian assembly' that would consist of forty-five representatives from each of the two colleges to represent the residents of the country before the governor general, as well as an 'Algerian council' that would carry out the decisions of the assembly. Article 2 of the Organic Law bill upheld the 7 March 1944 ordinance and stated: 'All residents of the *départements* of Algeria possessing French nationality exercise, without distinction of origin or religion, the rights associated with the quality of French citizens and are subjected to the same obligations. Particular laws define electoral procedures [*la régie électorale*] and the status of local assemblies.'[55] The final version of the Organic Law, presented by the Socialist Minister of the Interior Édouard Depreux, was adopted by the National Assembly in September 1947. The two colleges would now each elect forty-six members of the National Assembly (thirty deputies and sixteen *conseillers de la République* – i.e. members of the upper chamber).[56] The parity of the two colleges gave the Europeans in Algeria a *de facto* veto right, as a two-thirds majority in the Algerian Assembly was required, thus effectively blocking any of the reforms advocated by Algerian representatives such as citizenship for Algerian women or teaching in Arabic.[57]

---

53 Ibid., 13. 'Alsace' was clearly used by the author to refer to Alsace-Moselle. The two departments retained special legislation after their reintegration into the French territory after the First World War – the most notable exception to the principle of standardization and indivisibility in the metropole. See: Michel Verpeaux, 'L'unité et la diversité dans la République', *Les nouveaux cahiers du Conseil constitutionnel* 1, no. 42 (2014): 12–13.
54 Archives de Sciences Po, Fonds Julien, Ju 20: Service Français d'Information, Le Statut d'Algérie, 6 August 1947, 5.
55 Archives de Sciences Po, Fonds Julien, JU 20: Assemblée nationale, première législature, session de 1947, annexe au procès-verbal de la 2ème séance du 29 mai 1947: Projet de loi portant statut organique de l'Algérie . . . présenté par M. Paul Ramadier, M. Edouard Depreux . . .,10.
56 Archives de Sciences Po, Fonds Julien, Ju 20: Service Français d'Information, Le Statut d'Algérie, 6 August 1947.
57 McDougall, *A History of Algeria*, 184.

Certain Europeans' reactions to the new Organic Law followed the path of previous controversies. On 9 July 1947, the review *L'Africain* dedicated its first page almost entirely to the government bill on the status of Algeria. 'The Governmental Bill on the Status of Algeria Is Incompatible with French Sovereignty', read the main headline. The following article defined it as 'unacceptable' for the French in Algeria.[58] In the *Tam Tam* – a particularly vulgar settler mouthpiece – General Aumeran, deputy for Algiers, criticized the bill as incoherent, saying that while Algeria was defined as a 'grouping of *départements*' by the new Organic Law, the 'Algerian Assembly' proposed by the bill constitutes a mini parliament. He demanded that the Algerian Assembly should not have any powers overriding those of the French parliament and that the 'two collectives' of Algeria have complete parity, so one cannot override the other.[59] In July, mayors and deputy mayors throughout Algeria resigned over debates in the National Assembly, though not in such large numbers as during the campaign against the Blum-Viollette project in 1938.[60] They were joined by European members of the departmental council of Algiers led by the council's president who threatened that eleven European deputies of the *Liste de défense de l'Algérie française* would quit the National Assembly, not before delivering a protest statement 'like the one read at Bordeaux in 1871 by the deputies of Alsace and Lorraine'.[61] As the new Organic Law passed through the different debates and readings in the cabinet and parliament, settler representatives returned to the terminology of 'betrayal' by the metropole.[62] An article in the right-wing mouthpiece *Unir* stated: 'L'Accord s'est fait contre l'Algérie française'. The author, René Reygasse, wrote that 'a dark veil now covers the future of our beautiful Algeria.'[63]

However, the debates on the 1947 Organic Law also witnessed the emergence of a new strand of settler opposition which focused on dividing Algeria into separate administrative units of Algerian Muslims and Europeans. On the eve of the debate on the Organic Law in the cabinet in early July 1947, Algiers deputy, dean of the law faculty at the University of Algiers and founder of the review *Renaissances* Paul Viard, member of the *Mouvement républicain populaire*, asked

---

58 'Le Projet gouvernemental de statut algérien est incompatible avec la souveraineté française', *L'Africain*, 9 July 1947, 1. archived in: ANOM, GGA 8CAB 62.
59 In Interview for *Le Tam Tam*, quoted in: *L'Africain*, 9 July 1947, 1. archived in: ANOM, GGA 8CAB 62.
60 ANOM, GGA 8CAB 62: Report to Governor Chataigneau, 28 July 1947.
61 ANOM, GGA 8CAB 62: Note pour le ministre, 8 August 1947, unsigned.
62 ANOM, GGA 8CAB 62: Le Statut de l'Algerie, unsigned note, evidently September 1947.
63 René Reygasse, 'L'Accord s'est fait contre l'Algérie française', *Unir*, 12 July 1947, 1. Archived in: ANOM, GGA 8CAB 62.

in an article for *Le Pays*: 'Will the Metropole Abandon its Children?' He criticized above all the fact that Algerian Muslims who had been given the vote by the ordinance of 7 March 1944 would now belong to the first, 'European' electoral college – an arrangement which he described as 'an electorate where citizens of the original type [citoyens-types] would be mixed [mêlés] with Frenchmen of a local status'. 'We therefore face today the necessity to organise together the life of the two collectives living on the Algerian soil', Viard argued and concluded: 'The purity of the college is the indispensable condition [sine qua non] of a status [of Algeria] whose modalities we can then discuss.' Any other arrangement, he said, would mean 'abandoning' the Europeans in Algeria and subjecting them to a legal position even worse than that of the Capitulations (the special status granted to European nationals residing in the Ottoman Empire).[64] Tellingly, in a parliamentary debate on Algeria a year earlier, PCA secretary general Amar Ouzegane praised the ordinance of 7 March 1944 precisely for having created a 'mixed' electoral college.[65]

Viard's terminology and demands were picked up by the *Comité d'Entente*, a group that gathered the Algiers branches of several political parties and which vehemently rejected the extension of Algerians' share in the country's political life. In a brochure from 1 August 1947, the *Comité d'Entente* argued that the populations in Algeria should remain separate from one another. Accordingly, the signatories demanded to redraw the boundaries of the two electoral colleges in what amounted to be an ethnoreligious division: to establish one college composed exclusively of Europeans and a second composed exclusively of Algerian Muslims, regardless of whether they had previously been granted the vote by the ordinance of 7 March 1944.[66] Furthermore, the signatories demanded that the metropole continue to exercise direct control over the Algerian administration and that the 'Algerian assembly' be subordinated to the vote of the French parliament in case of conflict between the two electoral colleges. Such demands were by no means marginal. Many of them were endorsed by no lesser a figure than De Gaulle himself.[67] Moreover, settler opposition to political reform was not confined to resignations and protests in the press. Settler militias, which had played a key role in the repression and reprisals of May 1945, were

---

64 Paul Viard, 'La Métropole abandonnera-t-elle ses Enfants?', *Le Pays*, 9 July 1947, archived in: ANOM, GGA 8CAB 62. For details on Viard see: ANOM, GGA 8CAB 62: Le Statut de l'Algerie, unsigned note, evidently September 1947.
65 Journal officiel de l'Assemblée nationale constituante, 6 April 1946, 1520.
66 Archives de Sciences Po, Fonds Mécheri, MEC 501: 'Appel aux élus de la Nation.' Brochure signed by the *Comité d'Entente*, Algiers, 1 August 1947.
67 ANOM, GGA 8CAB 62: Governor Chataigneau to Minister of the Interior, 13 August 1947.

still active and seeking to gain support.[68] In July 1947, the settler newspaper *Unir* reported that various 'official or clandestine committees' operated in Algeria and were raising 'tens of millions' of francs with the declared goal of 'saving French Algeria'.[69]

The government's insistence on the two-college system and the settler attempts to block Algerian Muslims' representation did not remain unchallenged. An alternative proposal, submitted by Bendjelloul and others, sought to hold general elections in Algeria in one electoral college in order to elect a 'constituent Algerian assembly' that would draw a constitution for the country. They avoided any mention of the French Union or indeed France.[70] Two other bills, proposed by two groups of Algerian deputies, sought to make Algeria an 'associated territory' within the French Union, as a step towards the founding of an Algerian republic.[71] Abderrahmane Bentounès, deputy of Algiers, suggested creating a new, Algerian citizenship that would apply to every individual born in Algeria to French parents.[72] Neither did the settler campaign remain unnoticed. Algerian councillors protested over the 'campaign of provocations' in the summer of 1947 and demanded an urgent vote on the Organic Law of Algeria that would 'uphold and extend' the ordinance of 7 March 1944.[73] In July 1947, municipal councillors in Algiers and Blida condemned the resignation of European mayors and departmental councillors.[74] In September, after the Organic Law was approved in a restrictive manner that gave Europeans a veto on all decisions concerning Algeria, Ferhat Abbas published an article in *Égalité* in which he attacked the settler deputies for their position.[75] Further criticism came from the AUMA president al-Ibrahimi, who rejected the procedures set in the Organic Law in an 'Address to the Arab Algerian Nation' in March 1948.[76]

It was out of the 'dynamism and paralysis of politics' that the FLN emerged, as James McDougall has trenchantly analysed.[77] On the one hand, the decade between 1945 and 1954 saw the coming of Algerian mass party politics, of

---

68 On the role of settler militia see: Martin Evans, *Algeria: France's Undeclared War* (Oxford: Oxford University Press, 2012), 88–9.
69 'Où va l'agent ?' *Unir*, 12 July 1947, 1. Archived in: ANOM, GGA 8CAB 62.
70 Archives de Sciences Po, Fonds Julien, Ju 20: Service Français d'Information: Le Statut d'Algérie, 6 August 1947, 24.
71 Ibid., 13, 17.
72 ANOM, GGA 8CAB 62: Aberrahmane ben Tounès, 'Projet de statut pour organiser la vie sociale et le progrès politique de l'Algérie' (Blida, 1947), 8.
73 Telegrams sent to governor general, archived on 30 July 1947, archived in: ANOM, GGA 8CAB 62.
74 ANOM, GGA 8CAB 62: Mairie de la Ville d'Alger: Extrait du procès-verbal, 29 July 1947; Bureau municipal de la municipalité de Blida: Motion, evidently late July 1947.
75 ANOM, GGA 8CAB 62: Le Statut de l'Algérie, unsigned note, evidently September 1947.
76 Courreye, *L'Algérie des oulémas*, 80.
77 McDougall, *A History of Algeria*, 182.

open debates, and inevitably of divisions and splits. On the other hand, the ongoing repression of Algerian political life, the restriction of participation and a constant manipulation of election results by the colonial apparatus curtailed much of the efficacy of party politics. It was as a response to the frustration of party politics in a system that blocked any meaningful political participation that the FLN demanded complete loyalty from all political groups and dedicated itself to armed resistance rather than debates on the character of a hypothetical state.[78]

Following the outbreak of the FLN uprising in November 1954, separation along ethnoreligious lines became the ultimate French response to the 'Algerian problem'. The 1950s saw a series of administrative reforms that included the creation of new *départements* and the redrawing of boundaries between different communes.[79] In a carefully worded radio broadcast statement from January 1957, the Socialist prime minister Guy Mollet, rejecting any demand for independence, formulated the guiding principles of the government's policy in Algeria amid continued warfare and mounting international pressure. While conceding to the demand of a single electoral college and promising 'an equal distribution of resources, of labour and of responsibilities between all inhabitants of Algeria', Mollet nevertheless reiterated the vocabulary of power-sharing along ethnoreligious lines and France's attempt to establish a symmetry between the demands and rights of 'the two communities': 'None of the two collectives ought to be oppressed by the other. Each of them must be able to retain its *originalité propre* [and] its own social norms [règles sociales particulières].' To guarantee this, there would be a 'regional and territorial division of Algeria'. New communes would be delineated according to 'ethnic realities'. Algeria would gain an enhanced level of autonomy over its own local affairs within the French Union, while France would assume the role of an 'arbiter'.[80]

A year later, in February 1958, the National Assembly adopted a law on 'the institutions of Algeria'.[81] This was a renewed attempt to accommodate both the old settler demand for complete administrative integration in the metropole

---

78 Ibid., 195–200.
79 For a concise list of these measures see: AN, F/60/4005: Service d'Information du cabinet du Ministre de l'Algérie: Action du Gouvernement en Algérie – mesures de pacification et réformes, Algiers, 1957, 473–80.
80 AN, F/60/4007: 'La Déclaration de M. Guy Mollet', in *Connaissance d'Algérie*, January 1957, 4–5. As Martin Evans notes, this statement represented a consensus amongst the coalition parties: Evans, *Algeria: France's Undeclared War*, 192–7.
81 *Journal officiel de la République française – Textes d'intérêt général – Algérie, 1958*: Loi no. 58-95 du 5 Février 1958.

and the demands for autonomy. It declared Algeria to be an 'integral part of the French Republic' while at the same time guaranteeing its autonomy. The Republic's role was to 'guarantee to all citizens in Algeria without distinction of race, religion or descent the equal exercise of their liberties and rights' and to 'safeguard the rights and liberties of the different communities'.[82] Moreover, Algeria was to be subdivided into different territories that would administer their local affairs 'freely and democratically'. However, the model for this 'democracy' was based on an equal representation of the two communities – Europeans and Algerian Muslims – in each territory, regardless of their actual numbers.[83] In the final days of the Algerian War, the French government turned to consider even territorial partition plans in a last-ditch attempt to maintain its presence in Algeria and allow Europeans to remain there.[84]

There were, of course, other voices. André Mandouze, a history lecturer at the University of Algiers, sought to promote dialogue between Algerian nationalists and reform-minded Europeans. Deputy for Algiers Jacques Chevallier 'sought to include [Algerian] nationalists in the political process in the 1940s and 1950s'.[85] Most famously, Albert Camus made the case for a 'civil truce' in late 1955 and early 1956, only to be greeted with a crowd shouting 'Camus to the Gallow' in his visit to Algiers in January 1956.[86] But such voices were few and isolated. Long before 1954, the vision of Algerians and Europeans sharing a common polity had lost not only credibility but, more significantly, its transformative appeal. What remained of French citizenship, we shall now see, was a powerful propaganda tool in the hands of colonial officials and generals seeking to give a facade of political legitimacy to a sweeping and ruthless state of exception.

Citizenship staged and deformed

In March 1956, almost a year and a half after the beginning of the FLN's uprising, the French parliament adopted a law 'authorising the government to undertake [mettre en oeuvre] in Algeria a programme of economic growth, of social

---

82 Conseil de la République – session ordinaire de 1957–1958, annexe au procès-verbal de la séance du 3 décembre 1957: Projet de loi . . . sur les institutions de l'Algérie . . . Articles. 1–2.
83 Ibid., Articles 3–4.
84 Arthur Asseraf, '"A New Israel": Colonial Comparisons and the Algerian Partition that never happened', *Fr Hist S* 41, no. 1 (2018): 95–120.
85 Evans, *Algeria: France's Undeclared War*, 93.
86 Horne, *A Savage War of Peace*, 124–7.

progress and of administrative reforms and allowing it to take any exceptional measure required for the re-establishment of order, the protection of people and property and the safeguarding of the territory'.[87]

It is hardly surprising that a context of anti-colonial insurgency and colonial repression should produce such an extreme state of emergency, where lawmakers all but ceded their authority and oversight to that which the government would deem as 'required by the circumstances', as the 1956 law put it.[88] Contemporary accounts and historical analyses have documented the extreme, often stomach-turning levels and practices of violence in both France and Algeria during the Algerian War. Systemic torture, arbitrary arrests, demolition of entire villages and killing of protesters, as well as sexualized violence were the most immediate and brutal forms of state violence. At the same time, forced resettlement saw the dislocation of 3 million Algerians – a measure originally designed to empty potentially strategic villages of their inhabitants and which came to exemplify the radical violence of the colonial state in its quest to dissolve and 'modernize' Algerian society.[89]

What is less widely acknowledged is the process by which decades of colonial policies and legal acrobatics around the issue of citizenship were undone within a few years – a rapid political change that eradicated even the deeply asymmetrical frames of political negotiation that had existed throughout the colonial period. Viewed through the lens of citizenship, the French war effort in the late 1950s aimed not at preserving the status quo but at disentangling any frame for negotiation, any platform of political participation – in short, any possibility of a political compromise. What was at work in the 1950s was a unique interplay of a French understanding of the conflict in Algeria as an essentially apolitical issue that could be solved through social and economic reforms, and an orchestrated staging of Algerian participation in the French institutions.

Of course, choreographed demonstrations of Algerian consent to French rule had accompanied every military campaign and every visit of a French head of state to Algeria since the 1840s.[90] And manipulation of elections – be it through

---

87 *Journal officiel de la République française – lois et décrets*, 17 March 1956, 2591.
88 Ibid.
89 Literature on colonial violence during the Algerian War is abundant. For a study of the origins of violence in the early stages of the war see most notably: Raphaëlle Branche, *L'Embuscade de Palestro: Algérie 1956* (Paris: Armand Colin, 2010). On continuities of state violence throughout the colonial period see: Sylvie Thénault, *Violence ordinaire dans l'Algérie coloniale. Camps interement, assignations à residence* (Paris: Odile Jacob, 2012). For a succinct account of counterinsurgency measures see: McDougall, *A History of Algeria*, 217–19. See also Evans, *Algeria: France's Undeclared War*, 226–57.
90 Çelik, *Empire, Architecture, and the City*, 216–26.

intimidation, omissions from electoral lists or pure fraud – had been widely used practices against Algerian Jews ever since the 1880s and through to the late 1930s. In the 1940s and 1950s, Algerian Muslims were subjected to the same practices, designed to curb the vibrant, unprecedentedly diverse party political sphere that emerged in the aftermath of the 7 March 1944 ordinance and the Organic Law of 1947. In 1948 and again 1951, in elections to the Algerian Assembly, candidates of the *Mouvement pour le triomphe des libertés démocratiques* ('Movement for the Triumph of Democratic Liberties – hereafter: MTLD) were arrested and maltreated, procedures manipulated and predominantly Muslim districts patrolled by soldiers. Similar frauds were repeated in the national legislative election of 1951 and the Algerian Assembly elections of 1954, thus eliminating the political representation of the MTLD and the *Union démocratique du manifeste algérien* ('Democratic Union of the Algerian Manifest' – widely known as the UDMA) in these assemblies.[91] Yet, the Algerian War produced new, unprecedented practices and logics of manipulation. As the FLN gained ascendency in Algeria and intensified its effort to achieve international recognition – it attended the Bandung conference in 1955, opened an office in New York and had a permanent delegation in Cairo – a certain facade of legitimacy through participation was deemed necessary by officials and generals in Algeria. It is in this context that the most remarkable staging of political participation and 'fraternization' between Algerians and Europeans was carried out by French officials and generals.

Perhaps the most remarkable occasion of orchestrated participation took place during the political crisis that brought the Fourth Republic to an end. In early 1958, tensions and suspicion between generals in Algeria and the government in Paris were mounting, as the former feared that the metropole, weakened by chronical political instability, might repeat the scenario of 1954 in Indochina and decide to negotiate with the FLN. A group of generals and officials therefore planned to force President René Coty to appoint as head of government Charles de Gaulle, whom they viewed as the only figure capable of leading France to a victory in the ongoing conflict. The political crisis reached its peak in mid-May. President Coty charged Pierre Pflimlin, who had previously suggested negotiating with the FLN, with forming a government. On 13 May, as the National Assembly was about to vote on the new government, a crowd stormed the headquarters of the Algerian administration while generals Jacques Massu and Raoul Salan seized power, announcing in a radio broadcast that the army had taken control over Algeria and openly called for the return of de Gaulle,

---

91 McDougall, *A History of Algeria*, 188.

who stated that he was willing to take power on 17 May. On 24 May, French paratroopers from Algeria landed in Corsica, ready to land in Paris to forcibly install De Gaulle as head of government. On 29 May, President Coty asked De Gaulle to become head of government. De Gaulle agreed on the condition that a new constitution would be written. He was sworn in on 1 June and was given a period of six months during which he could rule through ordinances.[92]

It was in these days of political vacuum and popular agitation that Massu and Salan staged their most widely noted propaganda activities as part of their attempt to consolidate their legitimacy: the 'westernization' campaigns of Algerian women. Between 18 and 28 May, military officers organized a series of what can only be described as public spectacles in various towns from Oran through Tizi Ouzou to Constantine. The scenes were almost identical: groups of veiled women would march the streets alongside Algerian servicemen and, upon arrival at the designated site – usually a highly symbolic place such as a town hall or a war memorial – would have their veil removed by European women who would refer to them as 'sisters'.[93] As Neil MacMaster notes, a small minority of these women were French-educated and belonged to Algerian families employed by the French administration – sometimes in very high positions. While the FLN's claim that these women were all recruited amongst prostitutes was most probably not accurate, many of them appear to have been recruited amongst domestic servants, and there can be no doubt that most of them were poor and illiterate.[94]

With De Gaulle's return to power in June 1958, this interplay of orchestrated participation and apolitical politics reached a new climax. On 4 June 1958, De Gaulle arrived in Algiers and addressed cheering crowds with his famously elusive declaration of *Je vous ai compris*. In the more concrete parts of this speech, he announced his intention to introduce a single electoral college in Algeria and voting rights for Algerian women. In the following months, as officials and politicians prepared the referendum on the constitution for a new, Fifth Republic, French officials in Algeria prepared to stage a mass participation of Algerians – particularly women – in order to buttress the legitimacy of de

---

92 Horne, *A Savage War of Peace*, chapter 13. For an hour-by-hour account of the events see: Philip Williams, 'How the Fourth Republic Died: Sources for the Revolution of May 1958', *Fr Hist S*, 3, no. 1 (1963): 1–40.

93 For an analysis of these spectacles as part of the broader French politics vis-à-vis Algerian Muslim women during the Algerian War see: Ryme Seferdjeli, 'French "reforms" and Muslim women's Emancipation during the Algerian War', *The Journal of North African Studies* 9, no. 4 (2004): esp. 43–7.

94 Neil MacMaster, *Burning the Veil: The Algerian War and the "emancipation" of Muslim Women, 1995–1962* (Manchester: Manchester University Press, 2009), 133–43.

Gaulle, the new constitution and *l'Algérie française*. As part of this effort, colonial and army officials in Algeria launched a propaganda manoeuvre to include Algerian women in the referendum. Algerian women were urged to participate in the referendum and support the new constitution by leaflets, radio broadcasts and films, as well as, in some cases, by their European employers. On the day of the referendum, voters were brought to the polls in army lorries and were requested to present unused 'No' ballots upon exiting. Complaints by the FLN were ignored.[95]

Such campaigns were part of a broader attempt to deny the FLN any legitimate claim to represent the Algerian people. As Martin Evans notes, a broad agreement across the French political spectrum saw the Algerian War not as a colonial conflict but as a struggle to maintain republican values against a criminal guerrilla organization.[96] In other words, this was a new incarnation of the colonial tradition that dismissed any Algerian demand for participation and insisted that the only areas of interest for 'the masses' were those of employment, housing and nourishment. (General Giraud had articulated this view most vividly in 1946, claiming that 'the Algerian Muslim' 'cares much less about the ballot which he cannot read than about sugar, coffee, tea and clothes'.)[97]

This was the guiding principle of a series of development and modernization plans which were formulated by the French administration from 1954 onwards and which culminated in the so-called Constantine Plan, named after De Gaulle's speech in Constantine in October 1958. Even within the areas it sought to address, the Constantine Plan shied away from addressing the structural cause of land shortage, poverty and famines: the unequal land ownership regime established over decades of colonization. As Martin Thomas notes, in 1958, 22,000 farms owned by Europeans yielded a volume of crops equal to the harvest of some 660,000 'smallholdings' in Algerian ownership.[98] Though it addressed some other pressing issues such as shanty towns and housing shortage, unemployment or agricultural reform, by avoiding any structural reform, the Constantine Plan rejected participation in the exercise of power in favour of a vast modernization and industrialization programme – now revolving around the Sahara as the epitome of an as-yet unexploited natural reserve – which reproduced previous

---

95 Ibid., 273–7.
96 Evans, *Algeria: France's Undeclared War*, 155–6.
97 *Journal officiel de l'Assemblée nationale constituante*, 23 August 1946, 3227.
98 Martin Thomas, *Fight or Flight: Britain, France, and Their Roads from Empire* (Oxford: Oxford University Press, 2014), 372.

patterns of appropriating land and natural resources.[99] As James McDougall observes, 'what this language [of reform] denoted in settler-colonial Algeria from the mid-1940s to the late 1950s was primarily an administrative process whose actual effect was the opposite of reform.'[100] Rather than an attempt at a fundamental change, the reforms of the 1950s represented the idea that France ought to accelerate its colonization efforts in Algeria and implement them on a much larger scale.

Ultimately, the only forms of meaningful participation and development to emerge during the years of the Algerian War were those which related to the prospect and coming of independent Algeria. One of the Constantine Plan's few meaningful measures was to open public posts, previously reserved for full French citizens, to all Algerians, thus qualifying a cadre of civil servants for the soon-to-be proclaimed Algerian Republic.[101] In a similar vein, the first time Algerians would vote without restrictions and discrimination was in the independence referendum of 1961. If generations of Algerian leaders had hoped that being French citizens would provide them with a meaningful platform for negotiation, this option had in effect disappeared in the 1940s. And if French politicians, generals and officials had any hope that offers of 'imperial' citizenship would defuse the Algerian conflict, the rapidly shifting horizons of participation and belonging in the age of decolonization proved them to have been fatally wrong.

---

99 On goals and scope of the Constantine Plan see: AN, F60/4011: Président du Conseil à Monsieur le Général d'Armée, délégué général du gouvernement et commandant en chef des forces en Algérie, 24 October 1958; Directives pour l'élaboration et la mise en œuvre du plan quinquennal de développement économique et social de l'Algérie (no date specified, evidently late 1958).
100 James McDougall, 'The Impossible Republic: The Reconquest of Algeria and the Decolonization of France, 1945–1962', *The Journal of Modern History* 89, no. 4 (2017): 783.
101 McDougall, *A History of Algeria*, 218.

Conclusion

In March 1959, President Charles De Gaulle gave his view of the prospects of integration and difference amid the ongoing Algerian War and recent independence of Indochina, Morocco and Tunisia. During a conversation with the young deputy Alain Peyrefitte, De Gaulle said:

> It is absolutely fine that there are yellow, black or brown Frenchmen. They show that France is open to all races and has a universal vocation. But under the condition that they remain a small minority. Otherwise, France will no longer be France. After all, we are a European people of white race, of Greek and Latin culture and of Christian religion . . . Have you seen the Muslims? Have you watched them with their turbans and jellabiyas? You see clearly that they are not French . . . Do you believe that the French body can absorb ten million Muslims who would become twenty million tomorrow and forty million the day after tomorrow? If we try integration, if the Arabs and Berbers of Algeria were to be considered as French, how can you prevent them from coming to settle in the metropole, given that the quality of life here is so much higher? My village would no longer be called Colombey-les-Deux-Églises, but Colombey-les-Deux-Mosquées.[1]

Like many texts and controversies concerning the Algerian War, it was not until the 1990s that these remarks came to light, when Peyrefitte included them in the first of three volumes of conversations with De Gaulle. The president, Peyrefitte remembered, impressed him with his 'foresight' and his determination to tell unpleasant truths.[2]

Of course, De Gaulle's remarks as recorded here represented the anxieties and confusion amid continued war in Algeria and the prospect of losing it. Peyrefitte would himself advocate partitioning the country in 1961 in a last-ditch attempt to save something of the rapidly collapsing colonial order.[3]

---

1   Quoted in: Alain Peyrefitte, *C'était de Gaulle*, vol. I (Paris: Fayard, 1994), 71–2. On De Gaulle's early vision of the nation as an ethnolinguistic entity see: Serge Berstein, *Histoire du Gaullisme* (Paris: Perrin, 2001), 20.
2   Ibid., 72.
3   Alain Peyrefitte, *Faut-il partager l'Algérie?* (Paris: Plon, 1961).

Upon Algerian independence, the French government issued a decree that stripped Algerian Muslims who were French citizens *dans le statut* of their French nationality, thus reintroducing the legal distinction between Europeans and Muslims in Algeria and preventing the latter from migrating to the metropole. The year before, a series of laws and decrees bestowed French civil legislation on all Algerian Jews who had hitherto conserved their 'Mosaic' *statut personnel* and prepared the 'reintegration' of 'repatriated' French nationals in the metropole.[4] At this historical moment, the quest of the French 'trans-Mediterranean state' to regulate the movement of people between Algeria and the metropole reached new levels of urgency. As the mechanisms of colonial domination and control were breaking down, it was precisely this ability to regulate movement across the Mediterranean that was at stake – and it was the anxieties caused by this development that De Gaulle referred to.

Yet, De Gaulle's terminology and reasoning represented a view of the French body politic which, as this book has argued, had emerged during decades of colonial rule and which the Algerian War merely rendered visible. It was no coincidence that for De Gaulle, Muslim clothing was such a significant marker of otherness and that it was possible for him to imagine, however reluctantly, 'yellow, black or brown' French citizens – but not 'Arabs', 'Kabyles' or 'Muslims'. Nor was it merely due to the raging war and the fear of mass migration from Algeria; after all, France had only recently withdrawn from Indochina, and migrant communities from Southeast Asia had belonged to the urban landscape of the metropole since the 1920s.[5] Rather, De Gaulle's remarks were a product and a particularly clear expression of the French idea of citizenship as shaped by decades of jurisdictional politics in Algeria.

That was the concept that this book has termed the ideology of French citizenship. Rather than viewing citizenship as a frame through which to negotiate questions of religious, cultural or linguistic difference, this concept relied on a predefined set of social and cultural norms and 'mores' to draw the boundaries of within and without. And since, as various historians have shown, the mainstream of French political thought in the late nineteenth and early twentieth centuries relied mainly on the idea of different stages of 'civilization'

---

4   Todd Shepard, 'Algerian nationalism, Zionism, and French laïcité: A History of Ethnoreligious Nationalisms and Decolonization', *International Journal of Middle East Studies* 45, no. 3 (2013): 448; Yann Scioldo-Zürcher, *Devenir métropolitain. Politique d'intégration et parcours de rapatriés d'Algérie en métropole: 1954–2005* (Paris: Éditions EHESS, 2010), 106–17.
5   Goebel, *Anti-Imperial Metropolis*.

to imagine hierarchies, it was often blind of its own bias. Loyal to the legacy of the French Revolution as the end of 'privileges', it identified equality before the law with uniformity. One of the clearest examples of this understanding of equality as uniformity stemmed from the struggle against the Blum-Viollette project, when European mayors in Algeria claimed that allowing Algerian Muslims to exercise rights while retaining their *statut personnel* would amount to 'excessive advantages that are incompatible with the equality which the year 1789 has sanctioned with a Revolution that eliminated all privileges to proclaim the equality of all citizens before the law, one and indivisible.'[6] Of course, mayors in Algeria were always at the forefront of the opposition against any attempt to reform the colonial order. But what De Gaulle's remarks show so clearly is how deeply and persistently the tenets of the legislation, jurisprudence, administrative praxis and political constellations in Algeria shaped metropolitan views of participation and exclusion. Ultimately, they suggest that France entered the post-colonial age of unprecedented ethnic, religious and linguistic heterogeneity lacking a concept of citizenship as a political frame through which to negotiate questions of difference, religion and the public sphere.

* * *

The turbulent months that saw the collapse of the Fourth Republic, De Gaulle's return to power and a rapidly crumbling metropolitan consensus over Algeria were shaking the fundaments of the legal borderland that France had created in Algeria in 1848 and fought to defend ever since. The Algerian War rendered the contradictions of this legal borderland visible and proximate to French public opinion after decades during which *l'Algérie française* was narrated and represented through colonial exhibitions, illustrated newspapers and mechanisms of exoticism. It was in the legal and political borderland where France was colonial, and it was this legal borderland which shaped the French idea of citizenship. Yet, that influence remained illegible to most French observers. It was this absence of Algeria from the public eye that allowed Charles-Robert Ageron to claim as late as 1978 that 'in its profundity, France was not colonial in the nineteenth and twentieth centuries.'[7] It was this mental dissociation between Algeria and the metropole that allowed Pierre Nora to refer to Algeria in 1961 as

---

6   ANOM, GGA: 3CAB 85: Fédération des maires d'Algérie: Congrès des maires du 27 janvier 1938, Oran.
7   Charles-Robert Ageron, *France coloniale ou parti colonial?* (Paris: Presse universitaire de France, 1978), 297.

'a land where law never reigned'.[8] Algeria was a stowaway in the French ship of state.

But a borderland is not a no man's land. Law – or better: a myriad of laws – did reign in Algeria, and as the violence and repression of the Algerian War spiralled, the construction of Muslimness and Europeanness as criteria of exclusion and inclusion was coming to haunt the Republic. When De Gaulle contrasted Muslims' and Arabs' 'turbans and jellabiyas' with the French 'European people', he was merely reiterating a caricature which decades of jurisdictional politics in Algeria had constituted as a norm. While various scholars have discussed in great detail the 'Mediterranean' and 'Latin' tropes as common denominators of an emerging settler community, this book has sought to demonstrate the centrality of European origin not just in settler identity but in French political theory and administrative praxis – most notably in the run-up to the major citizenship reform of 1889. Despite significant shifts in legislation and administrative praxis, the years 1865–89 marked a clear development which started with the definition of subjecthood and citizenship and culminated with the twin pairs of European-citizen and Muslim-subject.

Like so often in the modern history of European political thought, the clear-cut categories of within and without, of Europeanness and indigeneity as shaped in colonial Algeria, were disrupted by the unique position of the local Jewish minority. Exercising the rights of citizens since the Crémieux Decree of 1870 yet retaining and indeed reviving their Judeo-Arabic language, Algerian Jews defied the association of citizenship with Europeanness. As Pierre Birnbaum has trenchantly analysed, Jewish communities throughout Europe and the Mediterranean from the seventeenth century onwards entered 'vertical' (and precarious) alliances with rulers in search of protection from hostile 'masses'.[9] Perhaps nowhere else was this vertical alliance so clear, so important and so costly as in Algeria with the Jewish petition to Napoléon III in 1869 demanding full citizenship and the Crémieux Decree that accorded it. As Birnbaum argues, the Third Republic and the Dreyfus Affair – the first time in modern French history when state and society were at odds with one another – brought this vertical alliance into crisis. The settler leadership in Algeria now claimed the role of political avant-garde. Perhaps no statement captures the popular attack on the 'Jewish Republic' as Max Régis's statement upon his election as the mayor

---

8 Nora, *Les Français d'Algérie*, 43.
9 Pierre Birnbaum, *Prier pour l'État. Les Juifs, l'alliance royale et la démocratie* (Paris: Calman-Lévy, 2005), 12–24.

of Algiers in 1898: 'The town hall will become the People's House.'[10] Anti-Republicanism was now, almost automatically, anti-Semitism.

At the same time, Algerian Jewish participation in the Republic remains a fascinating testcase of the promise of citizenship in the age of empire. Even after the trauma of Vichy had shown all too poignantly the precarity of citizenship, Algerian Jewish leaders and notables gave all their energy to recover their political status. Benjamin Stora has aptly framed the history of Algerian Jews under colonial rule as that of three 'exiles': the Crémieux Decree of 1870, the stripping of citizenship in 1940 and the mass departure for the metropole following Algerian independence in 1962.[11] But as we have seen, it was in 1943 that Algerian Jews' choice of French citizenship appeared with particular vigour. While Ferhat Abbas described in the *Manifesto of the Algerian People* the abrogation of the Crémieux Decree as an opportunity to move from French to Algerian citizenship, the leadership of the Jewish minority reaffirmed its historical choice with its campaign to regain its citizenship. When in August 1956 the leaders of the FLN stressed at the Congress of Soummam that Algerian Jews were part of the nation, the latter had already made a very different choice.[12]

* * *

Did colonial reform ever stand a chance? Or, put differently: Was there a point in time when the French ideology of citizenship was seriously being reconsidered in order to accommodate religious difference? The question is explosive, as it touches some of the open wounds of colonial Algeria and its aftermath. All too easily can such discussions smack of *nostalgérie*, of entertaining counterfactual scenarios in which colonialism could have been saved. Yet, the question over the attempt to envisage a different idea of citizenship does not concern the flow of Algerian history or the Algerian War. After all, this book has sought to demonstrate the persistence and tenacity of ethnoreligious categories in French political thought since the late nineteenth century, to show the many ways in which citizenship as a meaningful frame of participation had been dissolved and made impossible in Algeria long before the 1950s.

Rather than speculating on the alleged 'missed opportunities' in the history of *l'Algérie française* or European expansionism more broadly, discussing reform

---

10 As quoted in: 'Max Régis, maire d'Alger', *Le Figaro*, 21 November 1898 [archived in: AN, F/7/16001/1].
11 Benjamin Stora, *Les trois exils: Juifs d'Algérie* (Paris: Stock, 2006).
12 Shepard, 'Algerian Nationalism, Zionism, and French laïcité', 460.

attempts in the 1930s and 1940s allows us to see the dramatic change in the meaning of citizenship as an institution and a promise: from political rights to national belonging. As Malika Rahal has stressed, when Ferhat Abbas wrote in 1936 'la France c'est moi', this was a subversive statement that challenged the ethnoreligious concept of citizenship.[13] The broader significance of Abbas's statement, in other words, was that Algerian Muslims could practise the religion, remember the history and speak the language that constituted their collective community while exercising their political rights as French citizens; that there was no contradiction between the two; and that political rights and sociocultural belonging did not have to be exercised within the same frame. Despite the considerable difference in the views expressed by Bendjelloul, Abbas, al-Uqbi, or Ben Badis during the fight for the Blum-Viollette plan, there was a broad agreement on this principle.

It was precisely this radical dissociation of political rights and cultural-religious belonging that underlay the Blum-Viollette plan, and it was precisely this dissociation that became impossible in the 1940s and 1950s – both in Algeria and in France. The firm views expressed by Algerian representatives to the reform commission of 1944 – on Arabic language, on the *statut personnel*, on the Algerian 'masses' – were symptomatic of how citizenship was seen and imagined amid the rapid decline of European colonial power. As Michelle Campos has argued, debates on citizenship at the end of empire were often prone to accentuating distinct identities rather than forging cross-communal solidarities.[14] The various plans to carve up sovereignty in Algeria in the 1940s and 1950s, to create political institutions that would run along the ethnoreligious categories of the colonial order show the impossibility of imagining citizenship as a common, cross-communal frame for participation in the late colonial age.

In this respect, France entered the post-colonial age with an idea of the body politic that shared much of the ethnoreligious logic that informed the citizenship concepts of new independent states such as India, Pakistan, Israel and not least Algeria. With the annulment of Algerian Muslims' recently obtained French citizenship (and its bestowal on the Jews of the M'zab), the ethnoreligious categories crafted over decades of colonial rule came to demarcate the boundaries of the body politic in the post-colonial age.[15]

---

13 Rahal, 'Ferhat Abbas, de l'assimilationisme au nationalisme', 444.
14 Michelle U. Campos, 'Imperial Citizenship at the End of Empire: The Ottomans in Comparative Perspective', *Comparative Studies of South Asia, Africa and the Middle East* 37, no. 3 (2017): 589, 598–9.
15 Shepard, 'Algerian nationalism, Zionism, and French laïcité', 448.

'Citizenship', Rogers Brubaker has aptly observed, 'is both an instrument and an object of closure'.[16] A closure which, as this book has argued, isn't exclusively or even primarily territorial. Citizenship as ideology, as we have seen, was a subtle yet effective tool of exclusion. Ultimately, the question that remains is how significant, if at all, citizenship as promise can be in a world still shaped by the institutionalized inequalities of the colonial age. Or, put more open-endedly, whether, in the early twenty-first century, citizenship can be reimagined.

---

16   Brubaker, *Citizenship and Nationhood*, 23.

Appendix

Translation of the French and Judeo-Arabic versions of the 1869 Algerian Jewish petition for citizenship.¹

Judeo-Arabic

(*Italics* denote words in Hebrew):

Sire, our sultan,

When in the year 1830 France, who is always great and noble, retained for the Jews their laws and their religion, she effected for us a work of justice.

And when, since then, she abolished our *tribunals* and gradually removed the authority of our *rabbis*² and diminished the jurisdiction of the seniors of our religion and established her laws in the transmission of our property and possessions from one person to another³ and admitted us to certain posts and services, she showed that she wishes to bring us closer to her and to give us her rules, magistrates and laws [and] advanced one more step so that we become equal to her in every aspect.

The sénatus-consulte of 14 July 1865 came and changed everything and taught us that the doors through which we shall enter in order to become French will not be opened but with caution.

The people who wish to demonstrate that the sénatus-consulte is just, say that we do not agree to become French and that imposing this on us would offend us in the religious sense and in the material⁴ sense.

The people who say this are mistaken about us and mislead France.

---

1   Source: ANOM F80/2043: Pétition des Juifs d'Alger, 5 December 1869.
2   In the original: 'חכמים'
3   In the original: 'מן יד ליד'
4   In the original: 'אומור אדוניא'

We ask to be equal to the French and subjected to their legislation in every aspect even though it will alter the structure of our families and will change the division of inheritance.

Sire, our sultan, please accept our request in this matter, which we desire and cherish so very much.

We beg Allah for this to happen[5] soon, when our request shall be accepted, and we shall become French.

As a fully integrated population,[6] which we have been for forty years, we will show that our *faith* is as strong and true as *the faith of the members of our people*,[7] the Jews of France. Like them, we shall learn from *our holy Torah* and from the people living amongst us the *good virtues* that are appropriate for acculturated residents and make them appropriate for their homeland to benefit from them.

Sire, our master, in the year 1860, the Jews of Algeria already wrote to your Majesty about what they desire and what they ask for from your benevolence. They do not seem to have persuaded you[8] in order for their demand[9] to be fulfilled.

We hope today to be more fortunate and that our request will be accepted, as your Majesty will believe us in the call that we utter and will recognize that we submit ourselves with sincere intentions and with all honesty to your authority.

May there remain no doubt in your heart and mind that we are obedient people, and may you do in the year 1870 for Algeria what France in the year 1789 and your uncle, may God have mercy on him, in the year 1807 did for our brothers the Jews of France and Italy.

Sire, the entire population asks for its right. Accept its request and your glory shall be our joy once our request will be accepted.

---

5   In the original: 'טציר', apparently derived from *sara* – 'happen'. This form is more common in the dialects of present-day Lebanon and Palestine, but such linguistic transfers were not uncommon. See: Ofra Tirosh-Boker, 'Linguistic Analysis of an Algerian Judeo-Arabic Text from the Nineteenth Century', *La Linguistique* 55 (2019): 203–7.
6   In the original: 'קום אלי מעאמן ראנא עאישין האדי ארבעין עאם'. This is a difficult phrase to translate. 'mu'amin' is clearly derived from ''ama' ('become all-embracing, common'), yet the syntax remains odd.
7   In the original: 'אמונת בני עמנו'.
8   In the original: 'ידכלו פי עקלך'.
9   In the original: 'דדהום/ר/רדהום/'. Translating this as 'demand' is merely an educated guess, identifying – despite inconsistent orthography – the Judeo-Arabic term with the Arabic ضغط ('pressure, emphasis'). On the problem of orthography see: Benjamin Hary, '*Il-'arabi dyalna* (Our Arabic): The History and Politics of Judeo-Arabic', in *Languages of Modern Jewish Cultures. Comparative perspectives*, ed. J. Miller and A. Norich (Ann Arbor, 2016), 302–3.

French

Sire,

When in 1830 France, always grand and magnanimous after her victory, retained for the Algerian Jews[10] their laws and religion, she accomplished an act of clemency and justice.

By abolishing since then our tribunals, by gradually taking all jurisdiction from our rabbis, by diminishing the authority of the administrators of our religious life,[11] by subjecting the division of our property to the general law,[12] by admitting us to certain [public] posts and functions, she has clearly manifested her will to bring us closer to her and to give us her laws, her magistrates, her institutions.

One more step in this direction of attachment and the assimilation would have been complete.

The Sénauts-Consulte of 14 July 1865, the last legal step which we have been seeking for forty years, cast doubt on all that and taught us that the gates of naturalization will not be opened to us but with discretion and reserve.

To try and justify this legislative act, it has been claimed that we reject emancipation and that imposing it upon us would mean offending our religious convictions and harming our material interests.

Those who use such language do not know us well, and, being themselves misled, unintentionally mislead France.

We request our assimilation, and, following this beneficence, we shall subject ourselves with no regret and no reserve to the rule of French legislation, despite its significant modifications concerning the constitution of our families and the division of our inheritances.

May your Majesty deign to accept this wish. It is the most cherished and legitimate wish we can utter. May it be realized soon and forever!

As full members of the French family, to which we belong for almost half a century, we shall prove that, unwavering though we are in the religious convictions that we share with our coreligionists of France, we will, like them, be able to draw on the principles of Judaism and the teachings surrounding us

---

10 In the original: 'Les Israélites algériens'. *Israélite* was a common and neutral term in French and German writing at the time. An 'old-fashioned and sometimes offensive' term in English (OED), I have chosen to translate it using the more common terms Jews/Jewish.
11 'Les chefs de notre culte'.
12 'Droit commun'.

to find the qualities and virtues that are appropriate for citizens and render them useful for their country.

Sire! Already in 1860, the Algerian Jews submitted to you the expression of their sentiments and of their patriotic aspirations.

They did not succeed in persuading you.

It is our firm hope that we shall be more fortunate today.

By doing in 1870 for Algeria what the Revolution in 1789 and the First Empire in 1807 did for our brothers in France and Italy, your Majesty, persuaded by the loyalty of our declarations and the sincerity with which we shall give up our prerogatives in order to obey the ordinary laws,[13] will acknowledge the long-standing devotion and sacrifice that inspire us.

Sire! An entire population asks for justice. Give us justice, and you shall render your reign glorious and fill us with joy and pride.

Algiers, 5 December 1869.

---

13 'Lois ordinaires'. Under the Second Empire, those laws were passed by the *Corps législatif*. See: Marcel Prélot, 'La Signification constitutionnelle du Second Empire', *Revue française de science politique* 3 (1953): 39–40.

Bibliography

Archives

Archives nationales d'outre-mer, Aix-en-Provence

Archives du Gouvernement général de l'Algérie.
Archives du Ministère de l'Intérieur – services de l'Algérie.
Archives des préfectures: Alger, Constantine, Oran.

Archives nationales, Pierrefitte-sur-Seine

Correspondance de la Division criminelle du Ministère de la Justice
Fonds Messimy
Ministère de l'Intérieur, fonds Panthéon: Dossier Max Régis
Secrétariat général du Gouvernement et services du Premier ministre

Central Archives for the History of the Jewish People (CAHJP), Jerusalem

Algérie (AL/A12)

Archives de Sciences Po, Paris

Fonds Charles-André Julien
Fonds Chérif Mécheri

La Contemporaine, Nanterre

Archives de la Ligue des droits de l'homme

Newspapers and periodicals

Alger-Républicain
Al-Islah

Al-Najah
L'Antijuif algérien
Bulletin officiel du Gouvernement général de l'Algérie.
Bulletin de la Société française pour la protection des indigènes des colonies
Le Constitutionnel
La Dépêche algérienne
La Dépêche de Constantine
Droit de l'Homme
L'Echo d'Alger
L'Entente franco-musulmane
Excelsior
Le Figaro
Le Gaulois
Journal des débats politiques et littéraires
Journal de Toulouse
La Libre parole
La Liberté
Le Matin
Le Nouvelliste
Oran républicain
Petit républicain
Qol Israel / La Voix d'Israël
Le Radical
Républicain de Constantine
La République algérienne
La Revue bleue
Revue des deux Mondes
La Revue indigène
La Revue de Paris
Le Sémaphore de Marseille
Le Siècle
Le Temps
L'Univers israélite
La Voix indigène

Published primary and secondary sources

Abi-Mershed, Osama W. *Apostles of Modernity: Saint-Simonians and the Civilizing Mission in Algeria*. Stanford: Stanford University Press, 2010.
Abitbol, Michel. 'L'Affaire Dreyfus et la montée de l'antisémitisme colonial en Algérie'. *Archives juives* 31, no. 1 (1998): 75–87.

Abitbol, Michel. *From Crémieux to Pétain: Antisemitism in Colonial Algeria 1870–1940*. Jerusalem: Zalman Shazar Centre, 1993. (Hebrew).

Abrevaya-Stein, Sarah. *Saharan Jews and the Fate of French Algeria*. Chicago: Chicago University Press, 2014.

Abu-'Uksa, Wael. 'The Construction of the Concepts of "Democracy" and "Republic" in Arabic in the Eastern and Southern Mediterranean, 1789–1878'. *Journal of the History of Ideas* 80, no. 2 (2019): 249–70.

Ageron, Charles-Robert. *Les Algériens musulmans et la France, 1871–1919*. Paris: Presses Universitaires de France, 1968.

Ageron, Charles-Robert. 'Une émeute anti-juive à Constantine (août 1934)'. *Revue des mondes musulmans et de la Méditerranée* 13, no. 1 (1973): 23–40.

Ageron, Charles-Robert. *France coloniale ou parti colonial?* Paris: Presse universitaire de France, 1978.

Ageron, Charles-Robert. *Histoire de l'Algérie contemporaine*, vol. II. Paris: Presses Universitaires de France, 1979.

Ageron, Charles-Robert. *L'Algérie Algérienne: De Napoléon III à de Gaulle*. Paris: Sindbad, 1980.

Ageron, Charles-Robert. 'Ferhat Abbas et l'évolution politique de l'Algérie musulmane pendant la Seconde Guerre mondiale'. In *Genèse de l'Algéria algérienne*, vol. II, 259–84. Saint-Denis: Èditons Bouchène, 2005.

Ahmed, Leila. *Women and Gender in Islam: Historical Roots of a Modern Debate*. New Haven: Yale University Press, 1992.

Amarana, M. *Note sur la colonisation de l'Algérie, présentant les moyens d'élever nos possessions d'Afrique à un haut degré de force et de prospérité*. Saint-Quentin: Imprimerie de A. Moureau, 1848.

Amin, Qasim. *The Liberation of Women. The New Woman. Two Documents in the History of Egyptian Feminism*. Translated by Samiha Sidhom Peterson. Cairo: The American University in Cairo Press, 2000.

Archives parlementaires de 1787 à 1860, vols. 25–6. Paris, 1862–1896.

Arendt, Hannah. 'Why the Crémieux Decree Was Abrogated'. *Contemporary Jewish Record* 6, no. 2 (1943): 115–23.

Asnky, Michel. *Les Juifs d'Algérie du décret Crémieux à la libération*. Paris: Éditions du Centre, 1950.

Assan, Valérie. *Les Consistoires israélites d'Algérie au XIXe siècle: l'alliance de la civilisation et de la religion*. Paris: Armand Colin, 2012.

Asseraf, Arthur. '"A New Israel"': Colonial Comparisons and the Algerian Partition that Never Happened'. *French Historical Studies* 41, no. 1 (2018): 95–120.

Asseraf, Arthur. *Electric News in Colonial Algeria*. Oxford: Oxford University Press, 2019.

Attal, Robert. 'Ha-'Iton Ha-Yehudi Ha-Rishon Ba-Magreb: L'Israélite algérien (A-Dazeeri), 1870'. *Pe'amim* 17 (1983): 88–95.

Ayalon, Ami. *The Arabic Print Revolution: Cultural Production and Mass Readership*. Cambridge: Cambridge University Press, 2016.

Aydin, Cemil. *The Idea of the Muslim World: A Global Intellectual History*. Cambridge, MA: Harvard University Press, 2017.

Bailly, Charles. *Le Départ pour l'Algérie*. Paris, 1848.

Bayoumi, Moustafa. 'Shadows and Light: Colonial Modernity and the Grand Mosque of Paris'. *The Yale Journal of Criticism* 13, no. 2 (2000): 267–92.

Benton, Lauren. 'Colonial Law and Cultural Difference: Jurisdictional Politics and the Formation of the Colonial State'. *Comparative Studies in Society and History* 41, no. 3 (1999): 563–88.

Berkovitz, Jay. *The Shaping of Jewish Identity in Nineteenth-Century France*. Detroit: Wayne State University Press, 1989.

Berstein, Serge. *Histoire du Gaullisme*. Paris: Perrin, 2001.

Berstein, Serge and Rudelle, Odile (eds), *Le modèle républicain*. Paris: Presses universitaires de France, 1992.

Betts, Raymond F. *Assimilation and Association in French Colonial Theory, 1890–1914*. New-York: Columbia University Press, 1961.

Birnbaum, Pierre. *Prier pour l'État. Les Juifs, l'alliance royale et la démocratie*. Paris: Calman-Lévy, 2005.

Birnbaum, Pierre. *L'Aigle et la Synagogue : Napoléon, les Juifs et l'État*. Paris: Fayard, 2007.

Birnbaum, Pierre. *The Anti-Semitic Moment: A Tour of France in 1898*. Translated by Jane Todd. London: University of Chicago Press, 2011.

Blanchemain, Prosper. *Chant des colons*. Paris, 1848.

Blévis, Laure. 'Sociologie d'un droit colonial: citoyenneté en Algérie (1865–1947): une exception républicaine?' (Doctoral thesis, Institut d'Etudes politiques, Aix-en-Provence, 2004).

Blévis, Laure. 'L'invention de l'« indigène », Français non citoyen'. In *Histoire de l'Algérie à la période coloniale*, edited by Abderrahmane Bouchène et al., 212–18. Paris: La Découverte, 2012.

Blévis, Laure. 'La Situation coloniale entre guerre et Paix: enjeux et conséquences d'une controverse de qualification'. *Politix* 4, no. 104 (Autumn 2013): 87–104.

Bonnardot, J. 'La presse algérienne sous la Seconde République (février 1848–décembre 1851)'. *1848 et les révolutions du XIXe siècle* 38, no. 180 (June 1948): 21–38.

Booth, Marilyn. 'Before Qasim Amin: Writing Women's History in 1890s Egypt'. In *The Long 1890s in Egypt: Colonial Quiescence, Subterranean Resistance*. Edited by Marylin Booth, 365–98. Edinburgh: Edinburgh University Press, 2014.

Bouzet, Charles du. *Les Israélites indigènes de l'Algérie. Pétition à l'Assemblée nationale contre le décret du 24 octobre 1870*. Paris: Imprimerie Schiller, 1871.

Boyer, Pierre. 'La Vie politique et les élections à Alger'. In *La Révolution de 1848 en Algérie*, edited by Marcel Emerit, 41–58. Saint-Denis: Éditions Bouchène, 2016 [Paris 1949].

Branche, Raphaëlle. *L'Embuscade de Palestro: Algérie 1956*. Paris: Armand Colin, 2010.

Brett, Michael. 'Legislating for Inequality in Algeria: The Senatus-Consulte of 14 July 1865'. *Bulletin of the School of Oriental And African Studies* 51, no. 3 (1988): 440–61.

Brubaker, Rogers. *Citizenship and Nationhood in France and Germany*. Cambridge, MA: Harvard University Press, 1992.

Bugéja, Marie. *Nos sœurs musulmanes*. Algiers: Éditions France-Afrique, 1931.

Cahiers algériens. Algiers: Imprimerie Duclaux, 1870.

Campos, Michelle U. *Ottoman Brothers: Muslims, Christians, and Jews in Early Twentieth-Century Palestine*. Stanford: Stanford University Press, 2011.

Campos, Michelle U. 'Imperial Citizenship at the End of Empire: The Ottomans in Comparative Perspective'. *Comparative Studies of South Asia, Africa and the Middle East* 37, no. 3 (2017): 588–607.

Camus, Albert. *Essais*. Paris: Gallimard, 1965.

Camus, Albert. *Le Premier homme*. Paris: Gallimard, 1994.

Carlier, Omar. 'Les Traminots algérios des années 1930: un groupe social médiateur et novateur'. *Le Mouvement Social*, no. 146 (1989): 61–89.

Carlier, Omar. 'Le Café maure: Sociabilité masculine et effervescence citoyenne (Algérie XVIIE-XXe siècles)'. *Annales. Economies, Sociétes, Civilisations*, no. 4 (1990): 975–1003.

Carlier, Omar. 'Medina and Modernity: The Emergence of Muslim Civil Society in Algiers between the two World Wars'. In *Walls of Algiers: Narratives of the City through Text and Image*, edited by Julia Clancy-Smith et al., 62–84. Seattle: University of Washington Press, 2009.

Carrey, Émile (ed.). *Recueil complet des actes du Gouvernement provisoire (février, mars, avril, mai 1848)*. Paris: Auguste Durand, 1848.

Çelik, Zeynep. *Urban Forms and Colonial Confrontations: Algiers under French Rule*. Berkeley: University of California Press, 1997.

Çelik, Zeynep. *Empire, Architecture, and the City: French-Ottoman Encounters, 1830–1914*. Seattle: University of Washington Press, 2008.

Chabal, Emile. *A Divided Republic: Nation, State and Citizenship in Contemporary France*. Cambridge: Cambridge University Press, 2015.

Chakrabarty, Dipesh. *Provincializing Europe: Postcolonial Thought and Historical Difference*. Princeton: Princeton University Press, 2008.

Clancy-Smith, Julia. *Rebel and Saint: Muslim Notables, Populist Protest, Colonial Encounters (Algeria and Tunisia, 1800–1904)*. Berkeley: University of California Press, 1997.

Clark, Christopher. *The Sleepwalkers: How Europe Went to War in 1914*. London: Penguin 2013.

Clayton, Anthony. *France, Soldiers and Africa*. London: Brassey's Defence, 1988.

Cohen, Hillel. *Year Zero of the Arab-Israeli Conflict 1929*. Waltham: Brandeis University Press, 2015)

Cohen, Jean-Louis. 'Casablanca: De la cité de l'énergie à la ville fonctionnelle'. In *Architecture française Outre-mer*, edited by Maurice Culot and Jean-Maurice Thiveaud, 108–20. Liège: Margada 1992.

Cohen, Marcel. *Le parler arabe des Juifs d'Alger*. Paris: H. Champion, 1912.

Cohen, William B. 'The Colonial Policy of the Popular Front'. *French Historical Studies* 7, no. 3 (Spring 1972): 368-93.

Cole, Joshua. *Lethal Provocation: The Constantine Murders and the Politics of French Algeria*. Ithaca: Cornell University Press, 2019.

Coller, Ian. *Muslims and Citizens. Islam, Politics and the French Revolution*. New-Haven: Yale University Press, 2020.

Collot, Claude and Henry, Jean-Robert (ed.). *Le Mouvement national algérien: textes 1912-1954*. Algiers: Office des publication universitaires, 1978.

Colonna, Fanny. *Instituteurs algériens, 1883-1939*. Paris: Presses de la Fondation nationale des sciences politiques, 1975.

Confer, Vincent. *France and Algeria: The Problem of Civil and Political Reform, 1870-1920*. Syracuse: Syracuse University Press, 1966.

Cooper, Frederick. *Citizenship between Nation and Empire: Remaking France and French Africa, 1945-1960*. Princeton: Princeton University Press, 2014.

Cooper, Frederick. *Citizenship, Inequality, and Difference: Historical Perspectives*. Princeton: Princeton University Press, 2018.

Coquery-Vidrovitch, Catherine. 'Nationalité et citoyenneté en Afrique occidentale française'. *The Journal of African History* 42. no. 2 (2001): 285-305.

Courreye, Charlotte. *L'Algérie des oulémas: une histoire de l'Algérie contemporaine (1931-1991)*. Paris: Éditions de la Sorbonne, 2020.

Crémieux, Adolphe. *Réfutation de la pétition de M. du Bouzet*. Paris: Imprimerie Schiller, 1871.

Dain, Alfred. *Étude sur la naturalisation des étrangers en Algérie*. Algiers: Adolphe Jourdan, 1885.

Davidson, Naomi. 'La mosquée de Paris. Construire l'islam français et l'islam en France, 1926-1947'. *Revue des mondes musulmans et de la Méditerranée*, no. 125 (2009): 197-215.

Davidson, Naomi. *Only Muslim. Embodying Islam in Twentieth Century France*. Ithaca: Cornell University Press, 2012.

Davis, Diana K. *Resurrecting the Granary of Rome: Environmental History and French Colonial Expansion in North Africa*. Athens: Ohio University Press, 2007.

Delpech de Saint-Guilhem, E. *Adresse de la délégation de l'Algérie aux Chambres*. Paris: Imprimerie de Rignoux, 1847.

Dermenjian, Geneviève. *La crise anti-juive oranaise: 1895-1905, l'antisémitisme dans l'Algérie coloniale*. Paris: L'Harmattan, 1986.

Derrida, Jacques. *Le Monolinguisme de l'autre*. Paris: Galilée, 1996.

Dewhurst-Lewis, Mary. *The Boundaries of the Republic: Migrant Rights and the Limits to Universalism in France, 1918-1940*. Stanford: Stanford University Press, 2007.

Dewhurst-Lewis, Mary. *Divided Rule: Sovereignty and Empire in French Tunisia, 1881-1938*. Berkeley: University of California Press, 2014.

Dodman, Thomas. *What Nostalgia Was: War, Empire, and the Time of a Deadly Emotion*. Chicago: Chicago University Press, 2018.

Dominique, L.-C. *Un Gouverneur général de l'Algérie: L'Amiral de Guyedon*. Algiers: Typ. Adolphe Jourdan, 1908.

Drumont, Édouard. *La France juive: Essai d'histoire Contemporaine*. Paris: C. Marpon & E. Flammarion, 1887.

Dubois, Laurent. *Avengers of the New World: The Story of the Haitian Revolution*. Cambridge, MA: Harvard University Press, 2005.

Dubois, Laurent. *A Colony of Citizens: Revolution and Slave Emancipation in the French Caribbean, 1787–1804*. Chapel Hill, NC: University of North Carolina Press, 2012.

Dunwoodie, Peter. *Writing French Algeria*. Oxford: Clarendon Press, 1999.

Emerit, Marcel. 'Les Déportés du Juin'. In *La Révolution de 1848 en Algérie*, edited by Marcel Emerit, 59–68. Saint-Denis: Éditions Bouchène 2016 [Paris 1949].

Estoublon, Robert. *Bulletin judiciaire de l'Algérie. Jurisprudence algérienne de 1830 à 1876*. Algiers: A. Jourdan, 1890–1891.

Evans, Martin. *Algeria: France's Undeclared War*. Oxford: Oxford University Press, 2012.

Fanon, Frantz. *A Dying Colonialism*. Translated by Haakon Chevalier. 1959. Reprint, New York: Grove Press, 1965.

Febvre, Lucien. 'Civilization: Evolution of a Word and a Group of Ideas'. In *A New Kind of History. From the Writings of Lucien Febvre*, edited by Peter Burke, 219–57. London: Routledge, 1973.

Fédération des maires d'Algérie, *Les droits électoraux des indigènes algériens: Le projet Viollette*. Algiers: Imprimeries la Typo litho et Jules Cabonel, 1938.

Ferretti, Federico and Philippe Pelletier. 'Sciences impériales et discours hétérodoxes? Élisée Reclus et le colonialisme français'. *L'Espace géographique* 42, no. 1 (January 2013): 1–14.

Fischer, Fabienne. *Alsaciens et Lorrains en Algérie: histoire d'une Migration, 1830–1914*. Nice: Gandini, 1999.

Fitzpatrick, David. 'Ireland and Empire'. In *The Oxford History of the British Empire: Volume III: The Nineteenth Century*, edited by Andrew Porter, 494–521. Oxford: Oxford University Press, 1999.

Fogarty, Richard S. 'The French Empire'. In *Empires at War 1911–1923*, edited by Robert Gerwarth and Erez Manela, 109–29. Oxford: Oxford University Press, 2014.

Folleville, Daniel de. *Traité théorique et pratique de la naturalisation: Études de droit international privé*. Paris: A. Marescq aîné, 1880.

Forest, Louis. *La naturalisation des Juifs algériens et l'insurrection de 1871*. Paris: Société française d'imprimerie et de librairie, 1897.

Frégier, Casimir. *Les Juifs algériens [. . .]: leur naturalisation collective*. Paris: Michel Lévy Frères, 1865.

Gallois, William. *A History of Violence in the Early Algerian Colony*. New York: Palgrave Macmillan, 2013.

Gammerl, Benno. *Untertanen, Staatsbürger und Andere: Der Umgang mit ethnischer Heterogenität im Britischen Weltreich und im Habsburgerreich 1886–1918*. Göttingen: Vandenhoeck & Ruprecht, 2010.

Gardot, A. *De la Colonisation de l'Algérie par le concours politique de la France et de l'Espagne*. 1848.

De Gaulle, Charles. *Discours et Messages*, vol. I. Paris: Plon, 1970.

Geggus, David. 'Racial Equality, Slavery, and Colonial Secession during the Constituent Assembly'. *The American Historical Review* 94, no. 5 (1989): 1290–308.

Geggus, David (ed). *The Haitian Revolution: A Documentary History*. Indianapolis: Hackett Publishing, 2014.

Girardet, Raoul. *L'idée coloniale en France de 1871 à 1962*. Paris: Editions de la Table Ronde, 1972.

Goebel, Michael. *Anti-Imperial Metropolis: Interwar Paris and the Seeds of Third World Nationalism*. Cambridge: Cambridge University Press, 2015.

Gosewinkel, Dieter. *Einbürgern und Ausschließen: die Nationalisierung der Staatsangehörigkeit vom Deutschen Bund bis zur Bundesrepublik Deutschland*. Göttingen: Vandenhoeck & Ruprecht, 2001.

Gosnell, Jonathan K. *The Politics of Frenchness in Colonial Algeria, 1930–1954*. Rochester: University of Rochester Press, 2002.

Green, Abigail. *Children of 1848: Liberalism and the Jews from the Revolutions to Human Rights*, draft manuscript.

Guignard, Didier. 'Conservatoire ou révolutionnaire? Le sénatus-consulte de 1863 appliqué au régime foncier d'Algérie'. *Revue d'histoire du XIXe siècle* 2, no. 41 (2010): 81–95.

Guignard, Didier. *L'Abus de pouvoir dans l'Algérie coloniale (1880–1914): Visibilité et singularité*. Paris: Presses Universitaires de Paris Ouest, 2014.

Hanley, Will. *Identifying with Nationality: Europeans, Ottomans, and Egyptians in Alexandria*. New York: Columbia University Press, 2017.

Hary, Benjamin. 'Il-'arabi dyalna (Our Arabic): The History and Politics of Judeo-Arabic'. In *Languages of Modern Jewish Cultures. Comparative Perspectives*, edited by J. Miller and A. Norich, 297–320. Ann Arbor: The University of Michigan Press, 2016.

Hazan, Efraim. 'Po'alo HaSifruti shel Rabi Yitzhak Mer'ali VeTochnito LeKhinus HaShira VeHapiyut BeAljiria', ('Isaac Morali's Literary Activity and his Programme of Collecting Poetry and *Piyutim* in Algeria'). *Pe'amim*, no. 91 (2002): 65–78.

Hazareesingh, Sudhir. *From Subject to Citizen: The Second Empire and the Emergence of Modern French Democracy*. Princeton: Princeton University Press, 1998.

Herzfeld, Michael. 'Practical Mediterraneanism: Excuses for Everything from Epistemology to Eating'. In *Rethinking the Mediterranean*, edited by William Harris, 45–63. Oxford: Oxford University Press, 2005.

Hofmann, Tessa. 'Der radikale Wandel: Das deutsche Polenbild zwischen 1772 und 1848'. *Zeitschrift für Ostforschung*, no. 42 (1993): 358–90.

Horne, Alistair. *A Savage War of Peace: Algeria, 1954–1962*. New York: The Viking Press, 1977.

Jackson, Julian. *The Popular Front in France: Defending Democracy 1934–1938*. Cambridge: Cambridge University Press, 1990.

Jurquet, Jacques. *La Révolution nationale algérienne et le Parti communiste français*, vol III. Paris, Editions du Centenaire, 1979.

Jansen, Jan C. *Erobern und Erinnern. Symbolpolitik, öffentlicher Raum und französischer Kolonialismus in Algerien, 1830–1950*. Munich: Oldenburg Verlag, 2013.

Julien, Charles-André. *L'Afrique du nord en marche: nationalismes musulmans et souveraineté française*. Paris: Julliard, 1952.

Julien, Charles-André. *Histoire de l'Algérie Contemporaine: La conquête et les débuts de la colonisation 1827–1871*. Paris: Presses universitaires de France, 1964.

Julien, Charles-André. 'Léon Blum et les pays d'outre-mer'. In *Léon Blum chef de gouvernement, 1936–1937*, edited by Pierre Renouvin and René Remond, 377–90. Paris: A. Colin, 1967.

Kalman, Samuel. *French Colonial Fascism: The Extreme Right in Algeria, 1919–1939*. Basingstoke: Palgrave Macmillan, 2013.

Kateb, Kamel. *Européens, "Indigènes" et Juifs en Algérie (1830–1962): représentations et réalités des populations*. Paris: Institut national d'études démographiques, 2001.

Katz, Ethan B. 'Constantine Riots (1934)'. In *Encyclopedia of Jews in the Islamic World*, edited by Norman A. Stillman. Consulted online on 1 September 2020. First published online: 2010.

Katz, Ethan B. 'Crémieux's Children: Joseph Reinach, Léon Blum, and René Cassin as Jews of French Empire'. In *Colonialism and the Jews*, edited by Ethan Katz, Lisa Moses Leff, and Maud S. Mandel, 129–65. Bloomington: Indiana University Press, 2017.

Katz, Ethan B. 'An Imperial Entanglement: Anti-Semitism, Islamophobia, and Colonialism'. *American Historical Review* 123, no. 4 (2018): 1190–209.

Kenny, Kevin. 'Ireland and the British Empire: An Introduction'. In *Ireland and the British Empire*, edited by Kevin Kenny, 1–25. Oxford: Oxford University Press, 2005.

Kimble, Sara L. 'Emancipation through Secularisation: French Feminist Views of Muslim Women's Condition in Interwar Algeria'. *French Colonial History* 7, no. 1 (2006): 109–28.

Lafi, Nora. 'Petitions and Accommodating Urban Change in the Ottoman Empire'. In *Istanbul as Seen from a Distance: Centre and Provinces in the Ottoman Empire*, edited by E. Özdalga et al., 73–81. Istanbul: Swedish Research Institute, 2011.

Lagrosillière, Joseph. *Rapport présenté à la Commission de l'Algérie, des Colonies et Pays de Protectorat [. . .] sur les résultats des investigations de la Sous-Commission d'Enquête parlementaire en Algérie [. . .], mars–avril 1937*. Paris: Imprimerie E.P., 1937.

Lambert, Gabriel. *L'Algérie et le projet Viollette*. Oran: F. Plaza, 1938.

Laroui, Abdallah. *The History of the Maghrib: An Interpretative Essay*. Translated by Ralph Manheim. Princeton: Princeton University Press, 1977.

Lazard, Claude. *L'accession des indigènes algériens à la citoyenneté française*. Paris: Librairie technique et économique, 1938.

Le Cour Grandmaison, Olivier. *De l'indigénat. Anatomie d'un «monstre» juridique: le droit colonial en Algérie et dans l'empire français*. Paris: La Découverte, 2010.

Leff, Lisa Moses. *Sacred Bonds of Solidarity: The Rise of Jewish Internationalism in Nineteenth-Century France*. Stanford: Stanford University Press, 2006.

Le Foll-Luciani, Jean-Pierre. 'Les Actions judéo-musulmanes pour une réforme de la citoyenneté en Algérie'. In *La fabrique coloniale du citoyen: Algérie, Nouvelle-Calédonie*, edited by Eric Savarese and Eric de Mari, 79–100. Paris: Karthala, 2019.

Leroy-Beaulieu, Paul. *L'Algérie et la Tunisie*, 2nd ed. Paris: Guillaumin et cie, 1897.

Liautaud, Augustin Pierre Joseph Louis. *La République de 1848 en Algérie*. Algiers: Juillet Saint-Léger, 1873.

Lorcin, Patricia. 'Mediating Gender, Mediating Race: Women Writers in Colonial Algeria'. *Culture, Theory and Critique* 45, no. 1 (2004): 45–61.

Lorcin, Patricia. *Imperial Identities: Stereotyping, Prejudice and Race in Colonial Algeria*. Lincoln: University of Nebraska Press, 2014.

De Luna, Frederick A. *The French Republic under Cavaignac, 1848*. Princeton: Princeton University Press, 1969.

MacMaster, Neil. *Burning the Veil: The Algerian war and the 'emancipation' of Muslim Women, 1995–1962*. Manchester: Manchester University Press, 2009.

Maman, Aharon. *Mirqam Leshonot HaYehudim BiTzfon Afriqa* (The Fabric of Jewish Languages in North Africa). Jerusalem: Mossad Bialik, 2014.

Manela, Erez. *The Wilsonian Moment: Self Determination and the International Origins of Anticolonial Nationalism*. New York: Oxford University Press, 2007.

Marchal, Charles. *Les Troubles d'Alger: Opinion d'un témoin*. Algiers: Imprimerie Charles Zamith & Cie, 1898.

Marglin, Jessica M. 'Extraterritoriality and Legal Belonging in the Nineteenth-Century Mediterranean'. *Law and History Review* 39, no. 4 (2021): 679–706.

Marx, Karl. 'The Future Results of British Rule in India'. In *The Collected Works of Marx and Engels. Electronic Edition*, vol. 12. Charlottesville: InteLex Corporation, 2006.

Marynower, Claire. *L'Algérie à gauche (1900–1962): socialistes à l'époque coloniale*. Paris: PUF, 2018.

Mbembe, Achille. 'La République et l'impensé de la "race"'. In *La Fracture coloniale. La société française au prisme de l'héritage Colonial*, edited by Nicolas Bancel, Pascal Blanchard, and Sandrine Lemaire, 137–53. Paris: La Découverte, 2005.

McDougall, James. *History and Culture of Nationalism in Algeria*. Cambridge: Cambridge University Press, 2007.

McDougall, James. 'The Secular State's Islamic Empire: Muslim Spaces and Subjects of Jurisdiction in Paris and Algiers, 1905–1957'. *Comparative Studies in Society and History* 52, no. 3 (2010): 553–80.

McDougall, James. *A History of Algeria*. Cambridge: Cambridge University Press, 2017.

McDougall, James. 'A World No Longer Shared: Losing the *Droit de cite* in Nineteenth-Century Algiers'. *JESHO*, no. 60 (2017): 18–49.

McDougall, James. 'The Impossible Republic: The Reconquest of Algeria and the Decolonization of France, 1945–1962'. *The Journal of Modern History* 89, no. 4 (2017): 772–811.

De Ménerville, Charles-Louis Pinson. *Dictionnaire de la législation algérienne: code annoté et manuel raisonné des lois, ordonnances, décrets, décisions et arrêtés*, vol. II. Paris and Algiers: Challamel and A. Jourdan, 1877.

Merdaci, Abdellali. 'Kessous, Mohamed-Aziz'. In *Auteurs algériens de langue française de la période coloniale: dictionnaire biographique*, 156–7. Paris: L'Harmattan, 2010.

Meynié, Georges. *L'Algérie juive*. Paris: A. Savine, 1887.

Meynier, Gilbert. *L'Algérie révélée. La guerre de 1914–1918 et le premier quart du 20e siècle*. Geneva: Librairie Droz, 1981.

Meynier, Gilbert. 'Les Algériens et la guerre de 1914–1918'. In *Histoire de l'Algérie à la période coloniale 1830–1962*, edited by A. Bouchène, J.-P. Peyroulou, O. Siari Tengour, and Sylvie Thénault, 229–34. Paris: La Découverte, 2012.

Ministère de la Guerre, *Annuaire militaire de l'Empire français pour l'année 1870*. Paris: Veuve Berger-Levraut & fils, 1870.

Montesquieu. *Considérations sur les causes de la grandeur des Romains et de leur décadence, Texte établi par Édouard Laboulaye*. Paris: Garnier, 1876.

Montesquieu. *De l'esprit des lois, in Œuvres complètes*, vol. II. Paris: Gallimard, 1958.

Murray-Miller, Gavin. 'Imagining the Trans-Mediterranean Republic: Algeria, Republicanism, and the Ideological Origins of the French Imperial Nation-State, 1848–1870'. *French Historical Studies* 37, no. 2 (2014): 303–30.

Murray-Miller, Gavin. 'Bonapartism in Algeria: Empire and Sovereignty before the Third Republic'. *French History* 32, no. 2 (2018): 249–70.

Napoléon III, *Lettre sur la politique de la France en Algérie: adressée par l'Empereur au Maréchal de Mac-Mahon . . . gouverneur général de l'Algérie*. Paris: Imprimerie Impériale, 1865.

Noiriel, Gérard. *Le Creuset Francais: Histoire de l'immigration (XIXe-XXe siècle)*. Paris: Seuil, 1988.

Nora, Pierre. *Les Français d'Algérie*. Paris: R. Julliard, 1961.

Ofrath, Avner. "We Shall Become French': Reconsidering Algerian Jews' Citizenship, c. 1860–1900'. *French History* 35, no. 2 (2021): 243–65.

Peabody, Sue. *There Are No Slaves in France: The Political Culture of Race and Slavery in the Ancien Régime*. Oxford: Oxford University Press, 1996.

Pedersen, Susan. *The Guardians: The League of Nations and the Crisis of Empire*. Oxford: Oxford University Press, 2015.

Pedersen, Susan and Elkins, Caroline. 'Introduction: Settler Colonialism: A Concept and its Uses'. In *Settler Colonialism in the Twentieth Century: Projects, Practices, Legacies*, edited by Susan Pedersen and Caroline Elkins, 1–20. London: Routledge, 2005.

Pelet de Beaufranchet, A. *Projet de colonisation générale de l'Algérie*. Paris: Imprimerie de Poussielgue, 1848.

Pensa, Henri. *L'Algérie: Organisation politique et Administrative, Justice, sécurité, Instruction publique, travaux publics . . . Voyage de la délégation de la commission sénatoriale d'études des questions algériennes présidée par Jules Ferry*. Paris, 1894.

Pétition et projet de colonisation en Algérie par associations temporaires, présentés au nom de 20,000 familles. Paris: Typ. A. Appert, 1848.

Peyrefitte, Alain. *Faut-il partager l'Algérie?* Paris: Plon, 1961.

Peyrefitte, Alain. *C'était de Gaulle*, vol. I. Paris: Fayard, 1994.

Pitts, Jennifer (ed.). *Alexis de Tocqueville: Writings on Empire and Slavery*. Baltimore: Johns Hopkins University Press, 2001.

Pitts, Jennifer. *A Turn to Empire: The Rise of Imperial Liberalism in Britain and France*. Princeton: Princeton University Press, 2006.

Prélot, Marcel. 'La Signification constitutionnelle du Second Empire'. *Revue française de science politique* 3 (1953): 31–56.

Présidence du Conseil – Délégation en Algérie, *Documents algériens*. Algiers, 1958.

Prochaska, David. *Making Algeria French: Colonialism in Bone, 1870–1920*. Cambridge: Cambridge University Press, 1990.

Prochaska, David. 'History as Literature, Literature as History: Cagayous of Algiers'. *American Historical Review* 101, no. 3 (1996): 671–711.

Projet de colonisation en Algérie, adressé aux citoyens Représentants du Peuple par le citoyen Faure-Daniels. Riom: E. Leboyer, 1848.

Rabinow, Paul. *French Modern: Norms and Forms of the Social Environment*. Chicago: The University of Chicago Press, 2014.

Rahal, Malika. 'Ferhat Abbas, de l'assimilationisme au nationalisme'. In *Histoire de l'Algérie à la période coloniale 1930–1962*, edited by A. Bouchène, J.-P. Peyroulou, O. Siari Tengour, and Sylvie Thénault, 443–6. Paris: Éditions la Découverte, 2012.

Rahnama, Sara. 'Hijabs and Hats in Interwar Algeria'. *Gender & History* 32, no. 2 (2020): 429–46.

Recueil des actes du Gouvernement de l'Algérie, 1830–1854. Algiers: Imprimerie du gouvernement, 1856.

Régis, Max. *Pourquoi je me reitre de la lutte politique*. Algiers: Imprimerie P. Crescenzo, s.d.

Renault, Francois. *Cardinal Lavigerie: Churchman, Prophet and Missionary*. Translated by John O'Donohue. London : Athlone Press, 1994.

Rey-Golzeiguer, Annie. *Le Royaume arabe: La politique algérienne de Napoléon III, 1861–1870*. Algiers: Office des Publications Universitaries, 2014.

Ripley, William. *The Races of Europe: A Sociological Study* [. . .]. London: Kegan Paul, 1899.

Roberts, Sophie B. *Citizenship and Antisemitism in French Colonial Algeria, 1870–1962*. Cambridge: Cambridge University Press, 2017.

Rosenberg, Clifford. *Policing Paris: The Origins of Modern Immigration Control between the Wars*. Ithaca: Cornell University Press, 2006.

Saada, Emmanuelle. *Empire's Children: Race, Filiation, and Citizenship in the French Colonies*. Translated by Arthur Goldhammer. Chicago: Chicago University Press, 2012.

Sala-Molins, Louis (ed.). *Le Code noir ou le calvaire de Canaan*. Paris: Presses universitaires de France, 2018.

Schreier, Joshua. *Arabs of the Jewish Faith: The Civilizing Mission in Algeria*. New-Brunswick: Rutgers University Press, 2010.

Schroeter, Daniel J. 'Between Metropole and French North Africa: Vichy's Anti-Semitic Legislation and Colonialism's Racial Hierarchies'. In *The Holocaust in North Africa*, edited by Aomar Boum and Sarah Abrevaya Stein, 19–50. Stanford: Stanford University Press, 2018.

Schwarzfuchs, Simon. *Napoleon, the Jews and the Sanhedrin*. London: Routledge & Kegan Paul, 1979.

Schweitzer, Thomas Adrian. 'Le Parti communiste français, le Comintern et l'Algérie dans les années 1930'. *Le Mouvement sociale*, no. 78 (March 1972): 115–36.

Scioldo-Zürcher, Yann. *Devenir métropolitain. Politique d'intégration et parcours de rapatriés d'Algérie en métropole: 1954–2005*. Paris: Éditions EHESS, 2010.

Seferdjeli, Ryme. 'French "reforms" and Muslim Women's Emancipation during the Algerian War'. *The Journal of North African Studies* 9, no. 4 (2004): 19–61.

Semidei, Manuela. 'Les socialistes français et le problème colonial entre les deux guerres (1919–1939)'. *Revue française de science politique* 18, no. 6 (Autumn 1968): 1115–154.

Sessions, Jennifer E. *By Sword and Plow: France and the Conquest of Algeria*. Ithaca: Cornell University Press, 2011.

Sessions, Jennifer E. 'Colonizing Revolutionary Politics: Algeria and the French Revolution of 1848'. *French Politics, Culture & Society*, no. 1 (2015): 75–100.

Shaarawi, Huda. *Harem Years: The Memoirs of an Egyptian Feminist (1879–1924)*. Translated and edited by Margot Badran. New York: The Feminist Press, 1993.

Shepard, Todd. *The Invention of Decolonization: The Algerian War and the Remaking of France*. Ithaca: Cornell University Press, 2006.

Shepard, Todd. 'Algerian Nationalism, Zionism, and French laïcité: A History of Ethnoreligious Nationalisms and Decolonization'. *International Journal of Middle East Studies* 45, no. 3 (2013): 445–67.

Shinar, Pessah. 'A Controversial Exponent of the Algerian Salafiyya: The Kabyle 'Alim, Imam and Sharīf Abu Ya'la Sa'īd b. Muhammad al-Zawawī'. In *Studies in Islamic History and Civilization in Honour of David Ayalon*, edited by M. Sharon, 267–90. Leiden: Brill, 1986.

Shurkin, Michael. 'French Liberal Governance and the Emancipation of Algeria's Jews'. *French Historical Studies* 33 (2010): 259–80.

Sibeud, Emmanuelle. 'Une Libre pensée impériale? Le Comité de protection et de défense des indigènes (ca. 1892–1914)'. *Mil neuf cent. Revue d'histoire intellectuelle*, no. 27 (2009): 57–74.

Siblot, Paul. '"Cagayous antijuif". Un discours colonial en proie à la racisation'. *Mots*, no. 15 (October 1987): 59–75.

la Sicotière, Léon de. *Rapport fait au nom de la Commission d'enquête sur les actes du Gouvernement de la défense nationale – Algérie*, vol. 2. Versailles: Cerf et fils, 1875.

Sivan, Emmanuel. 'L'antisémitisme comme reflet de la situation coloniale en Algérie'. In *Pa'amei Ma'arav. Etudes judeo-maghrébines*, edited by Itzhak Bezalel, 58–74. Jerusalem: Ben-Zvi Institute, 1983.

Smith, Andrea L. *Colonial Memory and Postcolonial Europe: Maltese Settlers in Algeria and France*. Bloomington: Indiana University Press, 2006.

De Solms, E. and de Bassano, E. *Pétition à l'Assemblée nationale. Projet de colonisation de l'Algérie par l'association*. Paris: Imprimerie. de É. Proux, 1848.

Sternhell, Zeev. *La Droite révolutionnaire, 1885–1914: Les origines françaises du fascisme*. Paris: Fayard, 2000.

Stora, Benjamin. *Les trois exils: Juifs d'Algérie*. Paris: Stock, 2006.

Surkis, Judith. 'Propriété, polygamie et statut personnel en Algérie coloniale, 1830–1873'. *Revue d'histoire du XIXe siècle* 41, no. 2 (Spring 2010): 27–48.

Surkis, Judith. *Sex, Law and Sovereignty in French Algeria, 1830–1930*. Ithaca: Cornell University Press, 2019.

Tengour, Ouanassa Siari. 'Constantine 1887: des notables contre la "naturalisation"'. In *Histoire de l'Algérie à la période coloniale 1830–1962*, edited by A. Bouchène, J.-P. Peyroulou, O. Siari Tengour, and Sylvie Thénault, 235–8. Paris: La Découverte, 2012.

Thénault, Sylvie. *Violence ordinaire dans l'Algérie coloniale. Camps Interement, Assignations à residence*. Paris: Odile Jacob, 2012.

Thomas, Martin. 'Albert Sarraut, French Colonial Development, and the Communist Threat, 1919–1930'. *The Journal of Modern History* 77, no. 4 (2005): 917–55.

Thomas, Martin. *Fight or Flight: Britain, France, and Their Roads from Empire*. Oxford: Oxford University Press, 2014.

Tirosh-Boker, Ofra. 'Linguistic Analysis of an Algerian Judeo-Arabic Text from the Nineteenth Century'. *La Linguistique* 55 (2019): 193–212.

Tobi, Yosef. 'Bekache, Shalom'. In *Encyclopedia of Jews in the Islamic World*. Executive Editor Norman A. Stillman. Consulted online on 22 March 2022.

Tobi, Yosef and Tsivia Tobi. *Judeo-Arabic Literature in Tunisia, 1850–1950*. Detroit: Wayne State University Press, 2014.

De Tocqueville, Alexis. 'Rapport fait à la Chambre des députés (. . .), 1847'. In *Œuvres complètes*, vol. 9. Paris: Imprimerie Simon Raçon, 1866.

Verpeaux, Michel. 'L'unité et la diversité dans la République'. *Les nouveaux cahiers du Conseil constitutionnel* 1, no. 42 (2014): 7–16.

Violette, Maurice. *L'Algérie vivra-e-elle? Notes d'un ancien Gouverneur général*. Paris: Alcan 1931.

Wahl, Alfred. *L'Option et l'émigration des Alsaciens-Lorrains: 1871–1872*. Paris : Ophrys, 1974.

Warnier, Auguste. *L'Algérie et les victimes de la guerre*. Algiers: Imprimerie Duclaux, 1871.

Weil, Patrick. *Qu'est-ce qu'un Français?Historie de la nationalité francaise depuis la Révolution*. Paris: Gallimard, 2004.

Weil, Patrick. 'Le statut des musulmans en Algérie coloniale'. *Histoire de la Justice* 1 (2005): 93–109.

Wilder, Gary. *The French Imperial Nation-State: Negritude and Colonial Humanism between the Two World Wars*. Chicago: The University of Chicago Press, 2005.

Williams, Philip. 'How the Fourth Republic Died: Sources for the Revolution of May 1958'. *French Historical Studies* 3, no. 1 (1963): 1–40.

Wippermann, Wolfgang. '"Gesunder Volksegoismus": Vorgeschichte, Verlauf und Folgen der Polendebatte in der Paulskirche'. In *1848. Revolution in Europa: Verlauf, politische Programme, Folgen und Wirkungen*, edited by Heiner Timmermann, 351–65. Berlin: Duncker & Humblot, 1999.

Index

1795 constitution (Constitution of the Year III) 25
1848 Second Republic Constitution 34, 35
1848 revolution 30, 31
1876 Ottoman constitution 96
1946 Fourth Republic constitution 35, 139
1905 law 111

Abbas, Ferhat 115, 116, 125, 127, 131, 136, 139–41, 143–5, 150, 163, 164
Abbo, Gabriel 134
Abd al-Qadir ibn Muhyi al-Din al-Hasani 22, 28, 38, 107
Abdul Hamid II 96
Abi-Mershed, Osama 3, 29
Abitbol, Michel 69
A-Daziri/L'Israélite algérien (newspaper) 51, 72
Ageron, Charles-Robert 56, 133, 161
Algeria 1, 22, 23, 28, 41, 42, 44, 91–3, 102, 104, 107, 108, 110, 116, 146. *See also* France/French; French citizenship
    administration 11, 23, 28, 29, 42, 45, 55, 57, 60, 79, 96, 97, 99, 109, 133, 134, 141, 149, 154–7
    Algerians 4, 7, 17, 28, 37, 38, 45, 64, 66, 88, 94–101, 105–7, 109, 115, 126, 130, 138, 146, 152–4, 157
    Assembly and Assembly elections 147, 148, 150, 154
    Algerian autonomy proposals (1950s) 151, 152
    colonialism/colonization 1, 2, 7, 5, 14, 15, 19, 26, 28, 33, 36–8, 40–4, 46, 49, 51, 54–6, 58–61, 64–6, 88, 89, 94, 97, 107–10, 116, 121, 122, 125, 127, 133, 136, 137, 142, 145, 153, 156, 157, 160, 163
    colonial lobby/lobbyists 72, 93, 94, 109, 122, 130, 132, 136
    colonial subjecthood/subjects 2, 7–9, 11, 40, 42–9, 56, 63, 94, 99, 102–4, 109, 162
    consistorial system 49, 52, 53
    electorate 105, 125–6, 131
    Europeans in (*see also* settler population) 2, 6, 7, 12, 14, 18, 27–9, 31, 34, 38, 45, 51, 55–60, 65, 66, 69, 70, 79, 80, 82, 83, 86–8, 95, 107, 108, 115, 116, 118, 126, 130–2, 139, 143, 144, 146–50, 152, 154, 160
    family structures 7, 8, 48, 103, 118, 125
    Francophone press 88, 117, 121, 122, 133
    independence 14, 112, 160, 163
    Italians 57–60, 79, 87
    Jews 2, 8, 16, 31, 34, 44–6, 49, 51–5, 67, 69–73, 75–8, 84–7, 98, 132, 133, 143–6, 154, 160, 162, 163
    jurisdictional politics 2, 4, 5, 11, 15, 42, 44, 49, 55, 103, 160
    land ownership 5, 38, 44, 156
    land seizure 42, 49, 55
    as legal borderland 1, 3, 5, 10, 11, 13, 18, 21–40, 161
    legal reform 88, 99, 105, 115
    legal status 6, 23, 25, 26, 45, 49, 56, 63, 66, 88, 103, 130
    Maltese population 58, 60
    mayors in 106, 116, 133, 134, 148, 161
    municipal councillors 77, 100, 133, 141, 146, 150
    municipal elections 34, 56, 93
    Muslims 2, 5, 7, 8, 12, 13, 16, 27, 34, 43, 44, 47, 49, 51, 55–7, 60–3,

65, 66, 74, 75, 77, 81–3, 88, 89, 94, 97–106, 118, 121, 129, 131, 133, 134, 136, 138–40, 142, 143, 145–50, 152, 154, 156, 160, 161, 164
  nationalism   18, 113, 120
  national legislative election (1951)   154
  Organic Law (1947)   147, 148, 150, 154
  parliamentary elections   32, 78, 87
  political reforms   2, 99–100, 105, 115, 126, 129, 131, 146, 149
  public opinion   127, 128, 141
  racial segregation   1, 9
  republicanism   23, 27, 30, 35, 134, 151
  right to vote   138, 141, 155
  secularization   124
  settler population   2, 11, 30–5, 37, 55, 57, 58, 79
  society   8, 18, 23, 29, 59, 83, 97, 117, 121, 125, 143, 145, 153
  sovereignty   1, 23, 24, 28–31, 33, 36, 46, 55, 92, 106, 133–5, 146, 164
  Spaniards   57, 79, 81, 87
  taxation   99–101, 105, 106
  women   17, 81, 82, 84, 120–5, 128, 130, 147, 155, 156
Algerian War   1, 5, 10, 13, 14, 17, 128, 152–4, 156, 157, 159–63
Algiers   1, 16, 21, 22, 27, 30, 32, 35, 48, 53, 59, 70–2, 78–81, 83, 85, 126, 150, 152, 155
  Bab el Oued   80, 86
  Place du gouvernement   31, 86
Al-Islah (newspaper)   119, 120
Alliance israélite universelle   132
Al-Muntaqid (newspaper)   119
Al-Najah (newspaper)   112, 117
Alsace-Lorraine settlement project (1870s)   42, 62, 109
Al-Shihab (newspaper)   119, 120
Amin, Qasim   119
al-Amin al-'Amudi, Muhammad   120, 129
anti-Imperialism   107
anti-Islamism   12

anti-republicanism   87, 116, 163
anti-Semitic/anti-Semites/anti-Semitism   14, 19, 69–71, 76, 78–89, 98, 106, 116, 132, 144, 163
  crisis (1890s)   19, 71, 74–7, 81, 91, 98, 106, 132
  movement   79, 87, 88
  politics   69, 70, 77, 86
  press   76, 78, 88
  violence   77–84
'Arab kingdom' policy   44, 51
Arabs/Arabic   46, 82, 89, 133
  language   16, 125, 164
  press   125
  conflict with Jews   132–3
  women's rights   118–20
Arendt, Hannah   145
Armée d'Afrique   22, 27, 36, 39, 95, 102
Armée métropolitaine   94
Asseraf, Arthur   4, 32, 93
assimilation and association   2, 8, 16, 28–32, 35, 36, 40, 44, 46, 49, 51, 53, 54, 64, 69, 70, 97, 120, 124, 142
Association des étudiants musulmans d'Afrique du Nord ('Association of North African Students')   112
Association des 'ulama musulmans algériens ('Association of Algerian Muslim 'ulama/ AUMA)   112–13, 119, 141. *See also* 'ulama
Atlantic Charter   140
Aumeran, Adolphe   148
Aydin, Cemil   43, 93

Bandung conference (1955)   154
Barrès, Maurice   95
Batna insurrection (1916)   101, 102
Beccache, Shalom   72
Ben Badis, Abd al-Hamid   119, 125, 126, 129, 130, 164
Bendjelloul, Mohamed-Salah   139, 141, 142, 150, 164
ben Gharbit, Si Kaddour   110, 111
Benisti, Nessim   51
Benthami, Belkacem   109

Benton, Lauren 15
Bentounès, Abderrahmane 150
Bet Yisrael (newspaper) 72
Birnbaum, Pierre 53, 162
Blévis, Laure 3, 43, 63
Blum, Léon 115, 126, 127, 132
Blum-Viollette plan 103, 113, 116, 117, 125–36, 140, 141, 148, 161, 164
Bonaparte, Napoléon I 25, 27, 49, 52, 53, 55
Bonaparte, Napoléon III 43–6, 91, 162
Bourdarie, Paul 95, 97, 98, 109, 110, 112
Brett, Michael 46
Britain 93, 108 10
Brubaker, Rogers 9, 56, 165
Bugéja, Marie 123
Bureaux arabes 29

Cagayous (fictional figure) 59, 78, 79
Campos, Michelle 4, 164
Camus, Albert 17, 58, 128, 152
Caribbean 23, 26, 27
Carlier, Omar 4
Catholicism 62, 135
Cavaignac, Eugène 22, 30, 32–4
Çelik, Zeynep 16
Central Powers 101
Chakrabarty, Dipesh 7
Chamber of Deputies 28, 30, 66, 87, 133
Chaze, Lucien 78
Chevallier, Jacques 152
child marriage 48, 118
chrétiens musulmans 63
citizenship reform (1889) 44, 55–63, 71
'civilizing mission' 97, 122
civil rights 47, 94–102
Clemenceau, Georges 96, 101
Code civil (1804) 8, 11, 48, 53–5, 61, 62, 98, 102, 103, 105, 130, 135
Code de l'indigénat (1881) 12, 13, 41, 62, 63, 66, 67, 71, 88, 93–7, 101, 109, 112
Code noir (1685) 25, 28
Colin, Maurice 87
collective naturalization 52, 60, 71, 87, 94
Coller, Ian 12, 27
Colonna, Fanny 4, 12
Colrat, Maurice 110
Comité d'Afrique française 109

Comité d'Entente 149
Comité français de libération nationale ('French Committee of National Liberation/CFLN) 138, 142, 144
Commission du suffrage universel 116, 133
Commission of Foreign Affairs 101, 102, 104, 105
Committee for Social Studies 144
Committee for the Defence of Muslim Interests 99
communal violence 133, 146
communes mixtes 62, 125
communist propaganda 126
Congrès musulman 125–7, 130–2
Congress of Mediterranean Women 122
Congress of Soummam 163
conscription 5, 19, 37, 56, 80, 94–102, 108, 109, 129
Conseil supérieur (Algerian administration) 42, 57, 60, 66, 133
Constantine 35, 48, 58, 59, 66, 78, 87, 88, 130, 137, 138, 144
Constantine Plan 156, 157
Contemporary Jewish Record (review) 145
Cooper, Frederick 3, 139
cooperative associations (1848 colonization schemes) 3, 15, 37, 38
Corps législatif 52
Coty, René 154, 155
coup d'état
 1799 25
 1851 30
 1936 (Spain) 132
Courreye, Charlotte 4, 142
Crémieux, Adolphe 31, 51, 54, 55, 75
Crémieux Decree (1870) 8, 63, 69, 71, 73–8, 87, 89, 98, 132, 143–5, 162, 163
Cuttoli, Paul 110

Dain, Alfred 56, 57
Daladier government 131, 134
Davidson, Naomi 43, 109
decolonization 5, 157
de Folleville, Daniel 61, 62

Index

de Gaulle, Charles 138, 139, 149, 154–6, 159–62
de Gueydon, Louis-Henri 74
de Lamoricière, Louis Juchault 33, 38, 39
de Lamothe, Henri 14, 41–2, 64, 97, 98
Delangle, Claude-Alphonse 46, 47, 51
de la Rocque, François 132
Délégations financières 105, 110, 125, 133, 140, 141
de MacMahon, Patrice 47, 52
de Maupassant, Guy 13
democracy 152
Democracy in America (Tocqueville) 28
Depreux, Édouard 147
Derrida, Jacques 143
Dewhurst-Lewis, Mary 3, 92
Diagne, Blaise 104
Diection des Affaires musulmanes 141
Doriot, Jacques 132
Dreyfus Affair 70, 71, 76, 162
Dreyfus, Alfred 85
Droit de l'Homme (newspaper) 80
Drumont, Eduard 70, 75, 76, 81, 83–5, 87–9, 98
du Bouzet, Charles 73, 74
Dunwoodie, Peter 17

écoles israélites françaises 52
education
   girls 119, 120, 122, 123
   law 59
   system 56, 80
Educational Club 112
Égalité (newspaper) 143, 150
Egypt 16, 27, 118, 119, 122, 135
Egyptian Feminist Union 118
electoral colleges 100, 106, 139, 147, 149–51, 155
Emerit, Marcel 39
emir Khaled 107, 109
Enfantin, Prosper 29
Enlightenment 7, 65
ethnoreligious categories 5, 19, 44, 56, 151, 163, 164
Etienne, Eugène 57
Étoile nord-africaine ('North African Star'/ENA) 112, 113
Europeanness 2, 43, 44, 56, 60, 162
Europe/European
   citizenship 7
   origin 60, 63, 77–84, 162
   settlers 23, 30
   women 155
Evans, Martin 156

Fanon, Frantz 18
federalism 139
Femmes d'Alger (Delacroix) 82
Ferry, Jules 89
First Internationale 65
First World War 14, 19, 66, 91, 92, 94, 126, 144
Flandin, Louis-Hugues 46
'Four Communes' (Senegal) 104
France/French 8, 10, 25–8, 30, 31, 33, 37, 42–8, 51, 52, 56, 59, 65, 75, 81, 84, 85, 91, 93, 94, 102, 108–11, 124, 129, 132, 135, 136, 144, 146, 151–3, 159–61, 164. *See also* Algeria
   army 54, 65, 103, 107
   authority 54, 88, 91, 101, 129, 154
   citizens 7, 9, 12, 31, 32, 34, 38, 43–9, 51, 75, 94, 95, 100–2, 105, 139–40, 147, 157, 160, 164
   citizenship (*see* French citizenship)
   courts 25, 52
   empire 13–15, 18, 24, 89, 92, 93, 102, 104, 107–9, 138–40
   feminists 122
   Fifth Republic 155
   Fourth Republic 2, 35, 138, 146, 154, 161
   Freemasonry 96
   government 1, 26, 66, 101, 117, 134, 144, 145, 147, 152, 160
   legislation 7, 8, 29, 30, 45–8, 51–5, 60, 62, 72, 98, 102, 103, 105, 131, 160
   parliament 125, 148, 149, 152
   public opinion 13, 30, 88, 89, 94, 96, 97, 117, 120, 121, 124, 129, 161
   Second Empire 12, 42, 44, 46, 48, 54, 64, 74
   Second Republic 2, 21–6, 28, 30, 31, 35, 37, 46, 132
   socialism 65, 127
   Third Republic 3, 12, 38, 42, 43, 86, 162

Vichy government 138, 143, 163
women 122, 124, 130
Franco-Prussian war 38, 42, 54
free people of colour (Saint-Domingue) 25, 26
French aristocracy 42, 109
French citizenship 1, 2, 11, 23, 26, 30, 35, 36, 40, 42, 47, 56, 61, 66, 70, 73–4, 76, 78, 80, 87, 92, 97, 98, 103, 104, 109, 117, 126, 129, 131, 132, 136–9, 143, 144, 146, 147, 150, 152, 160–5. *See also* Algeria
and empire 3–5
as institution and ideology 5–10
limits 15–19
French feminist movement 121
French metropole 1–3, 11, 15, 16, 23–5, 28, 30, 33, 34, 48, 55, 61–4, 69, 70, 78, 79, 80, 83–9, 92, 98, 100, 101, 106, 121, 122, 132–4, 138, 149, 151, 154, 160, 163
French Revolution 24, 25, 27, 161
'French Union' 15, 139, 146, 147, 150, 151
Front de Libération nationale ('National Liberation Front'/FLN) 18, 150–2, 154, 156, 163

Gaulier, Alfred 65
Geiser, Jean 82
Germany 14, 38, 42, 92, 134
Giraud, Henri 156
Girault, Arthur 99
Gosnell, Jonathan 120
Government of National Defence 54, 55, 75, 144
Grand Sanhedrin (1807) 53
Green, Abigail 51
Guadeloupe 11, 61
Guernut, Henri 134
Guignard, Didier 13

Hacene, Seghir 122
Haiti 11, 26. *See also* Saint-Domingue
Hamed, Larguehce 122
Haskalah 2
Hazareesingh, Sudhir 48

Henley, Will 6
Hijaz 119
Hitler, Adolf 134

al-Ibrahimi, Rachid 141, 150
Imperial Court of Algiers 47
India 62, 164
'indigenous'/'indigenes'/indigeneity 2, 8, 9, 43–7, 49, 55, 60, 62–4, 66, 67, 69, 71, 72, 76, 87, 89, 96, 98, 100, 101, 116, 121, 132, 162
individual naturalization 9, 46–8, 52–4, 56, 57, 59, 60, 62, 65, 66, 69, 72, 74, 76, 93, 96–8, 101–5, 131, 142
Indochina 3, 11, 159, 160
industrialization 156
Institut musulman (Paris) 109
Ireland 10, 13
islah 2, 119
Islam(ic) 7, 43, 44, 46, 64, 95, 104, 110–12, 117, 135, 136. *See also* Muslim(s)
law 8, 9, 27, 45, 47, 48, 54, 62, 97, 98, 101, 102, 109, 118, 120, 121, 124, 129, 130, 142
Israel 164
Italy 134

Jaurès, Jean 70, 89
Jean-Darrouy, Lucienne 122
Jews/Jewish 29, 34, 44–6, 77, 143. *See also* anti-Semitic/anti-Semites/anti-Semitism
campaign for citizenship 49–55
congregations 49
immigration 132
journalism 51, 71–3
law 53
jihad 101
Jonnart, Charles 96, 105, 106
Jonnart law (1919) 105–7, 109
Judaism 50
Judeo-Arabic language 50–1, 53, 72–3, 162
Julien, Charles-André 116
July Monarchy 22, 27
jus sanguinis ('right of blood') 3, 9, 36, 55

jus soli ('right of land')   3, 9, 11, 36, 44, 55–63

Kabylia(n)   137
  revolt (1871)   38, 55, 74–6, 102
  woman   120
Katz, Ethan   8
Kessous, Muhammad al-Aziz   127, 128, 141–3

La Coloniale (French army)   95
La force noire (Mangin)   95
'*La France c'est moi*' (Abbas)   140, 164
La France juive (Drumont)   75, 82, 85
L'Africain (review)   148
Lagrossilière, Joseph   102–4, 127, 129–31
L'Akhbar (newspaper)   31
L'Algérie juive (Meynié)   76
L'Algérie vivra-t-elle? (Viollette)   123
La Libre parole (newspaper)   82, 83
Lambert, Gabriel   134
Lambrecht, Félix   74
Lamine-Guèye, Amadou
Lamine-Guèye Law   139
l'Antijuif algérien (newspaper)   83, 85
La Réunion   23, 61
Laroui, Abdallah   15
La Seybouse (newspaper)   31
Latin identity   78, 79, 85
La Voix des humbles (newspaper)   120
La Voix indigène (newspaper)   121
League of Nations   92, 108
L'Echo d'Alger (newspaper)   124
L'Echo d'Oran (newspaper)   31
Le Foll-Luciani, Pierre-Jean   117
legal pluralism   15, 28, 48, 144
Le Hon, Léopold   52
Le Matin (newspaper)   91
Lenin, Vladimir   93, 107
l'Entente franco-musulmane (newspaper)   115
Le Pays (newspaper)   149
Le Petit Républicain (newspaper)   89
Lépine, Louis   79
Le Radical (newspaper)   80
Leroy-Beaulieu, Paul   59, 64
Les Français d'Algérie (Nora)   14
Le Temps (newspaper)   89, 95, 96

'Letter to an Algerian Militant' (Camus)   128
Lévy, Emmanuel   79, 80
Leygues, Georges   101
Ligue des droits de l'homme ('League of Rights of Man'/LDH)   96, 121, 134
Liste de défense de l'Algérie française   148
London   10, 92
Loubet, Emile   85
Louis-Philipp (King)   22
L'Univers israélite (newspaper)   80
Lutaud, Charles   88, 100
Lyautey, Hubert   91, 108, 111

McDougall, James   4, 8, 59, 94, 120, 130, 150, 157
MacMaster, Neil   155
Maghrib/Maghribi   2, 4, 16
  architecture   111
  community in France   94, 112, 121
  Islam   112, 129
  saint-worshipping   121
Malaterre-Sellier, Germaine   122
mandates system   107
Mandouze, André   152
Manela, Erez   92
Mangin, Charles   95
Manifesto of the Algerian People (Abbas)   140, 143, 163
Marchal, Charles   86, 87
Marglin, Jessica   6
Margueritte Affair (1901)   88, 89
Maritian, Jacques   144
Marseillaise antijuive   86
Martinique   26, 61, 103
Marynower, Claire   117
Massu, Jacques   154, 155
Mbembe, Achille   10
Mediterranean   2, 4, 5, 17, 27, 59, 117, 118, 135, 162
Messali Hadj   127, 140, 143
Messimy, Adolphe   91, 93–6, 99, 100, 108
Meynié, Georges   76
Meynier, Gilbert   94, 101, 112
Michelin, Henri   65
Ministry of Interior   145
Ministry of Justice   60, 61

Ministry of War   106
Mobacher (newspaper)   31–2
modernity   98, 119, 120, 124
modernization   108, 156
Mollet, Guy   151
monogamy   48
Montesquieu   6, 27, 46
Moreau de Saint-Méry, Louis-Élie   26
Morinaud, Emile   87, 88, 106, 110
Morocco   91, 94, 95, 102, 107, 108, 110, 159
Mosque of Paris   107–13
Mostaganem   77, 78
Moutet, Marius   105
Mouvement pour le triomphe des libertés démocratiques ('Movement for the Triumph of Democratic Liberties'/MTLD)   154
Mouvement républicain populaire   148
Muhammad 'Ali   118
al-Muqrani, Muhammad al-Hajj   38, 42, 74, 75
Muslim(s)   27, 34, 45, 46, 110, 111, 135, 136. *See also* Islam(ic)
  Muslimness   2, 7, 43, 44, 162
  origin   62, 63
  society   103, 118, 123, 124, 145
  soldiers   101
  women   121, 124, 130
Mussolini, Benito   134

Nahda   2
National Assembly   13, 23, 25, 26, 30, 32–4, 36–8, 41, 63, 77, 103, 109, 116, 147, 148, 151, 154
National Convention   26
nationality   4, 6, 48, 57, 58, 62, 144, 147, 160
National Workshops   36, 37
naturalization   *See* collective naturalization individual naturalization, naturalization dans le statut, 'partial naturalization'
naturalization *dans le statut*   101–4, 116, 129, 160
Noiriel, Gérard   3
Nora, Pierre   14, 162
North Africa   28, 80, 98, 99, 108, 119, 140
Nos soeurs musulmanes (*Our Muslim Sisters*, Bugéja)   123

Old Regime   25, 27
'one and indivisible' maxim   24–9
Oran   30, 32, 34, 35, 39, 57, 59, 71, 73, 77, 78, 81, 95, 144
Oran républicain (newspaper)   128
Organisation de l'armée secrète ('Secret Army Organization'/OAS)   14
Ottoman Empire   4, 95, 96, 99, 107
Ouzegane, Amar   142, 149

Pakistan   164
Palestine   132, 133
pan-Islamism   95, 126
Paris   25, 26, 29, 31, 32, 36, 39, 60, 71, 76, 79, 83–7, 92, 96, 110, 146, 154
'partial naturalization'   105
Parti communiste algérien ('Algerian Communist Party'/PCA)   140, 142
Parti communiste français ('French Communist Party'/PCF)   113
Parti du peuple algérien ('Algerian People's Party'/PPA)   127, 137
Parti Populaire Français   132
Parti Social Français   132
pataouète dialect   59, 60
Pedersen, Susan   92
Pelet de Beaufranchet family   37
Permanent Mandates Commission   92
Persian Letters (Montesquieu)   27
Pétion de Villeneuve, Jérome   26
Peyrefitte, Alain   159–60
Pflimlin, Pierre   154
Pierrey, Alfred   47, 48
Pitts, Jennifer   27
Poincaré, Raymond   99
political participation   3–5, 43, 49, 93, 124, 136, 138, 151, 153
political rights   9, 26, 64, 95–7, 101, 104, 106, 115, 116, 138, 139, 164
polygamy   18, 48, 102, 118, 120, 124, 128–30, 146
Popular Front   14, 103, 113, 115, 117, 125, 127, 134, 135
Portalis, Jean-Marie   48
Pourcet, Joseph   54
Pradelle, Louis   76
Principes de la domination coloniale (Girault)   99

Prochaska, David   17, 58
provisional government (Algerian Republic)   115
provisional government (French Second Republic)   23, 27, 31, 32

Qol HaTor (newspaper)   73
Qol Israel/La Voix d'Israël (newspaper)   71–3
Quran   16, 120, 135
Quranic law   129

rabbinical jurisdiction   49, 51, 53
race   1, 17, 41, 58, 62, 65, 108, 152
racialization   43, 44, 56
radicalism   2, 16, 39, 125–31
Radio-Alger   133
Rahal, Malika   140, 164
Reclus, Élisée   65
Regency of Algiers   27
Régis, Max   70, 71, 76, 79–87, 98, 134, 162
religion/religious
   as descent   56, 57
   difference   12, 46, 103, 104, 131
   faith   50
   legislation   2, 62
'The Representation of the Indigenes' (de Lamothe)   41
'restricted occupation' strategy   28
Revue indigène   95–9, 109
Reygasse, René   148
Roberts, Sophie   77
Robespierre, Maximilien   26
Rome   75
Roosevelt, Franklin D.   140
Rozet, Albin   88, 107

Saada, Emmanuelle   3
Saint-Domingue   11, 25, 26, 28. See also Haiti
Saint-Simon, Henri de   29
salafiyyah   119
Salan, Raoul   154, 155
Saraffe, Prosper   71–2
Sarraut, Albert   93, 110, 133
Saurin, Paul   135
Schreier, Joshua   3, 54
Schroeter, Daniel   145

secessionism   24, 30, 57, 59, 82
Section française de l'Internationale ouvrière ('French Section of the Workers' International'/SFIO)   127–8
sénatus-consulte (imperial law, 1865)   8, 9, 44–9, 51–3, 55, 56, 61, 63, 71
Senegal   23, 104, 139
Service des affaires indigènes   121
Sessions, Jennifer   27, 35
Sétif   137, 146
Sha'arawi, Huda   118, 119
Shahada   88
Shari'a   120
Shepard, Todd   5, 43
shikayat   22
Siblot, Paul   59
Siècle (newspaper)   80
slavery   7, 11, 23, 25–7, 75, 129
Smith, Andrea L.   58
Société de protections des indigènes des colonies   13, 63–5
Société des habous des lieux-saints de l'Islam   110, 111
Southeast Asia   160
Soviet Union   107
Spain   26, 57, 134
Spirit of Laws, The (Montesquieu)   6
statut personnel   8, 62, 63, 66, 96, 98, 101, 104, 126, 129–31, 134, 135, 139, 142, 160, 161, 164
Sternhell, Zeev   70
Stora, Benjamin   163
Sublime Porte   22
Surkis, Judith   48, 118
Syria   16, 107

Tahrir al-Mar'a (The Liberation of Women, Amin)   119
Tam Tam (newspaper)   148
Theoretical and Practical Treaty on Naturalisation (de Folleville)   61
Thomas, Martin   156
Thomson, Gaston   88, 110
Tirailleurs algériens   102
Tirman, Louis   42, 57, 66
Tocqueville, Alexis de   28
Torah   50

Tunisia   91, 92, 94, 107, 110, 159
Turkey   93, 123
two-college system   150

'ulama   21, 23, 119, 121, 125, 129, 141, 142
Union démocratique du manifeste algérien ('Democratic Union of the Algerian Manifest'/UDMA)   154
Union française pour le suffrage des femmes ('French Union for Women's Suffrage'/UFSF)   122
Unir (newspaper)   148, 150
United States   27, 33, 36, 107
University of Algiers   148, 152
al-'Uqbi, Tayeb   119–21, 125, 129, 141, 142, 164
Urbain, Thomas Ismaÿl   29, 63
usines de défense nationale   94

Vérone, Maria   122, 128
Versailles conference (1919)   92, 107
Viard, Paul   148, 149

Viollette, Maurice   14, 16, 18, 102–4, 113, 116, 123, 125–7, 132, 135
Viollette, Thérèse   124

Waldeck-Rousseau, Pierrre   88
Weil, Patrick   3, 63
Westernization campaign   155
Wilder, Gary   15, 92
Wilhelm II (German Kaiser)   93
Wilson, Woodrow   92, 93, 107
women
   Algerian   17, 81, 82, 84, 120–5, 128, 130, 147, 155, 156
   Arab   118–20
   emancipation   121–3, 128
   European   155
   French   122, 124, 130
   Muslim   121, 124, 130
   oppression of   117, 119
   seclusion of   17, 118, 119
workers' uprising (1848)   39

Zola, Emile   76, 78
Zouwawi, Abu-Ya'la   120

www.ingramcontent.com/pod-product-compliance
Lightning Source LLC
Chambersburg PA
CBHW061831300426
44115CB00013B/2330